Access 2002 For Dummies®

Cheat Sheet

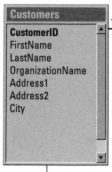

Customers

- **CustomerID**
- FirstName
- LastName
- OrganizationName
- Address1
- Address2
- City

Items

- **ItemID**
- ItemName
- Description
- CustomerID
- DateIn
- DateOut
- AuctionID

Auctions

- **AuctionID**
- Location
- AuctionType
- StartDate
- EndDate
- AuctioneerID
- Status

Auctioneers

- **AuctioneerID**
- LastName
- FirstName
- SocialSecurityNumber
- Address
- City
- StateOrProvince
- PostalCode

Primary key (Bold)

Each table contains one or more fields.

Foreign key (AuctioneerID on the Auctions table is a Foreign key related to AuctioneerID on the Auctioneers table.)

One-to-many relationship (For each Auctioneers record there can be many Auctions records but for each Auctions record there can be only one Auctioneers record.)

Customers: Table

	ID	First	Last	Address1
+	18	Clyde & Carmen	White	P.O. Box 3387
+	19	Paula	Ritter	229 Waterbury Cir
+	20	Erika	Whitechurch	3872 E. Sedlak Tr.
+	21	Bruce	Yatsak	1 Captain's Square
+	22	Sam	Gregory	1620 Edmondson Ave
+	23	Amanda	Tillery	6 E. Market

Customer 22 (Sam Gregory) has four items in the auction. The Customers and Items tables are related by the common field CustomerID. The two tables form a one-to-many relationship—for each customer there can be many items but for each item there is only one customer. The Customers table is said to be the parent while the Items table is the dependent because you cannot have an item without a valid customer. In other words, before you can add items for Customer 22, the customer must already exist on the Customers table.

Items: Table

Item ID	Min Bid	Description	ID
3	$30.00	Box of assorted hardback books. Printing dates range from 1930 to 1940.	22
4	$30.00	Box of assorted hardback books. Printing dates range from 1940 to 1950.	22
5	$30.00	Box of assorted hardback books. Printing dates range from 1950 to 1960.	22
6	$30.00	Box of assorted hardback books. Printing dates range from 1960 to 1970.	22

P9-CAO-540

For Dummies®: Bestselling Book Series for Beginners

Access 2002 For Dummies®

Cheat Sheet

Access 2002 Telephone Support Numbers

When all else fails, there's nothing like picking up the phone and yelling *help me!* at some innocent soul on the other end of the connection. Here's where to dial for assistance:

Telephone Number	Who You Reach
800-936-4100	The FastTips hotline for free recorded help 24 hours a day
425-635-7056	Access 2002 support in the United States; first two incidents are free
905-568-3503	Access 2002 support in Canada; first two incidents are free
800-668-7975	Access 2002 usability support in the U.S. and Canada — $35 U.S./$45 Canada per incident
800-936-5800	Access 2002 development and programming support in the U.S. and Canada — $245 U.S. per incident (Other countries refer to `http://support.microsoft.com/directory/Default.asp`)
800-892-5234	Microsoft text telephone (TT/TDD) services for customers with hearing disabilities

Field Types to Know and Love

Each field (or column) of your datasheet can hold only one type of information. Here are the basic Access information types:

Field	Contents
Text	Any kind of text (letters, numbers, and even letters and numbers)
Memo	Really long text entries (such as descriptions and reports)
Number	Any number you intend to use for counting or doing math
AutoNumber	Automatically fills in a unique number for every record
Currency	Numbers and symbols that represent quantities of money
Date/Time	Contains dates, times, or both
Yes/No	Binary (two-option) logic values, such as Yes/No, True/False, or Male/Female
Hyperlink	Clickable links to World Wide Web pages on the Internet or your company's intranet
OLE object	Highly technical, complex objects that can do everything but wash your car

Hungry Minds™

For Dummies®: Bestselling Book Series for Beginners

™

References for the Rest of Us!®

BESTSELLING BOOK SERIES

Are you intimidated and confused by computers? Do you find that traditional manuals are overloaded with technical details you'll never use? Do your friends and family always call you to fix simple problems on their PCs? Then the For Dummies® computer book series from Hungry Minds, Inc. is for you.

For Dummies books are written for those frustrated computer users who know they aren't really dumb but find that PC hardware, software, and indeed the unique vocabulary of computing make them feel helpless. For Dummies books use a lighthearted approach, a down-to-earth style, and even cartoons and humorous icons to dispel computer novices' fears and build their confidence. Lighthearted but not lightweight, these books are a perfect survival guide for anyone forced to use a computer.

"I like my copy so much I told friends; now they bought copies."

— *Irene C., Orwell, Ohio*

"Quick, concise, nontechnical, and humorous."

— *Jay A., Elburn, Illinois*

"Thanks, I needed this book. Now I can sleep at night."

— *Robin F., British Columbia, Canada*

Already, millions of satisfied readers agree. They have made For Dummies books the #1 introductory level computer book series and have written asking for more. So, if you're looking for the most fun and easy way to learn about computers, look to For Dummies books to give you a helping hand.

Access 2002
FOR
DUMMIES®

Access 2002
FOR
DUMMIES®

by John Kaufeld

Revised by Michael MacDonald

Hungry Minds™

HUNGRY MINDS, INC.

New York, NY ◆ Cleveland, OH ◆ Indianapolis, IN

Access 2002 For Dummies®

Published by
Hungry Minds, Inc.
909 Third Avenue
New York, NY 10022
www.hungryminds.com
www.dummies.com

Library of Congress Control Number: 2001086264

ISBN: 0-7645-0818-0

Printed in the United States of America

10 9 8 7 6 5

1B/RV/QV/QS/IN

Distributed in the United States by Hungry Minds, Inc.

Distributed by CDG Books Canada Inc. for Canada; by Transworld Publishers Limited in the United Kingdom; by IDG Norge Books for Norway; by IDG Sweden Books for Sweden; by IDG Books Australia Publishing Corporation Pty. Ltd. for Australia and New Zealand; by TransQuest Publishers Pte Ltd. for Singapore, Malaysia, Thailand, Indonesia, and Hong Kong; by Gotop Information Inc. for Taiwan; by ICG Muse, Inc. for Japan; by Intersoft for South Africa; by Eyrolles for France; by International Thomson Publishing for Germany, Austria and Switzerland; by Distribuidora Cuspide for Argentina; by LR International for Brazil; by Galileo Libros for Chile; by Ediciones ZETA S.C.R. Ltda. for Peru; by WS Computer Publishing Corporation, Inc., for the Philippines; by Contemporanea de Ediciones for Venezuela; by Express Computer Distributors for the Caribbean and West Indies; by Micronesia Media Distributor, Inc. for Micronesia; by Chips Computadoras S.A. de C.V. for Mexico; by Editorial Norma de Panama S.A. for Panama; by American Bookshops for Finland.

For general information on Hungry Minds' products and services please contact our Customer Care Department within the U.S. at 800-762-2974, outside the U.S. at 317-572-3993 or fax 317-572-4002.

For sales inquiries and reseller information, including discounts, premium and bulk quantity sales, and foreign-language translations, please contact our Customer Care Department at 800-434-3422, fax 317-572-4002, or write to Hungry Minds, Inc., Attn: Customer Care Department, 10475 Crosspoint Boulevard, Indianapolis, IN 46256.

For information on licensing foreign or domestic rights, please contact our Sub-Rights Customer Care Department at 212-884-5000.

For information on using Hungry Minds' products and services in the classroom or for ordering examination copies, please contact our Educational Sales Department at 800-434-2086 or fax 317-572-4005.

For press review copies, author interviews, or other publicity information, please contact our Public Relations Department at 317-572-3168 or fax 317-572-4168.

For authorization to photocopy items for corporate, personal, or educational use, please contact Copyright Clearance Center, 222 Rosewood Drive, Danvers, MA 01923, or fax 978-750-4470.

Hungry Minds is a trademark of Hungry Minds, Inc.

About the Authors

John Kaufeld got hooked on computers a long time ago. Somewhere along the way, he discovered that he really enjoyed helping people resolve computer problems. John finally achieved his BS degree in management information systems from Ball State University and he became the first PC support technician for what was then Westinghouse near Cincinnati, Ohio.

Since then, he's logged nearly a decade of experience working with normal people who were stuck with a "friendly" PC that turned on them. He's also trained more than 1,000 people in many different PC and Macintosh applications. Today, John is president of Access Systems, a computer consulting firm. He still does troubleshooting, conducts technical and interpersonal skills seminars for up-and-coming computer gurus, and writes in his free moments.

His other titles include *FoxPro2.6 For Windows For Dummies, Paradox 5 For Windows For Dummies, Games Online For Dummies,* and the bestselling *America Online For Dummies,* 5th Edition. John lives with his wife, two children, and a tolerable American Eskimo dog in Indianapolis.

Michael MacDonald has been living a double life for years. He's your average, I-have-a-life sort of guy, but he's also a geek with the Microsoft certifications to prove it. Like Bob Newhart, Mike started out as an accountant and also like Bob, Mike quickly realized that accounting was not exciting enough. He migrated to the much more exciting world of databases and programming. Mike has been working with relational database products, such as Access, since 1984.

After working at a couple of real jobs, Mike had some business cards printed and launched an independent consultancy in 1996. Besides forays to clients throughout the northeast, Mike is a senior instructor for Worcester Polytechnic Institute and is author of various books on subjects from Windows to Visual Basic to music software.

Mike lives in the booming metropolis of Whitinsville, Mass., where he likes to join his neighbors on Saturday nights and watch the traffic signal turn from green to yellow to red to green. . . .

Dedications

John Kaufeld: To Jenny, because without you, I'd be completely nuts. To J.B. and the Pooz for reminding Daddy to smile when all he could do was write. To Hungry Minds, Inc., for the opportunity of a lifetime. My sincere thanks to you, one and all.

Michael MacDonald: To my family — each of you is like a breath of fresh air on those stressful days. To all those people in my professional and personal lives who saw fit to share a little of themselves, I am in awe.

Authors' Acknowledgments

John Kaufeld: As with any good magic trick, there's more to putting out a book than meets the eye. Kudos to my Project Editor, Pat O'Brien, and Copy Editor, Christine Berman, for their diligent efforts to make my ramblings follow commonly accepted semantic guidelines. Equally significant thanks goes to Technical Editor Michael Gibson for seeing that I'm not making this stuff up.

My sincere thanks goes to Diane Steele, the Executive in Charge of a Bewildering Array of Problems, for her support and encouragement.

Michael MacDonald: When you look at the cover of a book, you see the author's name. But so many more names should be there. I'm humbled by the talent of people who put this book together. For the people at Hungry Minds, these books are a mission. Sort of makes somebody like me want to get out of bed in the morning.

The first person I have to acknowledge is the original author, John Kaufeld. Next are those who shepherd a book from when it's a twinkle in some editor's eye to when it's in your hands. Steven Hayes is the acquisitions editor who asked, "Mike, would you?" Pat O'Brien, the project editor, is the guy who asked, "Mike, could you?" Christine Berman is the copy editor and is the single reason that any two sentences in this book make semantic sense. Christine was also there for me with a lot of advice. Michael Gibson, the tech editor, is the guy responsible for making sure that I'm not lying to you.

More people worked on this book and space precludes me from addressing their accomplishments and the gratitude owed each, but be sure you flip to the Publisher's Acknowledgments.

One other very special person needs to be acknowledged and that's you, the reader. Without your patronage and feedback (good, bad, or indifferent), books like this simply would not happen.

Publisher's Acknowledgments

We're proud of this book; please send us your comments through our Hungry Minds Online Registration Form located at www.dummies.com.

Some of the people who helped bring this book to market include the following:

Acquisitions, Editorial, and Media Development

Project Editor: Pat O'Brien

Acquisitions Editor: Steve Hayes

Copy Editor: Christine Berman

Technical Editor: Michael A. Gibson, MCP

Editorial Managers: Kyle Looper, Constance Carlisle

Media Development Manager: Laura Carpenter VanWinkle

Media Development Supervisor: Richard Graves

Editorial Assistant: Amanda Foxworth, Jean Rogers

Production

Project Coordinator: Nancee Reeves

Layout and Graphics: Amy Adrian, Brian Drumm, John Greenough, Jackie Nicholas, Jill Piscitelli, Brian Torwelle, Jeremey Unger

Proofreaders: John Greenough, Andy Hollandbeck, Susan Moritz, Nancy Price, Angel Perez, TECHBOOKS Production Services

Indexer: TECHBOOKS Production Services

General and Administrative

Hungry Minds Technology Publishing Group: Richard Swadley, Vice President and Executive Group Publisher; Bob Ipsen, Vice President and Group Publisher; Joseph Wikert, Vice President and Publisher; Barry Pruett, Vice President and Publisher; Mary Bednarek, Editorial Director; Mary C. Corder, Editorial Director; Andy Cummings, Editorial Director

Hungry Minds Manufacturing: Ivor Parker, Vice President, Manufacturing

Hungry Minds Marketing: John Helmus, Assistant Vice President, Director of Marketing

Hungry Minds Production for Branded Press: Debbie Stailey, Production Director

Hungry Minds Sales: Michael Violano, Vice President, International Sales and Sub Rights

Contents at a Glance

Introduction 1

Part I: Which Came First: The Data or the Base? 7
Chapter 1: The 37-Minute Overview 9
Chapter 2: Finding Your Way around like a Native 23
Chapter 3: Calling the Online Saint Bernard and Other Forms of Help 33

Part II: Truly Tempting Tables 43
Chapter 4: Designing and Building a Home for Your Data 45
Chapter 5: Relationships, Keys, and Indexes (And Why You Really Do Care) 69
Chapter 6: New Data, Old Data, and Data in Need of Repair 79
Chapter 7: Making Your Table Think with Formats, Masks, and Validations 89
Chapter 8: Making Your Datasheets Dance 103
Chapter 9: Table Remodeling Tips for the Do-It-Yourselfer 117

Part III: Finding the Ultimate Answer to Everything (Well, Not Everything) 125
Chapter 10: Quick Searches: Find, Filter, and Sort 127
Chapter 11: Pose a Simple Query, Get 10,000 Answers 139
Chapter 12: Searching a Slew of Tables 153
Chapter 13: The Ands and Ors of Dr. Boole 163
Chapter 14: Teaching Queries to Think and Count 171
Chapter 15: Calculating Your Way to Fame and Fortune 179
Chapter 16: Automated Editing for Big Changes 191

Part IV: Turning Your Table into a Book 201
Chapter 17: AutoReport: Like the Model-T, It's Clunky but It Runs 203
Chapter 18: Wizardly Help with Labels, Charts, and Multilevel Reports 215
Chapter 19: It's Amazing What a Little Formatting Can Do 229
Chapter 20: Headers and Footers for Groups, Pages, and Even (Egad) Whole Reports 247

Part V: Wizards, Forms, and Other Mystical Stuff 263

Chapter 21: Spinning Your Data into (And onto) the Web 265

Chapter 22: Making Forms That Look Cool and Work Great 277

Chapter 23: If Love Is Universal, Why Can't I Export to It? 289

Chapter 24: The Analyzer: Your Data's Dr. Freud, Dr. Watson, and Dr. Jekyll 297

Chapter 25: Talking to Your Computer 305

Part VI: The Part of Tens 315

Chapter 26: Ten Timesaving Keyboard Shortcuts 317

Chapter 27: Ten Common Crises and How to Survive Them 321

Chapter 28: Ten Tips from the Database Nerds..................................327

Index 331

Cartoons at a Glance

By Rich Tennant

page 201

page 43

"Our classroom PCs have created a challenging atmosphere where critical analyzing, synthesizing, and problem solving skills are honed. I think the students have gotten a lot out of them too."

page 7

"This isn't a quantitative or a qualitative estimate of the job. This is a wish-upon-a-star estimate of the project."

page 315

"I've been in hardware all of my life, and all of a sudden it's software that'll make me rich."

page 125

"You ever get the feeling this project could just up and die at any moment?"

page 263

Cartoon Information:
Fax: 978-546-7747
E-Mail: richtennant@the5thwave.com
World Wide Web: www.the5thwave.com

Table of Contents

Introduction 1

You Don't Need to Be a Nerd to Use This Book 1
Sneaking a Peek at What's to Come 2
    Part I: Which Came First: The Data or the Base? 2
    Part II: Truly Tempting Tables 2
    Part III: Finding the Ultimate Answer to Everything
       (Well, Not Everything) 2
    Part IV: Turning Your Table into a Book 2
    Part V: Wizards, Forms, and Other Mystical Stuff 3
    Part VI: The Part of Tens 3
What the Funny Text Means 3
Finding Points of Interest 4
Setting Sail on the Voyage 5

Part 1: Which Came First: The Data or the Base? 7

Chapter 1: The 37-Minute Overview 9

In the Beginning, There Was Access 2002 (But It Wasn't Running) 9
Opening an Existing Database 11
Touring the Database Window 13
Finding Candy amongst the Grass Clippings 15
Making a Few Changes 17
Reporting the Results 18
Saving Your Hard Work 19
The Great Backup Lecture 20
Making a Graceful Exit 21

Chapter 2: Finding Your Way around like a Native 23

Making Sense of the Sights 24
Windows Shopping for Fun and Understanding 25
    The database window 26
    The datasheet window 27
    The form window 28
    The query window 29
Belly Up to the Toolbar, Folks! 30
Menus, Menus Everywhere (And Keystrokes That Work as Well) 31
Playing with the Other Mouse Button 32

Chapter 3: Calling the Online Saint Bernard and Other Forms of Help 33

Pressing F1 for Assistance 33
    Combing the contents 36
    Asking the Answer Wizard 37
    Inspecting the index 38
The Whatzis Menu Option 39
Your Modem Knows More Than You May Think 39
Talking to a Human 41

Part II: Truly Tempting Tables 43

Chapter 4: Designing and Building a Home for Your Data 45

Database Terms to Know and Tolerate 46
    Data (your stuff) 46
    Fields (the rooms for your stuff) 47
    Records (the rooms in one house) 47
    Table (the houses of a neighborhood) 47
    Database (a community of neighborhoods) 48
Frolicking through the Fields 48
A Smattering of Fields to Get You Started 50
Flat Files versus Relational Databases: Let the Contest Begin! 52
    Flat files: Simple answers for simple needs 52
    Relational databases: Complex solutions to bigger problems 53
    Figuring out what all this means 54
Great Tables Start with Great Designs 55
Building a Database 56
Creating Tables at the Wave of a Wand 61
Building Tables by Hand, Just like in the Old Days 65

Chapter 5: Relationships, Keys, and Indexes (And Why You Really Do Care) 69

The Joy (And Necessity) of a Primary Key 70
Divulging the Secrets of a Good Relationship 72
Linking Your Tables with the Relationship Builder Thingy 74
Indexing Your Way to Fame, Fortune, and Significantly
    Faster Queries 77

Chapter 6: New Data, Old Data, and Data in Need of Repair 79

Dragging Your Table into the Digital Workshop 79
Adding Something to the Mix 82
Changing What's Already in a Record 85
Kicking Out Unwanted Records 86
Recovering from a Baaaad Edit 87

Chapter 7: Making Your Table Think with Formats, Masks, and Validations 89

Finding the Place to Make a Change 89
To Format, Perchance to Better See 91
    Text and memo fields 92
    Number and currency fields 92
    Date/time fields 94
    Yes/No fields 95
What Is That Masked Data? 96
    Using the Input Mask Wizard 97
    Making a mask by hand 98
Validations: The Digital Breathalyzer Test 101

Chapter 8: Making Your Datasheets Dance 103

Wandering Here, There, and Everywhere 103
Seeing More (Or Less) of Your Data 105
    Changing the column width 106
    Changing the row height 108
    Reorganizing the columns 109
    Hiding a column 110
    Freezing a column 112
Fonting around with Your Table 114
Giving Your Data the 3-D Look 114

Chapter 9: Table Remodeling Tips for the Do-It-Yourselfer 117

This Chapter Can Be Hazardous to Your Table's Design 118
Putting a New Field Next to the Piano 118
Saying Good-bye to a Field (And All Its Data) 121
A Field by Any Other Name Still Holds the Same Stuff 122
    Changing a field name in Design view 122
    Changing a field name in Datasheet view 123

Part III: Finding the Ultimate Answer to Everything (Well, Not Everything) 125

Chapter 10: Quick Searches: Find, Filter, and Sort 127

Finding Stuff in Your Tables 128
    Finding first things first (and next things after that) 128
    Tuning a search for speed and accuracy 129
Sorting Out Life on the Planet 131
Filtering Records with Something in Common 132
    Filter For 133
    Filter by Selection 133
    Filter by Form 134
    Removing your mistakes (or when good criteria go bad) 137
    Filter by exclusion 137

Chapter 11: Pose a Simple Query, Get 10,000 Answers 139

Database Interrogation for Fun and Profit 140
On Your Way with a Simple Query — Advanced Filter/Sort 140
    Peering into the Filter window 142
    Building a simple query — er, filter 142
Plagued by Tough Questions? Try an Industrial Strength Query! 145
Build a Better Query and the Answers Beat a Path to Your Monitor ...146
Toto, Can the Wizard Help? 149

Chapter 12: Searching a Slew of Tables 153

Some General Thoughts about Multiple-Table Queries 153
Calling on the Query Wizard 155
Rolling Up Your Sleeves and Building the Query by Hand 158

Chapter 13: The Ands and Ors of Dr. Boole 163

Comparing AND to OR 163
Finding Things between Kansas AND Oz 164
Multiple ANDs: AND Then What Happened? 166
Are You a Good Witch OR a Bad Witch? 167
AND and OR? AND or OR? 168

Chapter 14: Teaching Queries to Think and Count 171

Totaling Everything in Sight 171
Counting the Good Count 173
Counting with Crosstab 175
There's More to Life Than Sum and Count 176

Chapter 15: Calculating Your Way to Fame and Fortune 179

A Simple Calculation 180
Bigger, Better (And More Complicated) Calculations 184
    Add another calculation — go ahead, add two! 184
    Using one expression to solve a different question 184
    Making Access 2002 ask 185
    Working with words 186
Expression Builder to the Rescue 188

Chapter 16: Automated Editing for Big Changes 191

First, This Word from Our Paranoid Sponsor 191
Quick and Easy Fixes: Replacing Your Mistakes 192
Different Queries for Different Jobs 194
You're Outta Here: The Delete Query 195
Making Big Changes 197

Part IV: Turning Your Table into a Book 201

Chapter 17: AutoReport: Like the Model-T, It's Clunky but It Runs 203

AutoReport Basics for High-Speed Information 204
Putting the Wheels of Informational Progress into Motion 204
Previewing Your Informational Masterpiece 206
    Zooming around your report 207
    Calling on the pop-up menu 208
Truth Is Beauty, So Make Your Reports Look Great 209
    The Margins tab 210
    The Page tab 210
    The Columns tab 212

Chapter 18: Wizardly Help with Labels, Charts, and Multilevel Reports 215

Creating Labels 215
Using the Chart Wizard in Your Report 220
Creating More Advanced Reports 222
    Starting the wizard and picking some fields 223
    Creating new groupings 225
    Sorting out the details 226
    Picking a layout style 227

Chapter 19: It's Amazing What a Little Formatting Can Do 229

Taking Your Report to the Design View Tune-Up Shop 230
Striking Up the Bands (And the Markers, Too) 230
Formatting This, That, These, and Those 233
    Colorizing your report 234
    Moving elements around 235
    Bordering on beautiful 237
    Tweaking your text 239
Taking a Peek at Your Report 240
AutoFormatting Your Way to a Beautiful Report 242
Lining Up Everything 243
Drawing Your Own Lines 244
Inserting Page Breaks 244
Sprucing Up the Place with a Few Pictures 245
Passing Your Reports around the (Microsoft) Office 246

Chapter 20: Headers and Footers for Groups, Pages, and Even (Egad) Whole Reports 247

Everything in Its Place 247
Grouping your records 251
Changing a section's size 254
Fine-Tuning the Layout 254
Dressing up your report as a whole 254
Formatting individual sections
of your report 256
Taking it one item at a time 257
Filling in Those Sections 258
At the head of the class 258
Expressing yourself in footers 259
These feet were made for summing 259
Page numbers and dates 261

Part V: Wizards, Forms, and Other Mystical Stuff 263

Chapter 21: Spinning Your Data into (And onto) the Web 265

Access 2002 and the Internet: A Match Made in Redmond 265
Can't Hyperlinks Take Something to Calm Down? 266
Adding a hyperlink field to your table 267
Typing and using hyperlinks 268
Pushing Your Data onto the Web 270
Advanced Topics for Your Copious Nerd Time 274

Chapter 22: Making Forms That Look Cool and Work Great 277

Tax Forms and Data Forms Are Very Different Animals 277
Creating a Form at the Wave of a Wand 279
Giving the Form Just the Right Look 282
Mass Production at Its Best: Forms from the Auto Factory 284
Ultimate Beauty through Cosmetic Surgery 285
Taking a form into Design view 285
Moving fields 286
Adding lines and boxes 286
Changing the field tab order 287

Chapter 23: If Love Is Universal, Why Can't I Export to It? 289

Importing Only the Best Information for Your Databases 290
Translating file formats 290
Importing or linking your files 292
Sending Your Data on a Long, One-Way Trip 293

Chapter 24: The Analyzer: Your Data's Dr. Freud, Dr. Watson, and Dr. Jekyll **297**

It Slices, It Dices, It Builds Relational Databases! 297

Documentation: What to Give the Nerd in Your Life 301

Performance: Toward a Better Database 302

Chapter 25: Talking to Your Computer **305**

What Is Speech Recognition (And What Can I Do with It)? 305

Installing Speech Recognition 306

Sending Access to Voice Training School 307

Speaking to Access 309

"Access, take a letter please" 309

Correcting dictation errors 311

Using Command mode 312

Improving Speech Recognition 314

Part VI: The Part of Tens *315*

Chapter 26: Ten Timesaving Keyboard Shortcuts **317**

Chapter 27: Ten Common Crises and How to Survive Them **321**

Chapter 28: Ten Tips from the Database Nerds **327**

Index *331*

Introduction

Being a normal human being, you probably have work to do. In fact, you may have *lots* of work piled precariously around your office or even stretching onto the Internet. Someone, possibly your boss (or, if you work at home, your Significant Other), suggested that Access 2002 may help you get more done in less time, eliminate the piles, and generally make the safety inspector happy.

So you picked up Access 2002, and here you are. Whee!

If you're confused instead of organized, befuddled instead of productive, or just completely lost on the whole database thing, *Access 2002 For Dummies* is the book for you.

This is a book with a purpose: to explain Access 2002 without turning you into a world class nerd in the process. What more could you want?

You Don't Need to Be a Nerd to Use This Book

Becoming a nerd is totally out of the question. In fact, you need to know only a few things about your computer and Windows to get the most out of *Access 2002 For Dummies.* In the following pages, I presume that you

- Have Microsoft Windows 98, 98 SE, ME, 2000, or NT 4, and Access 2002 for Windows on your computer (if you have the whole Office 2002 suite, that's fine, too). If you're still using Windows 95, I recommend that you upgrade.
- Know the basics of whichever flavor of Windows you're using
- Want to work with databases that other people have created
- Want to use and create queries, reports, and an occasional form
- Want to make your own databases from scratch every now and then

The good news is that you don't have to know (or even care) about table design, field types, relational databases, or any of that other database stuff to make Access 2002 work for you. Everything you need to know is right here, just waiting for you to read it.

Sneaking a Peek at What's to Come

To give you an idea of what's ahead, here's a breakdown of the six parts in this book. Each part covers a general topic of Access 2002. The part's individual chapters dig into the details.

Part I: Which Came First: The Data or the Base?

Right off the bat, this book answers the lyrical question "It's a data-*what?*" By starting with an overview of both database concepts in general and Access 2002 in particular, this book provides the information you need to make sense of the whole database concept. This part also contains suggestions about solving problems with (or even *without*) Access 2002. If you're about to design a new Access database to fix some pesky problem, read this section first — it may change your mind.

Part II: Truly Tempting Tables

Arguably, tables (where the data lives) are at the center of this whole database hubbub. After all, without tables, you wouldn't have any data to bully around. This part gives you the information you need to know about designing, building, using, changing, and generally coexisting in the same room with Access 2002 tables.

Part III: Finding the Ultimate Answer to Everything (Well, Not Everything)

If tables are at the center of the Access universe, then queries are the first ring of planets. In Access, queries ask the power questions; they unearth the answers you *know* are hiding somewhere in your data. In addition to covering queries, this part also explains how to answer smaller questions using Find, Filter, and Sort — Query's little siblings.

Part IV: Turning Your Table into a Book

Seeing your data on-screen just isn't enough, sometimes. To make your work *really* shine, you have to commit it to paper. Part IV covers the Access report system, a portion of the software entirely dedicated both to getting your information onto the printed page and to driving you nuts in the process.

Part V: Wizards, Forms, and Other Mystical Stuff

At some point, technology approaches magic (one look at the control panel for a modern microwave oven is proof of that). This part explores some of the mystical areas in Access, helping you do stuff faster, seek assistance from the wizards, get your computer to do what you want just by talking to it, and even venture into a bit of programming. If the Internet's limitless possibilities pique your online fancy, look in this part for info about the new Web connectivity features in Access 2002. They're really amazing!

Part VI: The Part of Tens

The words *For Dummies book* immediately bring to mind the snappy, irreverent Part of Tens. This section dumps a load of tips and cool ideas onto, and hopefully *into,* your head. You can find a little bit of everything here, including timesaving tips and the solutions to the most common problems awaiting you in Access 2002.

What the Funny Text Means

Every now and then, you need to tell Access to do something or other. Likewise, there are moments when the program wants to toss its own comments and messages back to you (so be nice — communication is a two-way street). To easily show the difference between a human-to-computer message and vice-versa, I format the commands differently.

Here are examples of both kinds of messages as they appear in the book.

This is something you type into the computer.

```
This is how the computer responds to your command.
```

Because this *is* a Windows program, you don't just type all day — you also mouse around quite a bit. Although I don't use a cool font for mouse actions, I *do* assume that you already know the basics. Here are the mouse movements necessary to make Access 2002 (and any other Windows program) work:

- ✔ **Click:** Position the tip of the mouse pointer (the end of the arrow) on the menu item, button, check box, or whatever else you happen to be aiming at, and then quickly press and release the left mouse button.

- ✔ **Double-click:** Position the mouse pointer as though you're going to click, but fool it at the last minute by clicking twice in rapid succession.

- ✔ **Click and drag *(highlight)*:** Put the tip of the mouse pointer at the place you want to start highlighting and then press and hold the left mouse button. While holding down the mouse button, drag the pointer across whatever you want to highlight. When you reach the end of what you're highlighting, release the mouse button.

- ✔ **Right-click:** Right-clicking works just like clicking, except that you're exercising the right instead of the left mouse button.

Of course, the Access 2002 menu comes in handy, too. When I want you to pick something from the main menu bar, the instruction looks like this:

Choose File⇨Open Database.

If you think that mice belong in holes, you can use the underlined letters as shortcut keys to control Access 2002 from the keyboard. To use the keyboard shortcut, hold down the Alt key and press the underlined letters. In the example above, the keyboard shortcut is Alt+F, O. Don't type the comma — it's just trying to make the command easier to read.

If you aren't familiar with all these rodent gymnastics, or if you want to learn more about Windows in general, pick up a copy of one of the many *Windows For Dummies* titles. Every version of Windows has one!

Finding Points of Interest

When something in this book is particularly valuable, I go out of my way to make sure that it stands out. I use these cool icons to mark text that (for one reason or another) *really* needs your attention. Here's a quick preview of the ones waiting for you in this book and what they mean:

Tips are *really* helpful words of wisdom that promise to save you time, energy, and perhaps some hair. Whenever you see a tip, take a second to check it out.

Some things are too important to forget, so the Remember icon points them out. These items are critical steps in a process — points that you don't want to miss.

Sometimes, I give in to my dark, nerdy side and slip some technical twaddle into the book. The Technical Stuff icon protects you from obscure details by making them easy to avoid. If you're in an adventuresome mood, check out the technical stuff. You may find it interesting.

The Warning icon says it all: *Skipping this information may be hazardous to your data's health.* Pay attention to these icons and follow their instructions to keep your databases happy and intact.

Setting Sail on the Voyage

Now nothing's left to hold you back from the wonders of Access 2002. Cleave tightly to *Access 2002 For Dummies* and dive into Access 2002.

- ✔ If you're brand new to the program and don't know which way to turn, start with the general overview in Chapter 1.
- ✔ If you're about to design a database, I salute you — and recommend flipping through Chapter 4 for some helpful design and development tips.
- ✔ Looking for something specific? Try the Table of Contents or the Index, or just flip through the book until you find something interesting.

Bon Voyage!

Part I
Which Came First: The Data or the Base?

The 5th Wave   By Rich Tennant

©RICHTENNANT

"Our classroom PCs have created a challenging atmosphere where critical analyzing, synthesizing, and problem solving skills are honed. I think the students have gotten a lot out of them too."

In this part . . .

*E*verything starts somewhere. It's that way with nature, with science, and with meatballs that roll down your tie. So what more fitting way to begin this book than with a look at where databases start — as a glimmer in someone's mind.

This part opens with a heretical look at problem solving, and then moves along to cover the new Access 2002 program itself. A little later in this part, you discover the secrets of good data organization and where to find help when the world of Access 2002 has you down.

All in all, this part is a pretty good place to start — whether you're new to the whole database concept, or just to Access 2002. Either way, welcome aboard!

Chapter 1

The 37-Minute Overview

In This Chapter

▶ Starting the program

▶ Opening a database that's already there

▶ A good database is more than tables

▶ Finding a record

▶ Changing a record

▶ Printing a report

▶ Saving your changes

▶ Getting out when you're done

*I*t's confession time. This chapter probably takes longer than 37 minutes to finish, if you read it all. Then again, you may spend *less* time than that if you're already somewhat familiar with the program or if you're a speed-reader. Either way, the chapter *does* give you a good overview of Access 2002 from start to finish (and I mean that literally).

Because the best way to get into Access 2002 is to literally *get into* it, this chapter leads you on a wild, galloping tour of the software, covering the highlights of what you and Access 2002 probably do together on a daily basis. This chapter is something of a "Day in the Life" story, designed to show you the important stuff while pointing you to other areas of the book for more information.

If you're new to Access 2002, this chapter is a good place to start. If you're already familiar with the older versions of Access, I recommend that you skim this chapter anyway to see the changes. Enjoy the trip!

In the Beginning, There Was Access 2002 (But It Wasn't Running)

To start Access, click the Start button and select Microsoft Access 2002 from the Start menu (see Figure 1-1). But what if Access hides from you? Look for a program group with a name like Office or Microsoft Office in the Start menu. If you still can't find Access on the Start menu, you have to create your own shortcut (egads!). Follow these steps to create a shortcut:

1. **Click the Start button and choose Find⇨Files or Folders.**

   The Find: All Files dialog box appears.

2. **Type** msaccess.exe **as the file name and click Find Now.**

   Windows finds the program file.

3. **Right-click (hold down the right mouse button) and drag the file from the Find Files result window onto the Start button.**

   The Start menu opens.

4. **Drag the file to Programs and release the mouse button where you want Access to appear (see Figure 1-2).**

   A pop-up menu appears, asking you what you want to do.

5. **Choose Create Shortcut Here.**

   Congratulations. You've just added a shortcut to the Start menu!

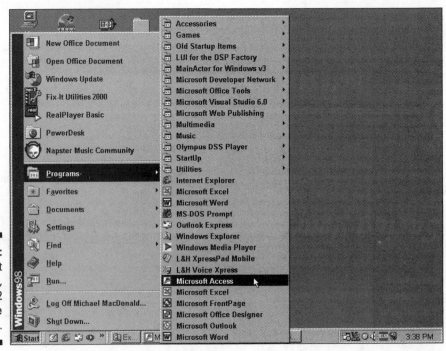

Figure 1-1:
For a smart program, Access 2002 doesn't hide very well.

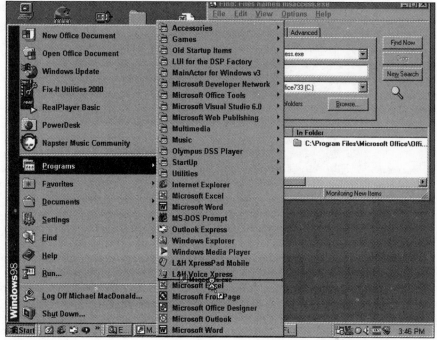

Figure 1-2:
You can
drag the
Access icon
onto the
Start menu
to unhide
the
program.

Opening an Existing Database

Access 2002 without a database file is like a CD player without a CD: Nice to look at, but you can't dance to it.

Database files fall into two distinct categories:

- **Database files that exist:** Odds are good that you're working with an existing database (after all, you build a database once, but use it forever). If so, read on — this section is for you.

- **Database files that don't exist:** If you're bound and determined to create a new database, flip to Chapter 4 for detailed help on design and creation.

If you just started Access 2002, your screen looks like Figure 1-3. By default, Access opens with the Task Pane displayed. The Task Pane sits on your screen, looking quite handsome, waiting for you to open an existing database, create a new one, and so on. Opening an existing database takes only a moment — simply select it from the list under "Open a file."

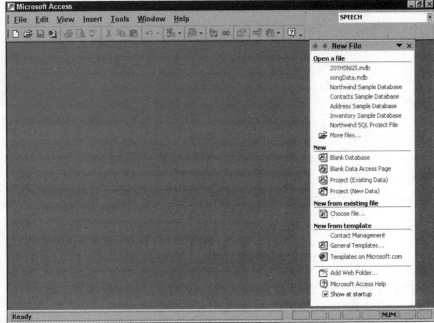

Figure 1-3:
Success at
last —
Access 2002
is running
and
displaying
the Task
Pane.

If you don't see the database you're looking for, follow these steps:

1. Click More Files under "Open a file."

The Open dialog box appears, as shown in Figure 1-4.

2. Double-click the database you're interested in.

The database loads and you're ready to work.

Figure 1-4:
The Open
dialog box,
in all its
glory.

If the database you want isn't listed in the Open dialog box either, the database is probably in some other directory folder. Skip to the sidebar in Chapter 6 for help with tracking down the database in your hard disk or network.

If you have already worked with Access for a while (printing reports, checking out a form or two, and generally keeping yourself busy), and now you want to open another database, follow these steps:

1. **Choose File⇨Open or click the Open button on the toolbar.**

   The Open dialog box (still appearing for your viewing pleasure in Figure 1-4) pops onto the screen.

2. **Double-click the name of the database you want to use.**

   If the database isn't listed, the database is probably in some other directory folder. Skip to the sidebar in Chapter 6 for help with tracking down the database in your hard disk or network.

Touring the Database Window

When a database opens, it usually appears on-screen looking like Figure 1-5. Click one of the buttons on the left side of the window under the Objects bar to display the various parts (Access 2002 calls them *objects*) of your database: Tables, Queries, Forms, and so on. The rest of the window lists whichever objects you select.

The top of the database window tells you the file format. In Figure 1-5, the format is Access 2002. You can use Access 2002 to open prior file versions (such as Access 2000 or Access 97) but you cannot use a prior version of Access to open an Access 2002 file.

Figure 1-5:
The database window gives you access to everything that makes up your, um, database.

After opening the database, you can fiddle with its parts:

- ✔ To open a table, click the Tables button and then double-click the table you want to see.

- ✔ To run a report, query, or form, click the appropriate button and then double-click the item you want to work with.

- ✔ When you get tired of a database, close it by clicking the Close Window button (the X box in the upper-right corner of the window) or by choosing File⇨Close. If you're a keyboard fan, Ctrl+W does the deed without disturbing the mouse.

If you want to know more about working with the cool Access 2002 interface, check out Chapter 2.

If some kind soul invested the time to make your life a little easier, a startup screen (or *switchboard*) resembling Figure 1-6 appears automatically when you open the database. The switchboard is basically a glorified menu of things to do with the database.

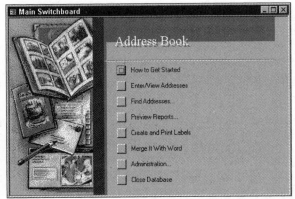

Figure 1-6:
A database
fronted by
a fancy
switchboard
screen.

If your startup screen has options like the ones in Figure 1-6, you're in luck. I *can* help you make sense of this startup screen because it was created using one of the many Database Wizard templates.

Chapter 4 has more information about startup screens.

Finding Candy amongst the Grass Clippings

If you want preschoolers to eat something, just let them take it outside and drop it into the yard first, preferably right after you cut the lawn with a mulching mower. Finding specific records in your Access table is a little like a toddler's method of whittling through sticky grass in search of candy. Whether you're looking for last names, first names, part numbers, or postal codes, Access 2002 makes finding your target records a whole lot easier — and infinitely less messy.

Here's one way to find records:

1. **Open the table you want to search.**

   If you don't know how to open a table, go back to the preceding section.

2. **Click in the field you want to search.**

   The blinking toothpick cursor leaps into the field, showing that Access 2002 really heard you.

 3. **Choose Edit⇨Find or click the Find toolbar button.**

   The Find and Replace dialog box appears (as shown in Figure 1-7).

   Access 2002 displays the name of the current field in the Look In section of the dialog box. To look in a different field, click the down arrow next to the field name, and then pick the field from the drop-down list.

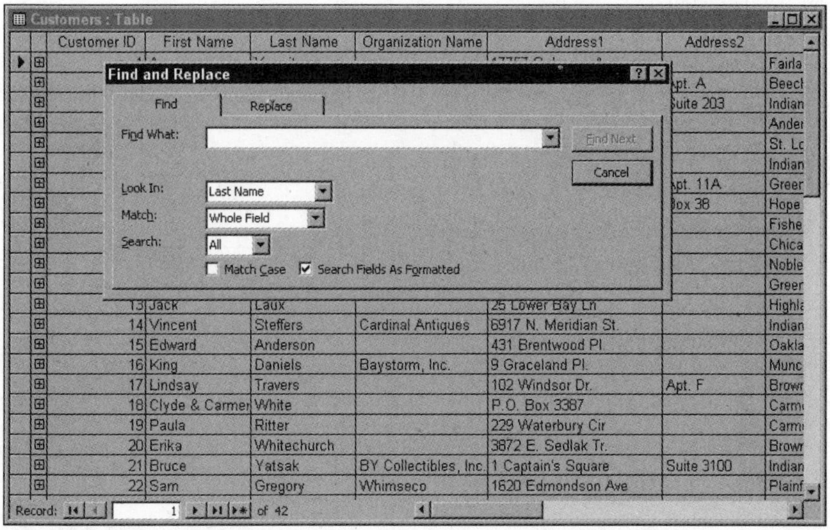

Figure 1-7:
The Find and Replace dialog box, at your service.

4. Type the text you want to find in the appropriately named Fi̲nd What text box.

Spell carefully, because Access 2002 looks for *exactly* what you type!

5. Press Enter or click the Fi̲nd Next button to start the search.

The search begins — and probably ends before you know it.

If the program finds a matching record, Access 2002 highlights the data (as shown in Figure 1-8).

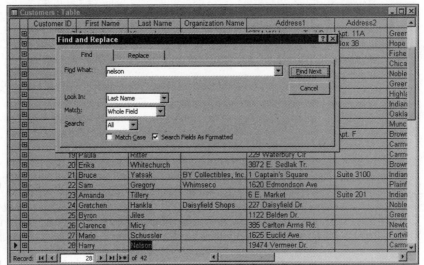

Figure 1-8:
Customer
Nelson is
found!

If no record matches your criteria, a big, officious dialog box informs you that Microsoft Access finished searching the records, but found no matches. (If the Office Assistant is on-screen, then instead of getting whacked by the big dialog box, the Assistant quietly tells you about the search results.) If this message appears, click OK and smile as the dialog box disappears; then double-check what you typed in the Find What text box. You probably just mistyped something. If so, fix it and try the search again.

Access 2002 automatically tries to match a *whole* field in the table with what you typed. So, if you type *Kaufeld* in the Find dialog box, Access 2002 *won't* find a record containing *Kaufeld School of Creative Writing*. Why? Because that entry is not an exact match for *Kaufeld* — it's only a partial match. To make Access 2002 accept partial matches as well as full ones, change the Match setting in the Find and Replace dialog box from Whole Field to Any Part of Field.

If you *still* can't find the record, Chapter 10 provides more details about the Find dialog box.

6. Click Cancel or press Esc to close the Find dialog box when you're done.

The right mouse button also provides some tricky ways to find records, but I'm saving those tricks for Chapter 10.

Making a Few Changes

Unfortunately for fruit growers and dairy farmers, life isn't always peaches and cream. Your customers move, the phone company changes an area code, and the digital gremlins mess up your typing skills. Whatever the cause, your job probably includes fixing the various problems in your database. Lucky you.

Changing the stuff in your tables isn't hard. In fact, making changes is almost too easy. I outline the precise steps in the following list. Keep in mind that your changes are *automatically* saved. When you finish working on a record, Access writes the new information to the database *right then*. If you make a mistake, *immediately* press Ctrl+Z to undo your changes — don't put it off until later.

Here's a quick word from the Society of the Perpetually Nervous: Be *very* careful when changing the records in your database. Making changes is easy; recovering from them can be tough. Access 2002 can help you undo only the *last change you made*.

When you're ready to change a record, follow these steps:

1. View the table on-screen as a data sheet or in a form.

Either way, your data is hanging out on the monitor and looking cool.

2. Click in the field you want to change.

A flashing toothpick cursor appears in the field, and the mouse pointer changes to an I-beam.

3. Perform whatever repairs the field needs.

All the standard editing keys (Home, End, Backspace, and Delete) work when you're changing an entry in Access 2002. See Chapter 6 for the key-by-key details.

4. When the field is *just right,* press Return to save the changes.

As soon as you press Return, the data is saved — and I do mean *saved.* If you immediately decide that you like the old data better, press Ctrl+Z or choose Edit⇨Saved Record.

Reporting the Results

Capturing all those wonderful details in your tables is nice, but what's even *nicer* is seeing those records fill a printed page. That's where the Access 2002 report system comes in.

Making your database look wonderful on paper is a cinch with Access 2002. The program has all kinds of report options, plus a reasonably strong Report Wizard to walk you through the hard stuff. Part IV tells you all you could ever want to know about the really cool report features.

Because printing a report is one of the most common tasks for Access 2002, I describe it here:

1. **In the Database window, click the Reports button, as shown in Figure 1-9.**

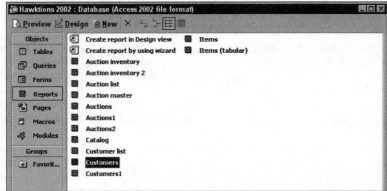

Figure 1-9: Click the Reports button to access all of your reports.

2. **Right-click the report you want to print.**

   A menu pops up wherever your mouse pointer is.

3. **Choose Print from the pop-up menu (see Figure 1-10).**

   Access 2002 puts a little dialog box in the middle of the screen to tell you how the print job is going. When the print job is complete, the dialog box vanishes without a trace.

   If you change your mind while the report is printing, click Cancel in the Print dialog box to stop the process.

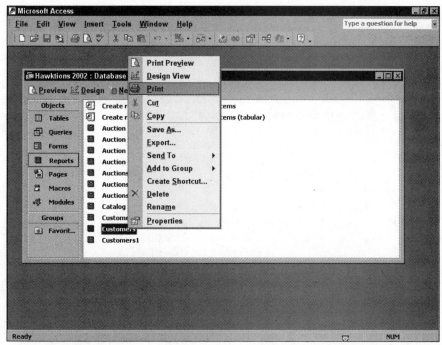

Figure 1-10:
Voila! An instant Print menu.

Saving Your Hard Work

The Access 2002 automatic save feature is good because it's one less detail left lying around to clutter up your life. Whether you entered a bunch of new records or simply fixed a couple that were ever so slightly wrong, your work is automatically safe and sound.

Help is always just a few clicks away

No matter where you are in Access 2002, help is always nearby. Chapter 3 covers all your help options in gory detail, but here's one to get you started.

If you're stumped for what to do next, press the F1 key; this is the Windows universal *help me* key. The F1 key brings up either the ever-helpful Office Assistant or a dialog box that's jam-packed with help topics ranging from an overview of the newest, coolest features of Access 2002 to phenomenally trivial explorations of macros.

Unless you're in the mood to browse, pose your question to the Office Assistant or click the Find tab at the top of the window and search for your topic of interest. Either way, your answer is only a moment away!

On the other hand, the automatic save feature *isn't* so good because Access 2002 doesn't pay any attention to what it's saving — it just saves everything that's there. If you accidentally wipe out 237 records and then make a couple of errant clicks, you can say *good-bye records, hello backups.*

I've said it before, but it bears repeating: When you change the records in your tables, *please* be careful. Messing up a record takes only a second. Don't let this tragedy happen to you.

The Great Backup Lecture

I know you've probably heard this before, but the PC support nerd in me won't let the chapter close without a few words about backing up your databases. Although I joke about it, regular backups are a *vital* part of using Access 2002 (or any program, for that matter).

Why is backing up so important? Take a minute and imagine life without your computer. Don't reminisce about business in the Good Old Days of the 1970s — think about what would happen if you walked in one morning and found *no* computer awaiting your arrival. None. Zippo. The desk is empty — no business letters, no receivables, no customer list, nothing. Everything was on the computer, but now the computer is history.

Unless you want to wave goodbye to your business, you need a formal backup plan. Even if it's just you and your computer, make some notes about how your backup process works:

- ✔ **How often is the computer backed up?** A better question is "How much data can you afford to lose?" If your information changes daily (like an accounting system, for example), you need to make backups every day or two. If you mainly play adventure games on your machine and use Access 2002 as infrequently as possible, back up every week or two. No universal rule is right for everyone.

- ✔ **Where are the backup disks or tapes stored?** If the backups are conveniently stored right next to the computer, they'll be conveniently destroyed along with the computer in the event of a fire. Keep your backups in another building, if possible, or at least in another room.

- ✔ **How do you back up the data?** Write down a step-by-step procedure, along with a method for figuring out what tape or disk set to use in the backup process.

- ✔ **How do you *restore* the data?** Again, create a step-by-step process. Your mind won't be particularly clear if tragedy strikes and you have to restore destroyed data, so make the steps simple and understandable.

After you settle into the backup routine, try restoring your data once to make sure that your system works. You're *much* better off finding out before the disk dies rather than afterward. Set aside a couple hours to ensure that your efforts pay off on that fateful day when the disk drive dies. You'll thank me later.

If you're in a corporate environment, it's possible that your local Department of Computer People automatically backs up your data. To find out for sure, give them a call and ask.

Making a Graceful Exit

When it's time to shut down for the day, do so the right way:

1. **If you have a database open, choose File⇨Close or click the Close Window button in the upper-right corner of the Database window.**

   I'm old-fashioned enough not to trust my program to close everything by itself without screwing something up. Whenever possible, I save and close my work manually before shutting down the program.

2. **Close Access 2002 by choosing File⇨Exit.**

Go ahead and shut down Windows as well if you're done for the night. To do so, click the Start button and then click Shut Down. When Windows asks whether you're serious about this shutdown, click Yes. After Windows does whatever it is that software does just before bedtime, turn off your computer and make your escape to freedom.

Chapter 2

Finding Your Way around like a Native

In This Chapter

▶ What's what with the interface

▶ Looking at the pretty windows

▶ Checking out the toolbars

▶ Ordering from the menu

▶ Performing tricks with the right mouse button

*C*ruising around an unfamiliar city is fun, exciting, and frustrating. Seeing the sights, recognizing famous landmarks, and discovering new places to exercise your credit card make it fun. Finding yourself lost deep within a neighborhood that's "in transition" makes it, uh, exciting. Being unable to find your way back in either case makes it frustrating.

If you're comfortable with earlier versions of Access, then driving your mouse through Access 2002 is much like steering your car through your hometown — 20 years later. The terrain looks somewhat familiar, but you're in for some surprises — "Where'd they move that menu item? It used to be right over, um . . . oh geez, half of the menu is gone — no, wait, it's back. Eeesh . . . I need more coffee."

I know the feeling. Nothing is worse than watching your work pile up while deciphering a new program. This chapter helps you out of that trap by presenting a tour of the sights and sounds of Access 2002. It covers the common features you see and deal with on-screen, from the main window to the toolbar and beyond. Kick back and enjoy the jaunt — it's a great way to get comfortable with Access 2002.

Making Sense of the Sights

Because Access 2002 is, after all, a Windows program, the first stop on this merry visual trip is the program's main window. Figure 2-1 shows Access 2002 in a common pose, displaying a database window (which I cover later in this chapter).

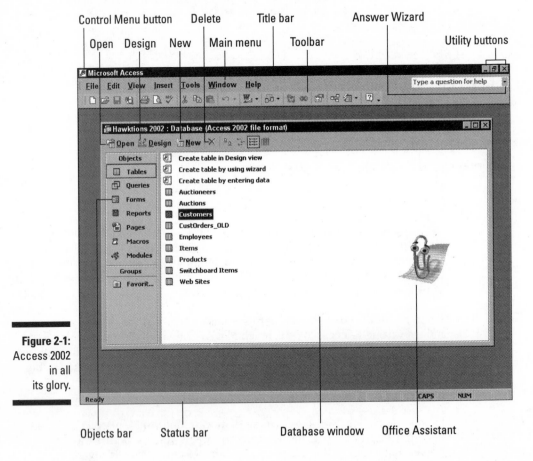

Figure 2-1: Access 2002 in all its glory.

To make the most of Access 2002, you need to be familiar with nine parts of the main window. I describe each part briefly in the paragraphs that follow. If you're *really* new to Windows, consider picking up a copy of *Windows 2000 For Dummies* (or *Windows Me For Dummies* or *Windows 98 For Dummies . . .* well, you get the picture) by Andy Rathbone (published by IDG Books Worldwide, Inc.).

✔ **Control Menu button:** Click the icon (the Access "key") in the upper-left corner to open the Control Menu. Double-click the icon to close Access 2002.

✔ **Title bar:** Every window comes complete with a space along the top for the title. This space has a second purpose, too: It changes color to let you know which program is currently active in Windows. Double-clicking the title bar alternately maximizes and restores Access 2002.

✔ **Main menu:** Between the title bar and the toolbar sits the Main menu. Aside from preventing fights between the two bars, this menu is also your main stopping point for Access 2002 commands and functions.

✔ **Toolbar:** Think of the toolbar as an electronic version of Lon Chaney, the Man of a Thousand Faces. Just about every time you do something in Access 2002, this bar does a quick change to serve up the tools you need. I tell you more about this slippery character later in this chapter.

✔ **Utility buttons:** These three buttons appear on every window. From left to right, these buttons

 • Reduce the current program to a button on the Taskbar

 • Make the current program either fit in a window or take up the whole screen (one button, two tasks)

 • Close the current window

✔ **Status bar:** Access 2002 is a talkative system, with words of wisdom to share about every little feature. Whenever Access wants to tell you something, a message appears on the Status bar. On the far right of the Status bar are indicators for keyboard settings such as Caps Lock.

✔ **Database window:** In the midst of this maelstrom sits a serene database window, explained in the next section.

✔ **Taskbar:** Across the bottom of the screen is the Windows taskbar, Microsoft's quick-and-easy tool for switching among programs. Each running program has a button on this bar. To use another program, just click its button.

✔ **Office Assistant:** This annoying little fellow shows up in all Office 2002 products, including Access 2002. When you have a question or want some help, give him a click and ask away. (And when you're bored, right-click it and select Animate for some brief entertainment.)

Windows Shopping for Fun and Understanding

There's more to Access 2002 than the big picture window. The program is chock-full of little windows for every need and occasion. This section looks at four of the most common windows.

To see how these windows work, what to do with them, and why you should even care, keep trekking through this book. Databases and datasheets appear in Part II, queries star in Part III, and forms have a supporting role in Part V.

The database window

Most of the time when you open a database, it appears in a window like Figure 2-2. This window gives you access to all the stuff in your database, provides tools to change displays or create new items, and generally helps you manage your database stuff. And it looks cool. Who can ask for more?

Figure 2-2: Well, this is another fine database that I've gotten myself into.

The Objects bar buttons down the left side of the window switch between lists of the *objects* (tables, queries, reports, and so on) that make up the database. Four toolbar buttons sit at the top of the database window to help you work with the database's objects:

- ✔ Open displays the current object
- ✔ Design lets you change the object
- ✔ New creates a new object
- ✔ The X deletes the current object (kiss that table good-bye!)

The other buttons to the right of the X change how Access 2002 lists the objects that your database contains. Your choices run the gamut from colorful, friendly icons to detailed mini-dossiers. Feel free to try the settings yourself — you can't hurt anything! (Just don't accidentally click the X, okay?)

Your database *may* start up looking like Figure 2-3. Don't let the pretty face fool you, though — this window is just a fancier front hung onto Figure 2-2's database. Seeing something like this window is a clue that you're working with a formal Access 2002 application. Most likely, the form was created by one of your in-house nerds. This special form is called a *switchboard*.

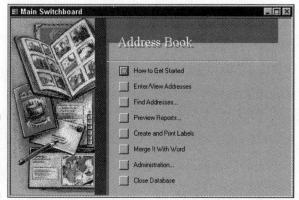

Figure 2-3:
An example
of a
switchboard.

The datasheet window

Is it a table or a spreadsheet? Only its owner knows for sure! Looking at Figure 2-4, it's easy to see why you may confuse the two. It's a table, but it looks like a spreadsheet. In datasheet view, an Access 2002 table appears (and arguably acts) like a simple spreadsheet. The resemblance is only skin-deep, though. This table is really a very different animal.

The datasheet window shows the table name across its top, just as it should. Below that, the table's *fields* are arrayed across the window. The table's *records* are laid out in rows. Don't worry if you're not exactly sure about the difference between a record and a field. Chapter 4 has all the details about that.

On the right side and lower-right corner are a pair of *scroll bars* which make moving through the table a real breeze. The *navigation buttons* hang out in the window's lower-left side. These buttons are a lot like the controls on a compact disc player or VCR. The buttons that have arrows pointing to a bar take you to the first or last record of the table. The arrow-only buttons move you to the next or preceding record. Clicking on the arrow and asterisk button adds a new record to the table.

Sometimes you see a little plus sign to the left of each record; the plus sign indicates a relationship between this table and some other table(s). (Not to worry, I show you how to create and use relationships between tables in Chapters 4 and 5.) When you click the plus sign next to a particular record, Access 2002 displays the related data. For example, Figure 2-5 displays all the items that Kevin Davis ordered.

Current record indicator   Table name   Fields

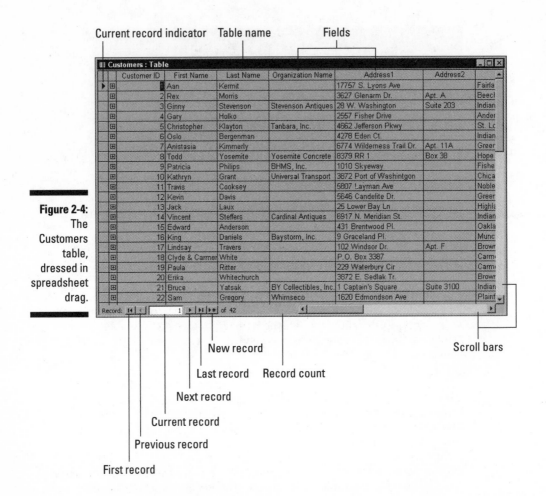

Figure 2-4:
The
Customers
table,
dressed in
spreadsheet
drag.

New record

Last record   Record count

Next record

Current record

Previous record

First record

Scroll bars

The form window

Form view is the other popular way to look at Access 2002 tables. With forms, the data looks more, well, traditional — none of that sissy spreadsheet-style stuff. A form usually shows the data in a table at the blinding rate of one record per screen, the same way that the nerds of the 1970s worked with their data, using million-dollar computers that had all the intelligence of today's microwave ovens.

Figure 2-6 is a very simple but classic example of an Access 2002 form. Along the top is the ever-anticipated title bar. The table's fields take up the middle of the form. In the lower-left corner are the same navigation buttons you saw and fiddled with in the datasheet window.

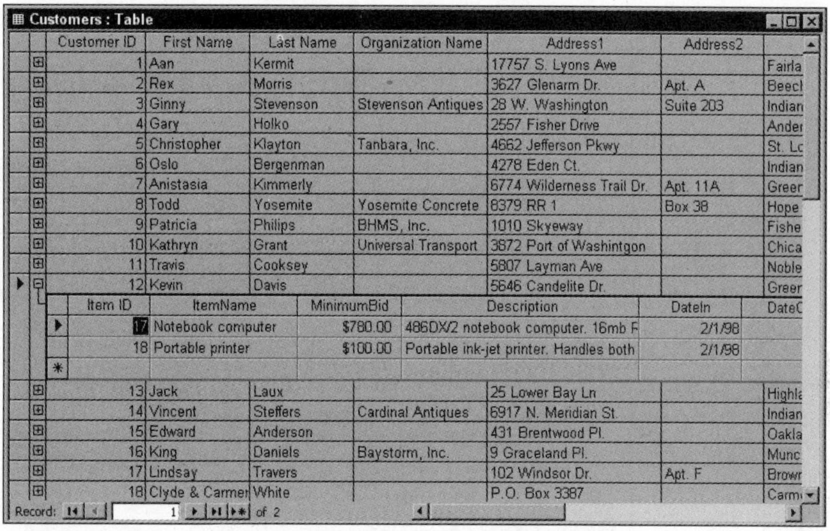

Figure 2-5:
Click the
plus sign
next to a
record to
"drill down"
to related
information.
Kevin sure
is a good
customer!

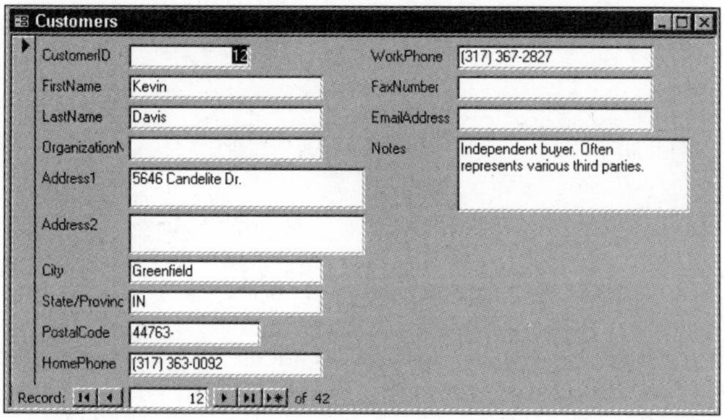

Figure 2-6:
There's
Kevin
again —
what a ham!

I show you how to create your very own forms in Chapter 22.

The query window

The heart of any database program is its capability of searching for information. In particular, the heart of Access 2002 is the query system. And sitting at the heart of the query system is the *query window,* lovingly reproduced in Figure 2-7. Here are the key pieces of the query window:

- ✔ The title bar displays the query's given name at the top of the window.

- ✔ *Tables* involved in the query appear in the window's upper half.

    If the query uses more than one table, this section also shows how t' tables are linked together (or *joined*).

✔ *Query criteria* — the instructions that make the query work — appear in the lower half of the window.

✔ Several *scroll bars* adjust panels to help you see everything clearly.

Tables in query

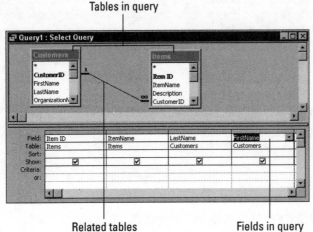

Figure 2-7:
The key
elements of
the query
window.

Related tables   Fields in query

When you run a query, Access 2002 usually displays the results in a datasheet.

Belly Up to the Toolbar, Folks!

Toolbars are the Office 2002 equivalent of sliced bread — they're *that* useful. Access 2002 has a bunch of them, too. You can't find yourself without a toolbar around to help.

So what *is* a toolbar? It's that row of cool buttons just below the menu at the top of the screen. Figure 2-8 shows the Database toolbar in action (as much action as any inanimate object ever shows).

The toolbars give you single-click access to the best features of Access 2002. The engineers designed the toolbars to contain the most common functions you need when working with your data. The Datasheet toolbar, for example, includes three buttons that control the Filter tools (tools that help you quickly find information in your database). Instead of working your way through a menu to find these Filter tools, they're out in the open, just a mouse click away.

Because a toolbar exists for literally every occasion, I describe the toolbars throughout the book. Don't worry if you can't remember what all the buttons do — neither can I. If you're button-challenged, just pause the mouse pointer over a button. After a moment, the button gets tired of that heavy pointer and, hoping that you'll go away, displays a *screen* tip — a small box with some text that describes the purpose of the button.

If you've waited a decent amount of time (like two seconds) and no quick help pops up, it has probably been turned off. Right-click on the toolbar and choose Customize. On the Options tab, make sure that "Show ScreenTips on Toolbars" is checked. While you're on the Options tab, check or uncheck the "Large Icons" check box to make the buttons large or small.

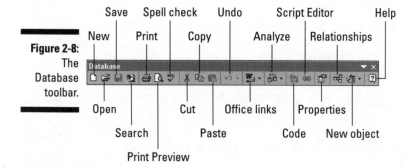

Figure 2-8:
The Database toolbar.

Menus, Menus Everywhere (And Keystrokes That Work as Well)

Truth be told, there isn't a lot to say about the Access 2002 menus. The main difference that you're sure to notice is that they change every time you do something new. Gone are the days of *one program, one menu*. Now you have *context-sensitive* menus that show different options depending on what you're doing at the moment.

Some features never change, though. Here's a brief rundown of generic menu truisms:

✔ If your mouse dies, you can get to the menu items from the keyboard. Just hold down the Alt key and press the underlined letter of the menu item you want.

For example, press Alt+F to open the File menu.

✔ Some menu items have a specific key assigned to them. The Copy command (Edit⇨Copy on the menu) also works without the menu by pressing Ctrl+C.

If an item has a keyboard equivalent, Access lists that key combination right next to the item in the pull-down menu.

Playing with the Other Mouse Button

Your mother probably told you to never play with your right mouse button. Well, she was wrong. Windows 95 introduced us to the raison d'etre for the right-mouse button: to display a pop-up or context menu of things you can do with or to the item you just clicked. In Figure 2-9, I right-click the Customers table. Access 2002 responds by offering a list of common processes for tables. Instead of working through the main menu to copy the current table, for instance, I can right-click and select Copy from the pop-up menu. Talk about a time-saver!

No matter what Windows application you work with, experiment with the right mouse button. If in doubt, right-click. Try right-clicking on everything in sight — see what happens.

Figure 2-9:
Too cool —
an instant
menu! In
this case,
I'm copying
a whole
table.

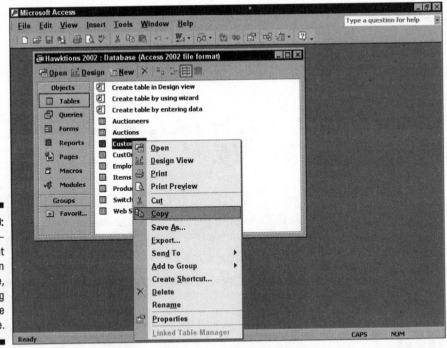

Chapter 3

Calling the Online Saint Bernard and Other Forms of Help

In This Chapter

▶ Introducing the Office Assistant

▶ Checking the Contents, Answer, and Index tabs

▶ Using the Whatzis menu option

▶ Modeming for help

▶ Querying humans

Getting in over your head is easy sometimes. For example, mountains are *much* taller after you start climbing them than they were when you looked up from the ground. Plus, your equipment *never* seems to fail when you're packing it. Instead, your trusty gear waits until you're in the middle of nowhere, dangling precariously from the crumbling edge of a craggy peak. Then and only then does your gear remember its mortal fear of heights and have heart failure.

That's what Saint Bernards are for. When you're lost in the alpine wilderness — cold, wet, and alone — it's reassuring to know that a Saint Bernard will be along soon. I'm a little unclear about precisely what the dog *does* when it finds you; but at that point, I'd probably settle for the companionship. Access 2002 has its own built-in Saint Bernard, although on-screen it looks more like a few dialog boxes than a husky canine. This chapter explores several different ways to find answers to your Access 2002 questions. Knowing where to look for information is as important as knowing the information itself, so browse through this chapter and discover your options.

Pressing F1 for Assistance

No matter where you are in Access 2002, help is available at the touch of a key. Just press F1, and the perky Office Assistant leaps into action (Figure 3-1). The Assistant shows up in all the Office 2002 applications. The Assistant replaces the old Answer Wizard and simplifies the help process even more. The Office Assistant even tosses in some entertaining animated moments at no extra charge.

When you call up the Assistant, it tries to figure out what you're trying to accomplish in Access 2002 and suggests ten Help topics that it thinks are relevant. If one of these topics hits the spot (which happens most of the time), click the button next to the topic and the Assistant presents the information to you.

Figure 3-1:
The Office
Assistant
reports for
duty (but
don't ask it
for coffee).

The Assistant is a good guesser but doesn't always come up with the right topics. For moments like that, the Assistant includes a do-it-yourself question box along the bottom of the window. Here's a step-by-step layout of how to use this marvel of modern technology to ask the Assistant a detailed question:

1. **Click the Office Assistant window or press F1.**

   The Assistant's dialog box pops up.

2. **Type your question in plain language in the box at the bottom of the window.**

   You read it right — in *plain language.* Can you believe it? A program that actually *understands* you. Who knows where this dangerous trend may lead? In Figure 3-2, I ask the assistant to tell me how to edit data.

3. **Click Search or press Enter when you finish typing.**

   The Assistant displays a list of Help topics that may answer your question (as shown in Figure 3-2). If none of the topics is quite what you had in mind, rephrase your question and give it another try.

4. **Click the Help topic that sounds like the best match.**

   If, after reading through some Help topics, you still aren't satisfied, close the Help window and then start again with Step 1 to ask the Assistant another question.

If you prefer, type your answer in the Ask A Question box in the upper-right-hand corner of the screen. Press Enter or click the down arrow to get a list of topics as shown in Figure 3-3.

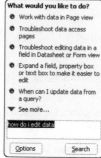
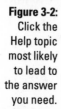

Figure 3-2:
Click the
Help topic
most likely
to lead to
the answer
you need.

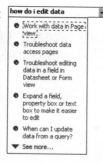

Figure 3-3:
If you really
don't want
to deal with
the Office
Assistant,
the Ask A
Question
box in the
top right
corner
displays the
same
information.

If you prefer to simply use the traditional Help system in Access 2002, you must first turn off the Office Assistant. Right-click the assistant and choose Options. Clear the Use the Office Assistant check box and click OK. Alternatively, you can choose Hide the Office Assistant from the Help menu.

To get the Assistant back, choose Show the Office Assistant from the Help menu.

The following sections explore each of the Help window tabs in order of usefulness.

Combing the contents

The Contents tab is for casual browsers or people who enjoy digging around in a book's table of contents in search of something. Here's how to use it:

1. **Click the <u>C</u>ontents tab.**

   The Help window lists the available master Help topics, complete with little manila folder icons next to each one.

   The book icon means that this entry leads to other Help topics or specific Help documents.

2. **Find a Help topic that looks interesting and double-click it (or press the right arrow).**

   The Help topic opens, changes the closed book icon to an open book, and shows you a list of specific Help documents (see Figure 3-4).

   A Help document is denoted by a page icon with a question mark in the middle.

3. **Repeat Step 2 until you find what you're looking for.**

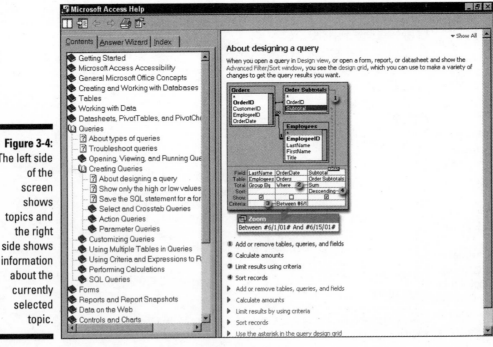

Figure 3-4:
The left side of the screen shows topics and the right side shows information about the currently selected topic.

Asking the Answer Wizard

The Answer Wizard uses a "natural language parser" to conjure up the information you need from the keywords you type. Follow these steps to call the Wizard into action:

1. **Click the <u>A</u>nswer Wizard tab.**

   As you expect, the Answer Wizard page appears on-screen.

2. **In the box at the top of the window, type a couple of key words that describe what you're looking for and then press Enter or click Search.**

   The Answer Wizard searches for topics that match your entry and displays a list of possible matches in the big window at the bottom of the screen.

3. **Scroll through the list at the bottom of the window until you find an item that looks like your topic.**

4. **When you find the topic, click it to see the Help document (see Figure 3-5).**

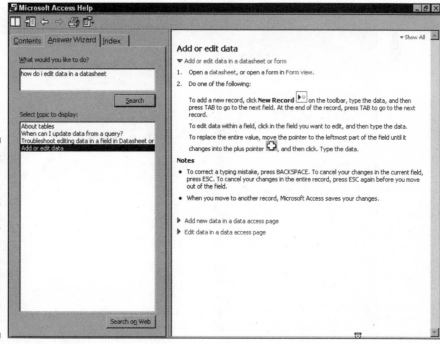

Figure 3-5:
Type a
question
and click
Search. The
Answer
Wizard
responds
with several
topics from
which to
choose.

Inspecting the index

You may prefer diving into the index rather than rattling through the table of contents. The Index tab works just like the index of a book, except that it's automated. Here's how to use it:

1. **Click the Index tab.**

   The Index page appears.

2. **Type the term you're looking for in the box at the top of the window.**

   As you type, Access 2002 suggests an alphabetical list of known terms from the existing help topics in a list in the middle of the window.

   Access 2002, like a savvy politician preparing for a televised debate, generates a list of responses or help topics near the bottom of the window that it thinks best suit your keyword phrase. Access 2002 offers a prioritized number of occurrences of your keyword phrase within the help topic (see Figure 3-6).

   At any point, you can stop typing your phrase and double-click a keyword in the list. Access 2002 pops the keyword into your keyword box.

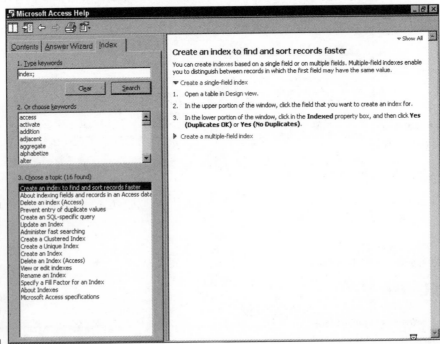

Figure 3-6:
On the Index tab, you can type search terms like you do with Web search engines.

3. **When you find the topic you're looking for, click to see the Help document.**

   If a couple of items match your topic, the Help system displays a dialog box.

4. **Double-click your choice to see it.**

The Office 2002 Help window works a little like a Web browser, mainly because Office 2002 is constructed with parts of a Web browser — specifically Microsoft Internet Explorer. If you've been "surfing" through Access 2002 Help a while and you want to get back to a topic you surfed over a few pages ago, click the left-pointing arrow on the Help toolbar to return to the preceding help topic. The left arrow toolbar button moves you back one help topic at a time. Likewise, you can click the right-pointing arrow on the Help toolbar to move back to where you were previously.

The Whatzis Menu Option

Whatzis isn't the technical term for this menu entry, but I think it should be (sometimes those programmers need more creative names). The item in question is the Help⇨What's This menu option (the one with a mouse pointer and question mark on it). I call this the *Whatzis* item — your tool for quickly finding out what any button or menu item in Access 2002 does.

Here's how the little bugger works:

1. **Choose Help⇨What's This?**

   The mouse pointer suddenly grows a large question mark on one side. Access 2002 is telling you that you're now in Whatzis mode.

2. **Select the menu item or click the button you want to know more about.**

   Access 2002 displays a Help screen with the name of the item and a brief description of what that item does.

3. **Click again to make the helpful little Help screen go away.**

Your Modem Knows More Than You May Think

If you have access (pardon the pun) to the Internet or an account on America Online, CompuServe, or Prodigy, then a world of answers waits at your modem.

Microsoft maintains official support areas on the major online services, plus a very complete World Wide Web page for the Internet crowd. A host of informal question and answer areas cover Microsoft products as well. Table 3-1 explains how to find the support areas on each system.

Table 3-1	Microsoft Support Online	
System	**Access Command**	**Notes**
America Online	keyword PCApplications	Look for MS Access Q&A in the message boards under Database Use and Development
CompuServe	go MSACCESS	Devotes a whole area to Access; lots of good stuff
Usenet	microsoft.public.access	Requires access to Internet newsgroups
Usenet	comp.databases.msaccess	Requires access to Internet newsgroups
World Wide Web		Requires Web access

A slew of *For Dummies* books can help you navigate the online world. Among them are *America Online For Dummies,* 7th Edition (written by yours truly); *CompuServe 2000 For Dummies,* (by R. Michele Phillips); and *The Internet For Dummies,* 7th Edition (by John Levine, Carol Baroudi, and Margaret Levine Young). Of course, Hungry Minds brings these fine books to you.

Drinking at the never-empty well of a mailing list

If you have an e-mail account, consider signing up for the Access mailing list to join a never-ending discussion of Access at all levels, from novice to nerd. Aside from filling your mailbox with important-looking messages, the list gives you a way to get answers quickly at any time.

To join the mailing list, send a message to LISTSERV@peach.ease.lsoft.com. You can write anything as the subject of your message (the computer on the other end doesn't

care). In the body of the message, type **SUBSCRIBE ACCESS-L** followed by your real name, *not* your e-mail address. The mailing list computer automatically picks up your e-mail address from the message itself.

After you subscribe, your first message explains how the list works, how to send messages to it, and how to get off of the list when you decide you've had enough. Give it a try — mailing lists are great tools!

Talking to a Human

Sometimes, you've had it up to *here* with computers and automation in general. At that point, you just want to talk to a human — any human — who can help solve your problem. Microsoft provides a variety of phone numbers for just such occasions.

On these numbers, you pay for the phone call, but the first two answers are free.

✔ To reach Access 2002 phone support, call 425-635-7056 from the United States. Human beings are available from 6 a.m. to 6 p.m. Pacific time, Monday through Friday (except holidays).

✔ In Canada, the number for free support is 905-568-2294. The Canada line is staffed from 8 a.m. to 8 p.m. Eastern time, Monday through Friday (except holidays).

After two calls, the free ride is over; it's time to get out your credit card and use the *per incident* line.

✔ For fast answers to your Access 2002 problems at any hour of the day or night, call 800-936-5700 from the U.S. or Canada. Unless your company purchased an annual support contract from Microsoft, solutions from this number cost a flat *$35 per incident*. So what's an incident? According to Microsoft, an *incident* is *all the calls related to the same problem* (or something close to that). The bottom line is that if you call several times trying to solve the same problem, you pay for only one call. Of course, the really nice reward of paying for support is that these numbers are staffed 24 hours a day. I guess you really *do* get what you pay for.

✔ If you have a light, fluffy question, such as "What's the current version number of Microsoft Access?" (or "What's the weather like in Redmond, Washington?"), call the Microsoft sales department at 800-426-9400. These folks are at the phones, waiting for your call, from 6:30 a.m. to 5:30 p.m. Pacific time, Monday through Friday.

✔ If you are deaf or hearing-impaired and have a TDD or TT modem, call 206-635-4948 between 6 a.m. and 6 p.m. Pacific time, Monday through Friday. This number works for all Microsoft products (Word, Excel, PowerPoint, and the others).

Part II
Truly
Tempting Tables

The 5th Wave   By Rich Tennant

WELL, OBVIOUSLY ONE OF THE
CELLS IN THE NAVIGATIONAL
SPREADSHEET IS CORRUPT!

In this part . . .

With Access 2002 well in hand, you begin a life of storing, managing, organizing, and reorganizing data. (By the way, welcome to your new life. I hope you enjoy your stay here.) Because data hangs out in tables, you need to know how to do the whole table thing if you have any hope of making your data do tricks.

This part eases you into the role of Commander of All Tables by covering the basics. You go from creating tables to using tables and on to maintaining and repairing tables. Heck, if you're not careful, you may find yourself attacking the dining room table by the end of Chapter 9.

Chapter 4

Designing and Building a Home for Your Data

In This Chapter

▶ Reviewing database terms

▶ Simplifying your day with sample fields

▶ Uncovering flat files and relational databases

▶ Designing your tables

▶ Creating a database

▶ Building a table with the Table Wizard

▶ Assembling a table by hand

*T*his may be the single most important chapter in this book. Why? Because really useful databases grow from carefully considered plans. The problem is that nobody ever explains stuff like how to successfully string a bunch of fields together and make a table out of them. For some unknown reason, they think you already know how to do it — that it's instinct, like birds flying south for the winter or my wife finding the best sales in the mall.

If you didn't pop from the womb muttering, "Phone numbers and postal codes are treated as text even though they're numbers" (and I'd worry about you if you did!), then this chapter is for you. The following pages divulge the secrets of fields, tables, and databases in Technicolor glory. The chapter covers the database terms you need to know, tips for choosing fields and designing tables, and details on assembling the pieces into great databases.

Although I hate making a big deal out of techie terminology, this time I must. Please, for your own sanity, get a good grip on the information in the first section of this chapter. The database terms described there appear *everywhere* in Access 2002. Whenever you build a query, design a form, or create a report, the terms stealthily await you, ready to leap out and befuddle the ill-prepared. Steel yourself for their attack by spending time in the terms section that follows.

Database Terms to Know and Tolerate

Wait! Don't skip this section just because it's about terminology. I keep the technoweenie content of this book to a minimum, but you simply *must* know a few magic words before your foray into database development.

If you just felt faint because you didn't realize that you are developing a database, just put the book down for a moment, take a few deep breaths, and remember that it's *only* a computer, not something really important like kids, kites, or chocolate mousse.

The few terms you need to know are listed in the following sections. There's a brief explanation of each one, plus a translation guide for people who have worked with other database software such as FoxPro, Oracle, Paradox, and so on.

The terms are listed in order, starting with the smallest piece of a database and advancing to the largest. It's much like a backward version of that "flea on the wart on the frog on the bump on the log in the hole in the bottom of the sea" song that my kids sing incessantly some days. The definitions kind of build on each other, so it makes the most sense if you start with *data* and work your way to *database*.

Data (your stuff)

Data is the stuff that Access stores, shuffles, and stacks for you. Every time you write your name on a form (last name first, of course), you're providing data. In a database program's skewed approach to the world, Your Name may be stored as one piece of data (your whole name, with or without the middle initial), two pieces (first and last name), or even more pieces (title, first name, middle initial, last name, and suffix). The details depend on how the database designer set up the database's fields (that's covered in the next section, so don't worry about it right now). Here are a couple of tidbits about data:

- ✔ Almost all database programs agree that data should be called data. Don't expect this degree of cooperation to continue much beyond the term data, because that's where it ends.

- ✔ Database programs view data differently than you and I do. If you see 16773, you know it's a number — it's intuitive. Access 2002 and the other database programs see 16773 as either a number or a group of characters, depending on what type of field it's stored in. There's more about this peculiar behavior in the section, "Frolicking through the Fields," later in the chapter. For the sake of your sanity, please make sure you're comfortable with this little oddity because it can *really* throw you for a loop sometimes.

Fields (the rooms for your stuff)

Because people don't want their data to wander around homeless, the technical wizards created *fields* — places for your data to live. Each field holds one kind of data. For example, to track information about a baseball card collection, your fields may include Manufacturer, Player Name, Position, Year, Team, Condition, and so on. Each of those items is a unique *field* in your database.

- ✔ As with the term *data,* programs such as FoxPro and Paradox all agree what a *field* is. However, larger database packages, such as Oracle and Microsoft SQL Server, use the term *column* instead of *field.*

- ✔ The programs mostly disagree when you talk about the specific types of fields available. Just because you *always used to do it this way in Paradox* doesn't mean the same method works in Access 2002. For more details, look at the section, "Frolicking through the Fields," later in this chapter.

Records (the rooms in one house)

Having fields is a good start, but if you stop there, how do you know which last name works with which first name? Something needs to keep those unruly fields in order — something like a *record.* All the fields for one baseball card, one accounting entry, or one of whatever it is you're tracking with Access 2002 are collectively known as a *record.* If you have two baseball cards in your collection, then you have two records in your database, one for each card. (Of course, you *also* have a mighty small card collection.)

- ✔ Again, FoxPro and Paradox concur on the term *record.* Oracle and Microsoft SQL Server use the term *row* instead.

- ✔ Each record in a *table* has the same fields, but (usually) different data inside those fields.

Table (the houses of a neighborhood)

A *table* is a collection of records that describe similar data. The key phrase to remember in that last sentence is *similar data.* All the records in a single table contain fields of similar data. The information about that baseball card collection may fit into a single table. So would the accounting data. However, a single table would *not* handle both baseball cards *and* accounting entries. Combining the two is a novel concept (and may even make accounting fun), but it doesn't work in Access 2002.

- Paradox and FoxPro basically agree with Access 2002 about what a table is, as do Oracle and Microsoft SQL Server.

- Did you notice that I said the baseball card collection *may* fit in one table? I'm not hedging my bet because I think that the table can't physically hold entries about all your cards. Instead, you may use a few *related* tables to hold the data. That's all you need to know for now, but understanding this topic is important. Be sure to peek at the section, "Flat Files versus Relational Databases: Let the Contest Begin!," later in this chapter for the whole scoop.

Database (a community of neighborhoods)

An Access 2002 *database* (or *database file* — the terms are interchangeable) is a collection of everything relating to a particular set of information. The database contains all the tables, queries, reports, and forms that Access 2002 helps you create to manage and work with your stuff. Instead of storing all those items *individually* on the disk drive, where they can become lost, misplaced, or accidentally erased, they're grouped into a single collective file.

Frolicking through the Fields

A field, you remember, is the place where your data lives; one field holds one piece of data such as Year or Team.

Because there are so many different kinds of stuff in the world, Access 2002 offers a variety of field types for *stuff storage*. In fact, Access 2002 puts ten different field types at your disposal. At first blush, ten choices may not seem like much flexibility, but believe me — it is. And if that weren't enough to satisfy the database connoisseur, Access 2002 provides a field by using the Lookup Wizard where you can define the possible contents of the field. Thanks to the field options, you also can customize the fields to suit your needs precisely. All this and it makes popcorn, too.

Each field offers a number of options to make customizing incredibly useful. You can ask for some information, test the entry to see whether it's what you're looking for, and then automatically format the field just the way you want. Everything you need to know about this cool stuff awaits your attention in Chapter 7.

All the field types appear in the following list. They're in the same order as they appear on-screen in Access 2002. Don't worry if you can't figure out why *anyone* would want to use one type or another. Just focus on the ones you need, make a mental note about the others, and go on with your work.

- **Text:** Stores text — letters, numbers, and any combination thereof — up to 255 characters.

  Numbers in a text field aren't numbers; they're just a bunch of digits hanging out together in a field. Be careful of this fact when you design the tables in your database.

  Text fields have one setting you need to know about: size. When you create a text field, Access 2002 wants to know how many characters the field holds. That's the field *size*. If you create a field called First Name and make its size 6, *Joseph* fits into the field, but not *Jennifer*. This can be a problem. A good general rule is to make the field a little larger than you think you actually need. It's easy to make the field even larger if you need to, but it's very dangerous to make it smaller. Surgery on fields is covered in Chapter 9.

- **Memo:** Holds up to 64,000 characters of information — that's almost 18 pages of text.

  This is a *really big* text field. It's great for general notes, detailed descriptions, and anything else that requires a lot of space.

- **Number:** Holds real, for-sure numbers.

  You can add, subtract, and calculate your way to fame and fortune with number fields. If you're working with dollars and cents (or pounds and pence), use a currency field.

- **Date/Time:** Stores time, date, or a combination of the two, depending on which format you use.

  Use a Date/Time field to track the whens of life. Pretty versatile, eh?

- **Currency:** Tracks money, prices, invoice amounts, and so on.

  In an Access 2002 database, the bucks stop here. For that matter, so do the lira, marks, and yen. If you're in the mood for some *other* kind of number, check out the number field.

- **AutoNumber:** Does just what it says: It fills itself with an automatically generated number every time you make a new record.

  AutoNumber is very cool. Just think, when you add a customer to your table, Access 2002 generates the customer number automatically! Although Microsoft SQL Server has something similar, the poor people who use Oracle have to jump through hoops to generate customer (or other types of) numbers.

✔ **Yes/No:** Holds Yes/No, True/False, and On/Off, depending on the format you choose. When you need a simple yes or no, this is the field to use.

✔ **OLE object:** Stands for Object Linking and Embedding, a very powerful, very nerdy technology, and is pronounced "O-Lay." An OLE object is something like a Word document, an Excel spreadsheet, a Windows bitmap (a picture), or even a MIDI song. By embedding an OLE object in your table, your database will automatically "know" how to edit a Word document or an Excel spreadsheet, play a MIDI song, and so on.

✔ **Hyperlink:** Thanks to this field type (and a little bit of Net magic provided by Microsoft Internet Explorer), Access 2002 now understands and stores the special link language that makes the Internet such a cool place.

If you use Access 2002 on your company's network or use the Internet extensively, this field type is for you. I show you more about hyperlinks and other neat Internet tricks in Chapter 21.

✔ **Lookup Wizard:** One of a database program's most powerful features is the *lookup*. It makes data entry go faster (and with fewer errors) by letting you pick a field's correct value from a preset list. No typing, no worry, no problem — it's quite a helpful trick. In some database programs, adding a lookup to a table is really hard. Luckily, the Access 2002 Lookup Wizard makes the process much less painful. Ask the Office Assistant for all of the details about the Lookup Wizard.

A Smattering of Fields to Get You Started

To give you a head start in the database race, Table 4-1 lists fields starring in databases around the world. Some oldies but goodies are in here, plus some examples especially for the new millennium.

Table 4-1	A Field for Every Occasion		
Name	*Type*	*Size*	*Contents*
Title	Text	4	Mr., Ms., Mrs., Mme., Sir
First Name	Text	15	Person's first name
Middle Initial	Text	4	Person's middle initial; allows for two initials and punctuation
Last Name	Text	20	Person's last name
Job	Text	25	Job title or position
Company	Text	25	Company name

Name	Type	Size	Contents
Address 1, Address 2	Text	30	Include two fields for address because some corporate locations are pretty complicated these days
City	Text	20	City name
State, Province	Text	4	State or province; apply the name appropriately for the data you're storing
Zip Code, Postal Code	Text	10	Zip or postal code; note that this is stored as text characters, not a number
Country	Text	15	Not needed if you work within a single country
Office Phone	Text	12	Voice telephone number; increase the size to 17 for an extension
Fax Number	Text	12	Fax number
Home Phone	Text	12	Home telephone number
Cellular Phone	Text	12	Cell phone or car phone
E-mail address	Text	30	Internet e-mail address
Web site	Hyperlink	*	Web page address; sized automatically
Telex	Text	12	Standard Telex number; use size 22 to include answerback service
SSN	Text	11	U.S. Social Security Number, including dashes

All these samples are *text* fields, even the ones for phone numbers. That's because Access 2002 sees most of the stuff you want to pack a database with as *text*. Remember that computers think that there's a difference between an actual *number* and a string of digits, such as the string of digits that makes up a phone number or government ID number.

When creating a field, Ask yourself, "Will I ever do *math* with this number?" If so, it goes in a number field. Otherwise, stuff it into a text field.

Later in this chapter, I describe the Table Wizard (see the section, "Creating Tables at the Wave of a Wand"), which is packed with ready-made fields for your tables.

Playing the (field) name game

Of all the Windows database programs out there, I think Access 2002 has the simplest field-naming rules. Just remember these guidelines to make your field names perfect every time.

✔ Start with a letter or number.

After the first character, you're free to use any letter or number. You can include spaces in field names, too!

✔ Make the field name short and easy to understand.

You actually have up to 64 characters for a field name, but don't even think about using all that space. But don't get stingy and create names like N1 or AZ773 unless they mean something particular to your company or organization.

✔ Use letters, numbers, and an occasional space in your field names.

Although Access 2002 lets you include all kinds of crazy punctuation marks in field names, don't do it. Keep it simple so that the solution you develop with Access 2002 doesn't turn into a problem on its own.

Flat Files versus Relational Databases: Let the Contest Begin!

Unlike ice cream, cars, and summer days, the tables in your database come in only two basic flavors: flat and relational.

A database is either flat file or relational — it can't be both.

These two escapees from the *Nerd Term of the Month Club* explain how tables store information in your database. And now for the cool part: When you build a new database, *you* get to choose which organizational style your new database uses! Don't let it worry you, though — you're not on your own in making the decision. The following paragraphs tell you a little about each kind of organization. (Chapter 5 goes into lots of detail on the subject, too.)

Flat files: Simple answers for simple needs

In a *flat* system (also known as *flat file*), all the data is lumped together into a single table.

A phone directory is a good example of a flat file database: Names, addresses, and phone numbers (the data) are crammed into a single place (the database). Some duplication occurs — if one person has three phone lines at home, her name and address are listed three times in the directory — but that's not a big problem. Overall, the database works just fine.

Relational databases: Complex solutions to bigger problems

The *relational* system (or *relational database*) uses as little storage space as possible by cutting down on the duplicated (the nerds call it *redundant*) data in the database. To accomplish this, relational databases split your data into several tables, with each table holding some portion of the total data.

Borrowing the preceding phone book example, one table in a relational database can contain the customer name and address information, while another can hold the actual phone numbers. Thanks to this approach, the mythical person with three phone lines only has *one* entry in the "customer" table (after all, it's *still* just one customer), but has *three* distinct entries in the "phone number" table (one for each phone line). By using a relational database, the system stores the customer's personal information only once, thus saving some space on the computer's disk drive (see Figure 4-1).

Figure 4-1: The key field here is (drumroll, please)... Cust No.

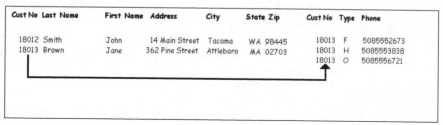

Cust No	Last Name	First Name	Address	City	State	Zip	Cust No	Type	Phone
18012	Smith	John	14 Main Street	Tacoma	WA	98445	18013	F	5085552673
18013	Brown	Jane	362 Pine Street	Attleboro	MA	02703	18013	H	5085553838
							18013	O	5085556721

The *key field* (or *linking field*) is the key to this advanced technology. All of the tables in a relational database system contain this special field. The key field's data identifies matching records from different tables. The key field works just like the claim stub you receive when you drop off film for processing at the local store. To join up with your film again, you present the claim check, complete with its little claim number. That number identifies (or *links*) you and your film so that the clerk can find it. Likewise, in the phone book example, each customer can have a unique customer ID. The "phone number" table stores the customer ID with each phone number. To find out who owns a phone number, you look up the customer ID in the "customer name" table. Granted, it takes more steps to find someone's phone number than the plain *flat file* system does, but the relational system saves storage space (no more duplicate names) and reduces the chance of errors at the same time.

If this process seems complicated, don't feel bad. Relational databases *are* complicated! That's why Chapter 5 explains the concept in infinitely more detail, complete with examples of how the process works and warning signs to watch for lest you turn into a full-fledged database nerd. For your own sanity, please be patient with yourself when wrestling with relational databases. There's no shame in asking for some help from your friendly neighborhood computer jockey, either.

Figuring out what all this means

Now you at least have an idea of the difference between flat file and relational databases. But do you care? Yes, you do. Each approach has its unique pluses and minuses for your database:

- ✔ Flat file systems are easy to build and maintain. (A Microsoft Excel spreadsheet is a good example.)

  Anyone can create a workable flat database system — and I *do* mean anyone. They're great for simple listings such as mailing lists, phone directories, and video collections. Flat systems are simple solutions for simple problems.

- ✔ Relational systems really shine in big business applications such as invoicing, accounting, or inventory.

  If you have a small project (such as a mailing list or membership database), a relational approach may be more solution than you need. Developing a solid relational database takes skill and practice (and, in some countries, a nerd license).

Your company probably has a lot of information stored in relational database systems. Understanding how to use relational systems is important for you, so that's covered just about everywhere you turn in this book. Specifically, check out Chapter 5 to find out about dealing with the relationships between tables.

On the other hand, I don't recommend that you set off to build a relational database system by yourself. If you're sure you need one, enlist either the Database Wizard or a friendly guru to help you bring the database to life. There's a lot to understand about how fields work together to form relations. Get some help the first time and then try it on your own later.

Although Access 2002 is a relational database program, it does flat systems quite nicely. Whether you choose flat file or relational for your database project, Access 2002 is the right program!

Great Tables Start with Great Designs

You're *almost* ready to start up the computer and run Access 2002 — but not quite. You need to design the tables for your database. I know this seems like a lot of paperwork, but it's absolutely necessary to build good databases. When I create systems for my clients, this is exactly how I do it:

1. **Get out a clean pad of paper and something to write with.**

   Despite the wonders of PCs and Windows, some jobs are easier on paper. Besides, if the database design work isn't going well, you can always doodle.

2. **Write brief descriptions of the reports, lists, and other outputs you want from the system.**

   Why start with the stuff that comes out? Because these reports and such are the *real* reason you're creating the database.

   Don't worry about making this a totally perfect and complete list. Settle for an *includes most everything* list, because you can always go back later and add new stuff to it.

3. **On another sheet of paper, sketch some samples of the reports, lists, and other outputs you listed in Step 2.**

   You needn't create detailed report designs at this point — that's not the goal. Right now, you're figuring out what you need to build the stuff that ultimately comes from your database (the reports, lists, mailing labels, and everything else). Just get a rough idea of what you want the most important reports to look like and write down the stuff that's on them. This list becomes the road map to your database's fields. (After all, you can't print a mailing label if your database doesn't store addresses somewhere.)

4. **For each field in your list, write a name and field type. For text fields, include a specific size.**

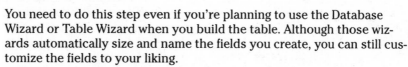

   You need to do this step even if you're planning to use the Database Wizard or Table Wizard when you build the table. Although those wizards automatically size and name the fields you create, you can still customize the fields to your liking.

5. **Organize the fields into tables.**

   Look for data that naturally goes together, like name, address, and phone number for a contact database, or product ID, description, distributor, cost, and selling price for an inventory system.

   If you have a lot of fields or if you run out of ideas for putting them together, get help from your friendly guru.

This last part is the hardest, but it gets easier with practice. To build your experience, create some sample databases with the Database Wizard and look at how they fit together. Pick a topic you know about (accounting, event scheduling, or compact disc collecting) and see how the pros at Microsoft did it.

Open the various tables in Design view (in the database window, right-click the table name, then select Design from the pop-up menu). Which fields went in each table? Why are tables organized that way? Get a big-picture view of how the tables interact within the database by clicking the Relationships button on the toolbar. Access 2002 displays the Relationships window (see Figure 4-2), which graphically shows how all the tables in the database link together. Follow the lines between the tables to unravel the connections.

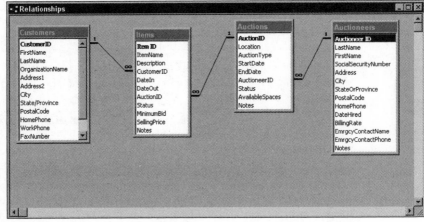

has to be tracked to -8 to fit on one line

Figure 4-2: The Relationships window.

Building a Database

After reading page after page of this book, writing reams of notes, and sucking down two or three cans of pop, the moment is finally here — it's time to build the database! Here's where you create the master holding file for your tables, reports, forms, and other stuff. Plus, if you use a Database Wizard, this step also creates all the tables, reports, and forms for you — it's one-stop shopping!

Without further ado, here's how to create a database:

1. **If it's not already running, take a moment to start Access 2002.**

2. **Choose File⇨New from the main menu (as shown in Figure 4-3) or click the New Object toolbar button.**

   The New File task pane opens. You can create a new database or open an existing one.

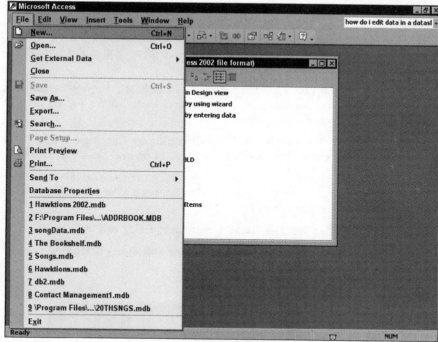

Figure 4-3:
It takes only
a quick click
to create a
database.

3. **Select General Templates (under New from template).**

The Templates window appears.

4. **Click the Databases tab.**

A list of database template wizards appears, as shown in Figure 4-4. If none of the templates meets your needs, you can select Templates On Microsoft.Com from the New File task pane to see more templates.

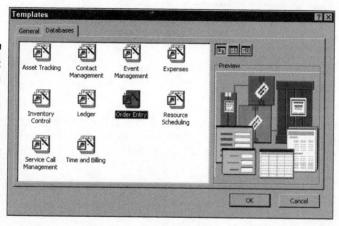

Figure 4-4:
Choose one
of the
Wizard
Templates
to give you a
head start
on creating
your
database.

To create a new database by hand, select Blank Database in the Task Pane. Access asks you for a file name for your database and voilà! One blank database is awaiting your command. Turn to "Creating Tables at the Wave of a Wand" for guidance on adding tables to your blank database.

If the Task Pane isn't open, you can get to it by right-clicking anywhere on the toolbar and choosing Task Pane. You can also choose View⇨ Toolbars⇨Task Pane.

5. **Scroll through the list until you find a Database Wizard template that seems most like what you want to do and then double-click it.**

   To create a database by hand, click the General tab of the New Database window and double-click the Database icon in the upper-left corner of the window.

   Either way, the File New Database dialog box appears.

6. **Type a name for your database and then click Create (as shown in Figure 4-5).**

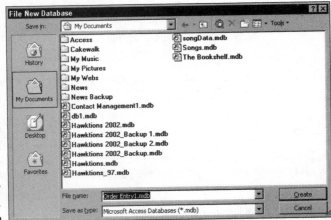

Figure 4-5:
Type a name
for the
database,
click Create,
and you're
on your
way.

To store the database somewhere other than in the default location (usually the My Documents folder), choose a different folder by clicking the down arrow beside Save In: and work through the directory tree until you find the folder you're looking for.

(Are you getting a headache from all this talk of folders, directory trees, and such? *Windows 2000 Professional For Dummies,* by Andy Rathbone and Sharon Crawford, and *Windows 98 For Dummies,* by Andy Rathbone, are the perfect remedy.)

If a dialog box pops up and asks whether you want to replace an existing file, Access 2002 is saying that a database with the name you entered is already on the disk. If this is news to you, click No and then come up with a different name for your new database. On the other hand, if you *intended* to replace that old database with a new one, click Yes and proceed.

7. **Skim the brief this-is-what-I'm-up-to window to see what the wizard has to say and then click Next to continue.**

   Access displays a list of tables and, for each table, a list of fields that you may want to include in your new database (see Figure 4-6).

Figure 4-6:
The Database Wizard asks you about adding optional fields in your database.

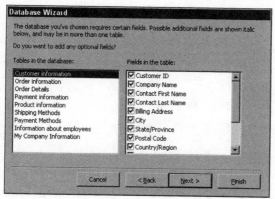

8. **If you want to add or remove standard fields from the database that the wizard is building for you, do so in the Fields dialog box and then click Next.**

9. **Click Next unless you're particularly moved to change something.**

   Now that the hard part is done, the wizard wants your opinion on some aesthetic questions.

10. **Click the on-screen display options to see what's available and then double-click the one you like.**

    Although my wife will accuse me of being bland again, I recommend the Standard option. The others are pretty, but most of them take more time to load. If you simply *must* add some diversity to your database, try the International, Sumi Painting, or Stone options — they don't slow you down.

11. **Pick the style for your reports (at last) and click Next.**

    Single-click the options to see what's available. I have no cool recommendations for you here — just pick something you like and move on.

12. **Name your masterpiece and click <u>N</u>ext.**

    The wizard kindly offers its own name, but you're free to change it by simply typing something new in the box at the top of the window.

13. **Tell the Database Wizard to add a picture to your reports if you're really into graphics.**

    To pick an image, check the Yes I'd Like to Include a Picture check box and then click the Picture button to choose the graphic you want to feature on the database's reports.

14. **Click <u>F</u>inish to build the database.**

    The wizard clunks and thunks for a while, giving you constant updates on how it's doing (see Figure 4-7).

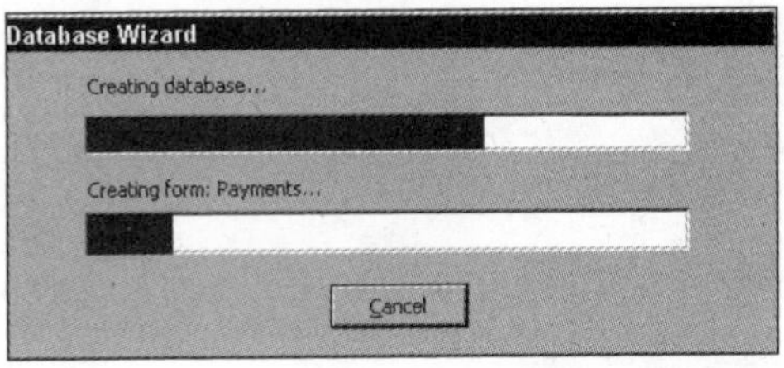

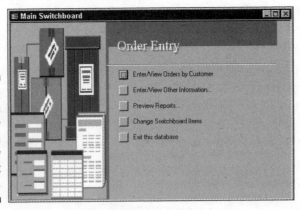

Figure 4-7: The Database Wizard, hard at work.

The Database Wizard lets you create a friendly switchboard screen, something like the one shown in Figure 4-8.

Figure 4-8: Access proudly displays the new database it built for you.

Now that the database is ready, flip through Chapters 6 and 7 for information on entering data, customizing the tables, and getting comfy with your new addition.

Creating Tables at the Wave of a Wand

Adding a new table to an existing database is easy with the Access 2002 Table Wizard. The Table Wizard offers a variety of ready-made fields to choose from, plus it does all the dirty work of table creation behind the scenes, so you can focus on important stuff.

With the Table Wizard, you don't so much *build* a table as *assemble* it. The wizard brings lots of pieces and parts — you pick out what you want and go from there.

The assembly approach is helpful when you're completely new at building tables. Instead of worrying about details like field types and sizes, you get to worry about bigger stuff, like field names and purposes. After you build a few tables, you probably won't use the Table Wizard. Instead of helping, the wizard starts getting in the way because you already know what fields you want and how to make them.

Without further ado, here's how to ask the wizard to help you build a table:

1. **Choose File⇨Open or click the Open Database button on the toolbar to open the database file that needs a new table.**

   The database pops into its on-screen window.

2. **Click the Tables tab under the Objects bar of the Database window and then double-click Create Table by Using the Wizard to start the creation process.**

   If everything works right, the Table Wizard dialog box shown in Figure 4-9 appears. If some other bizarre window appears, close that window and repeat this step.

Figure 4-9:
The Table Wizard suggests tables and fields and then builds the tables for you.

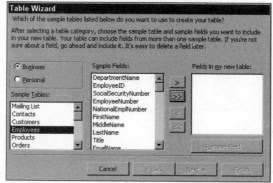

3. **Click a sample table to display the available fields.**

The Sample Tables list is a tad messy. Table names are listed in no particular order, forcing you to scroll through a long list to find what's available to you. Be patient — the effort is worth it.

The Table Wizard offers you all kinds of ready-made fields to assemble into a table.

4. **Double-click the fields you want for the table.**

The field name hops into the Fields in my new table column.

Select the fields in the order you want them to appear in the new table. Don't worry if you get one or two out of order — it's easy to fix that later (Chapter 9 tells you how).

- If you like *all* the fields from a particular table, click the >> button to copy the table's entire set of fields.

- To remove a field you chose by accident, click the field name and then click the < button.

- To remove *all* the fields and start over with a clean slate, click the << button.

- If you're not happy with the current name of a field in your new table, click the field name and then click Rename Field. Type the new field name into the dialog box and click OK to make the change. Too easy, eh?

5. **Repeat Step 4 until your table is full of fields (as shown in Figure 4-10).**

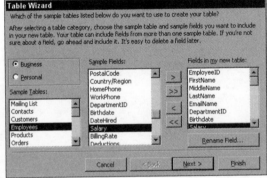

Figure 4-10:
Select the fields you want in your table.

6. **Click Next to continue.**

On-screen, the field information runs off to hide as the wizard asks some general stuff about the table.

7. **Type a name for the table and then click <u>N</u>ext.**

   The table name information vanishes, only to be replaced with the primary key screen.

   Leave the primary key settings alone for now. You can mess with the settings later (see Chapter 5).

8. **Click Next.**

   Access shows you a screen listing other tables in the database and whether it thinks your new table is related to them (see Figure 4-11). Access is often spectacularly bad in its assumptions about related tables, so look at the list closely.

9. **Click the Relationships button if the Table Wizard made an incorrect assumption about table relationships and you want to help it along.**

   The Relationships dialog box appears, as shown in Figure 4-12.

10. **Choose from one of the three options in the Relationships dialog box.**

    In Figure 4-12, I indicate that for each record in the Products3 table, there can be many in the Items table. (Chapter 5 has more about table relationships. Look in that chapter if you're a little foggy about the hows and whys of relating tables.)

11. **Click <u>F</u>inish to complete the task and build the new table.**

    Your table is now ready to be filled with data.

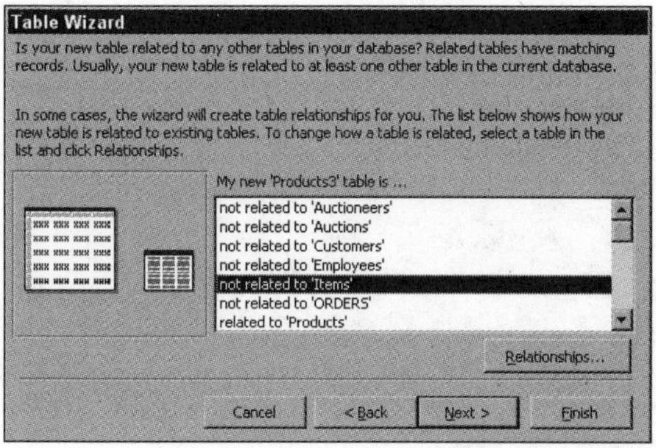

Figure 4-11:
The Table Wizard shows all of the existing tables and whether Access thinks they relate to your new table.

Table Wizard

Is your new table related to any other tables in your database? Related tables have matching records. Usually, your new table is related to at least one other table in the current database.

In some cases, the wizard will create table relationships for you. The list below shows how your new table is related to existing tables. To change how a table is related, select a table in the list and click Relationships.

My new 'Products3' table is ...

not related to 'Auctioneers'
not related to 'Auctions'
not related to 'Customers'
not related to 'Employees'
not related to 'Items'
not related to 'ORDERS'
related to 'Products'

Relationships...

Cancel   < <u>B</u>ack   <u>N</u>ext >   <u>F</u>inish

Highlights from the sample tables

For your convenience, I'm listing some of the more useful sample tables that the Wizard knows how to create and the purpose of each. Many of these tables link together to form relational databases. For example, Calls, Contacts, Contact Types, and "To Do's" work together as a single system. Don't bother trying to put the individual pieces together with the Table Wizard. Use the Database Wizard instead — it's a lot easier!

✔ Contacts: Very full-featured customer information table; stores details about your customers

✔ Customers: You guessed it — a customer information list, complete with a field for e-mail address

✔ Employees: Solid employee information table; good example of the detail you can include in a single table

✔ Events: Great for meeting planners or trainers setting up their own room information

✔ Mailing List: General information (name, address, and so on) geared toward seminar attendees

✔ Orders: Tracks customer order data

✔ Order Details: Covers the line items for each order

✔ Products: General product information for a catalog and sales system

✔ Reservations: Handles event reservations and pre-paid fees

✔ Service Records: Great example of a table that manages call information for a service business

✔ Tasks: Tracks to-do items

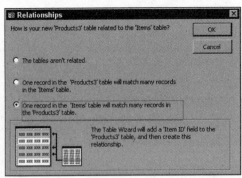

Figure 4-12:
Tell Access how your tables really relate in the Relationships dialog box.

Building Tables by Hand, Just like in the Old Days

Although automation is generally great, at times it just plain gets in the way. For example, I appreciate the fact that with the right automatic gizmo, I can clap my hands and turn off the television. This feat becomes a problem when I start keeping time with my favorite song and accidentally drive the TV insane.

Likewise, the Table Wizard makes life easy at first, but soon you know more about what you want than the wizard does. Don't worry — when you're ready for independence, Access 2002 is there with a straightforward way to build tables by hand.

Actually, *two* easy ways exist to build a table without the Table Wizard:

- *Datasheet view* displays a blank datasheet. You just start typing in data. After you've entered everything, Access 2002 looks at your entries and assigns field types based on the data it sees.

  The only problem is that Access 2002 frequently misunderstands your data, leaving you to tweak the field types by hand. The bottom line: For anything more complicated than a *really* simple table, don't use Datasheet view. It's a nice thought, but it drives you nuts in the end. Instead, use Design view.

- *Design view* is the formal, almost nerd-like way to build new databases. In this mode, you have full control over the new table's fields. Don't get all weirded out because the screen looks complicated — just go slow, follow the information in the steps, and everything turns out fine.

To create a new table by hand, cruise through these steps:

1. **Choose File⇨Open from the main menu; then double-click the database that needs a new table.**

   The database file appears on-screen.

2. **Click the Tables button on the left side of the Databases window and then double-click Create Table in Design View.**

   Access 2002 displays a blank table design form that looks a whole heckuva lot like Figure 4-13.

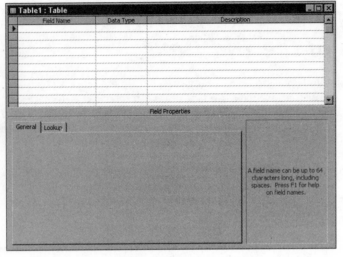

Figure 4-13:
A fresh,
clean Table
Designer
awaiting
your
instruction.

3. **Type the field name and then press Tab.**

   The cursor moves to the Data Type column.

4. **Click the down arrow to list all available field types. Click the field type you want (see Figure 4-14), and then press Tab to continue.**

   (Pressing the first letter of the field type scrolls you right to it. For example, if you tab into the Data Type column and press "A", the cursor scrolls to the "AutoNumber" entry.)

   The cursor moves into the Description field.

Figure 4-14:
You can
select from
all available
field (data)
types.

If you create a Text field, you probably need to adjust the field size (the default size is 50, which is too much field for almost anyone). Click in the Field Size box in the lower-left side of the screen *before* tabbing elsewhere; then type the correct field size.

5. Type a clear, concise description of what this field contains and then press Tab to move the cursor back into the Field Name column.

This step is *really* important! The Description information appears in the status bar at the bottom of the screen — it's automatic help text. *Please* take the time to write a quick field description. It makes your tables much easier to use.

6. Repeat Steps 3 through 5 until all the fields are in place (as shown in Figure 4-15).

What a feeling of achievement! Your new table is almost ready.

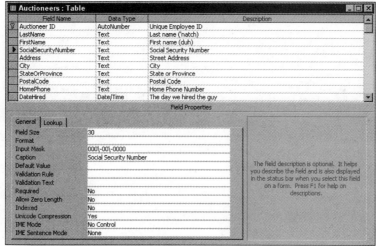

Figure 4-15: The fields are in place — time to give your table the stress test!

7. Select File⇨Save to write the new table to your disk drive or click the Save button on the toolbar.

8. In the Save dialog box, type the name that you want to use for the table and press Enter.

Access 2002 may send you a dialog box complaining "There is no primary key defined." This message means that your table won't automatically put itself into any order. Click Yes in the dialog box to create a key field and go to Chapter 5 for more about key fields.

9. Enjoy your new table!

That's not bad for working without automated intervention. Congratulations on a job well done!

Chapter 5

Relationships, Keys, and Indexes (And Why You Really Do Care)

. . . .

In This Chapter

▶ Getting organized with a primary key

▶ The scoop about relationships

▶ Building relationships between your tables

▶ Speeding up your life with indexes

. . . .

*E*very year, it's the same: Do more with less; work smarter not harder. They're not problems, they're *opportunities for achievement*. Why do I bring up such wonderful thoughts in a fun book like this? Because this chapter is at least a partial cure for these phrases that afflict you.

You need to get more done in less time, right? If that's you, then check out the index feature in Access 2002. This feature makes your queries fly, your sorts sing, and your hair hold firm in its current position. Are you plagued with *opportunities* because of all the duplicate data infesting your tables? Ferret out the problems with a well-placed key field. A good key field ensures that records appear once (and only once) in the table.

And what about relational databases? Can tables *really* have relationships, or do they just spend a lot of platonic time together? Thanks to the wonders of the Relationships tool in Access 2002, your tables work with each other better than ever. Of course, the matchmaking that leads to a successful relationship isn't any easier with tables than with humans, but don't let that worry you. With the tips in this chapter, you'll be a card-carrying Data Guru in no time.

The Joy (And Necessity) of a Primary Key

A table's primary key is a special field in your tables. Just about every table you create should have a primary key. Why?

- ✔ It organizes your data by *uniquely* identifying each record. For example, on a Customer table, the Customer Number would be the primary key — there is only one customer number 1, one customer number 2, and so on.

- ✔ Nerds pitch a fit if you don't.

You need to know a few rules about the primary key before running off to create one:

- ✔ A table can have only one primary key.

  A single table can have lots of indexes, but only one primary key.

- ✔ Access 2002 automatically indexes the primary key field (that's one reason that a primary key makes your database work a little faster). (I tell you more about indexes in the section, "Indexing Your Way to Fame, Fortune, and Significantly Faster Queries," later in this chapter.)

- ✔ If you create a new table without a primary key, Access 2002 automatically asks whether you want to add one.

  If you say yes, the program gleefully creates an AutoNumber field at the beginning of your table and sets it as the primary key. If the first field is an AutoNumber type, Access 2002 anoints it as the primary key without adding anything else to the table.

- ✔ Most of the time, the primary key is a single field, but in *very* special circumstances, two or more fields can share the job. The technical term for this type of key is a *multifield key*. The super-technical term for this type of key is *compound key*.

- ✔ You cannot use the Memo, OLE Object, or Hyperlink field types in a primary key.

- ✔ Although you *can* use the Yes/No field type in a primary key, you can have only two records (Yes and No) in such a table.

- ✔ The primary key automatically sorts records in the table. This just keeps your tables neat and tidy.

✔ Access 2002 doesn't care where the primary key field is in the table design. The key can be the first field, the last field, or in the middle. The placement choice is all yours. For your sanity's sake, I recommend putting the key field *first* in a table. In fact, make it a habit (you'll thank me later).

✔ All primary keys must have a name, just like the field has a name. This may come as a shock, so hold on to your seat, but Access 2002 automatically names all primary keys Primary Key.

To nominate a field for the job of primary key, follow these steps:

1. **Open the table in Design view.**

   If you're not familiar with this step, you probably shouldn't be messing with the primary key. Likewise, if you aren't comfortable with the content of Chapters 1 and 4, you aren't ready to tackle primary keys.

2. **Right-click the button next to the field you've picked for the primary key.**

   One of those cool pop-up menus appears. For some ideas on how to pick the right field for a primary key, see the following sidebar.

3. **Select Primary Key from the menu (as shown in Figure 5-1).**

   A little key symbol appears in the button. The primary key is set!

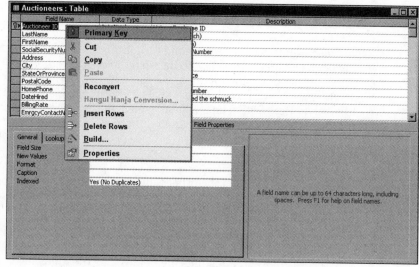

Figure 5-1: The primary key is created (and the records rejoice).

Picking the right field is a *key* issue

What makes a good key field? How do you find the right one? Good questions — in fact, they're the two most important questions to ask about a primary key.

The top criterion for a good key field is uniqueness. The values in a key field must be unique. Access 2002 won't tolerate duplicate key values. Each and every entry in the key field(s) must be the only one of its kind. If you see a lot of table creation in your future, then pin the phrase *Think unique* on your office wall.

With the word unique firmly imprinted in your mind, it's time to look for a natural key field in your table. Do you have any fields that always contain unique data? Is there a Customer Number, Stock Keeping Unit, Vehicle ID, or some other field that's different in every record?

If you have a natural key, that's great. Use it! If you don't, create a unique field by adding an AutoNumber field to your table. This field type automatically inserts a new, unique number into each record of your table. AutoNumber even keeps track of numbers that you delete so that Access won't use them again. Best of all, Access takes care of the details so that you don't have to worry about programming or any special tricks to make the program work. The AutoNumber field handles it for you.

Divulging the Secrets of a Good Relationship

Relational databases split data among two or more tables. Access 2002 uses a linking field, called a *foreign key,* to tie related tables together. For example, one table may contain customer names and addresses while another table tracks the customer's payment history. The credit information is tied to the customer's address with a linking field, which, in this example, is probably a customer number. Here are a few general thoughts to keep in mind when linking tables:

- Usually, the linking field is one table's primary key, but just an average, mild-mannered field in the other table. For example, the customer table in the example is probably arranged by customer number, whereas the credit data is likely organized by payment number.

- Tables don't magically begin relating to each other just because they're cooped up inside the same database file. You explain the relationships to Access 2002 and it handles the details. See the following section for details about explaining relationships to Access 2002.

- Linking fields must be the same data type. Remember, fields of a feather flock together in the weird world of databases. Try repeating that three times quickly.

When you link two tables together, they form one of four possible relation-ships. Although this information borders on the technical side, Access 2002 is particularly fond of these terms, so please take a minute to check them out.

- ✔ *One-to-one* relationships link one record in the first table to *exactly* one record in the second table.

  One-to-one relationships are the simplest, but they don't happen often. Tables that have a one-to-one relationship can be combined into one table, which usually happens.

- ✔ *One-to-many* relationships connect one record in the first table to *many* records in the second table.

  One sample customer may make many purchases at the store, so one customer record is linked to many sales records in the transaction table.

- ✔ *Many-to-one* relationships connect *many* records in the first table to *one* record in the second table.

  Many-to-one relationships are simply the reverse of one-to-many relationships.

- ✔ *Many-to-many* relationships link many records in one table to many records in another. Many-to-many relationships are bad, evil, and also not good. In fact, the database doesn't even allow you to create such a relationship. Instead, you must resolve it with something called a *linking table*.

So, what is this linking table stuff? Technoweenies walk around mumbling something about entity relationships. (And you thought Doctor Ruth was talking about people!) In technobabble, an entity is sort of like a table. Suppose, for example, that you have a table named Students and another table named Courses. Technoweenies ask themselves this question: "For each instance of the Student entity, how many instances of the Courses entity can there be?" The answer is many — each student can take many courses. Then, the technoweenie asks, "For each instance of Courses, how many Students can there be?" Again, the answer is many — each course can be taken by many students. This is a classic many-to-many relationship.

To fix a many-to-many relationship, you *must* create a linking table (some-times called a *joining table*) whose primary key is a combination of the pri-mary keys of the first two tables. So, suppose I have a table named Students with a primary key of Student Number, and another table named Courses with a primary key of Course ID. I need to create a third table (maybe Student Courses) with a primary key of Student Number *and* Course ID.

Linking Your Tables with the Relationship Builder Thingy

The mechanics of linking tables together in Access 2002 are quite visual. In Access 2002, you can look at tables, draw lines, and get on with your business. I hate to say this, but linking tables is actually kind of fun. Keep these three limitations in mind:

- You can only link tables that are in the same database.

- You can also link queries to tables, but that's unusual.

- You need to specifically tell Access 2002 how your tables are related. And you can't tell this stuff to Access on-the-fly — linking tables is a formal process (like ballroom dancing).

When you're ready to arrange some formal relationships among your more impassioned tables, here's how to do it:

1. **From the database window, choose Tools⇨Relationships or click the Relationships button on the toolbar.**

   The Relationships window appears, probably looking quite blank at the moment.

   If some tables are already listed in the window, someone (or some Wizard) has defined relationships for this database. If you're in a corporate environment, *please* stop at this point and seek assistance from your Information Systems folks before mucking around with this database.

2. **Choose Relationships⇨Show Table; click the Show Table button on the toolbar; or right-click and select Show Table.**

   The Show Table dialog box appears on-screen, listing the tables in the current database file.

3. **Click the first table involved in this would-be relationship and then click Add.**

4. **Repeat the process with the other tables you want to link.**

   As you add tables to the layout, a little window appears for each table, listing the fields in that table. You can see these windows next to the Show Table dialog box in Figure 5-2.

5. **Click Close after you're finished adding tables.**

   With the tables present in the window, you're ready to start the relationships!

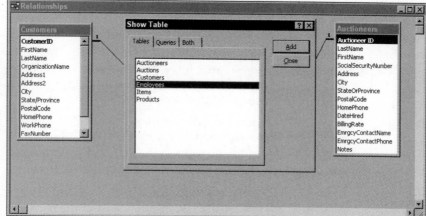

Figure 5-2:
Use the
Show Table
dialog box
to add
tables to the
Relation-
ships
diagram.

6. **Decide which two tables you want to link together.**

   In a one-to-many relationship, one of the tables is the *parent* and one is the *child*. In the parent, the linking field will be the primary key.

   In Access 2002, you need to see the two linking fields on-screen before you can make a relationship.

7. **Put the mouse pointer on the field you want to link in the *parent* table (which will be the primary key of that table) and hold down the left mouse button.**

8. **While holding down the mouse button, slide the mouse from one link-ing field to the other.**

   The pointer becomes a rectangle. When the rectangle is on the linking field, release the mouse button. A dialog box detailing the soon-to-be relationship appears, as shown in Figure 5-3.

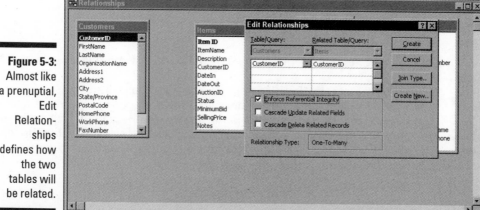

Figure 5-3:
Almost like
a prenuptial,
Edit
Relation-
ships
defines how
the two
tables will
be related.

Access 2002 is picky about your aim on this step. You must put the tip of the mouse pointer right on the field you're linking to. In Figure 5-3, I dragged CustomerID from the Customer table and dropped it on CustomerID in the Items table.

9. **Check Enforce Referential Integrity to enforce the relationship between the two tables (Access 2002 doesn't allow you to have an Item with a CustomerID that does not exist).**

   This creates a foreign key that technoweenies call the foreign key/primary key relationship *referential integrity*.

10. **Click Create after you're confident that the table and field names in the dialog box are correct (see Figure 5-4).**

    A line shows you that the tables are linked. If you checked Enforce Referential Integrity, Access places a "1" next to the parent in the relationship and an infinity symbol next to the child. This denotes a one-to-many relationship.

If the table names or field names listed in the dialog box are wrong, just click Cancel and try Steps 6 through 8 again.

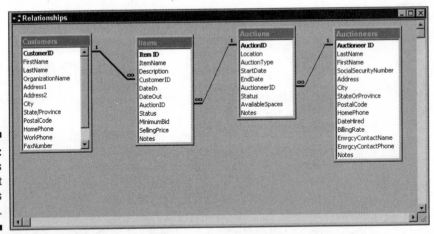

Figure 5-4:
Customers is the parent and Items is the child.

11. **To link another pair of tables, go back to Step 3 and begin again.**

When you're done, the Relationships window may look a little messy (because you'll have relationship lines crossing each other). To clean it up, put the mouse pointer on the title bar of a table window and then click and drag the table window to another part of the screen. It's traditional (although not always possible) to show parents above children. Figure 5-5 shows my final Relationships.

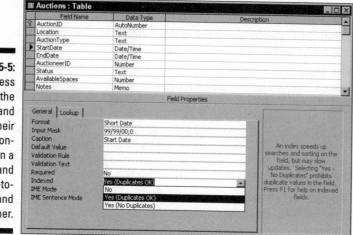

Figure 5-5:
Access
presents the
tables and
their
relation-
ships in a
neat and
easy-to-
understand
manner.

Indexing Your Way to Fame, Fortune, and Significantly Faster Queries

Psst — you with the book. Yeah, you. Want some inside information about your software? I've got a hot tip on a feature that'll blow you away. My tip speeds up your queries, makes sorting a snap, and prevents duplicate records in your tables. Pretty cool, eh? Oh, you *are* interested. Okay, then — here's the scoop.

The cool speed secret is an *index*. An Access 2002 table index works just like the index in a book. Using the index is a whole lot faster than flipping page after page in a hopeless search for the correct passage.

An Access 2002 index works just like a book index, but instead of listing page numbers, the index tracks *record* numbers. When you sort or query a table using an indexed field, the index does most of the work. That's why indexes dramatically speed up queries and sorts — the index lets the query zero in on the information without sifting through the whole table to find it.

Here are a few random thoughts about indexes:

- ✔ Each field in a table can be indexed as long as it's not one of these field types: hyperlink, memo, or OLE Object.

- ✔ Like the primary key, an index may have a unique name that's different from the field name.

- Although indexes make queries, searches, and sorts a whole lot faster, building too many indexes in a table actually *slows down* some tasks. Adding records to a table with several indexes takes a little longer than adding records to an unindexed table. Access 2002 spends the extra time updating all those indexes behind the scenes.

- Indexes either *allow* duplicate entries in your table or *prevent* them. The choice is yours. How do you choose the right one for your table? Most of the time, you want to *allow* duplicate records. The big exception is with primary key fields. Access 2002 always indexes primary key fields as *No duplicates* — after all, you don't want two customers with the same customer number. The *No duplicates* setting tells Access 2002 to make sure that no two records have the same values in the indexed field.

- To list the table's indexes, open the table in Design view and click the Indexes button on the toolbar.

The programmers at Microsoft made creating an index a pretty straightforward operation. Here's how you do it:

1. **With the table open in Design view, click the name of the field you want to index.**

   The blinking toothpick cursor lands in the field name.

2. **Click the Indexed box in the General tab of Field Properties.**

   The toothpick cursor, always eager to please, hops into the Indexed box. A down arrow appears on the right end of the box as well.

   If the *Indexed* display has no entry, this particular field type doesn't work with indexes. No matter how much you want to, you can't index hyperlink, memo, or OLE fields.

3. **Click the down arrow at the end of the box to list your index options.**

   A list of index options appears.

4. **Select the index you want from the list.**

   Most of the time, click Yes (Duplicates OK). In special cases when you want every record to have a unique value in this field (like Customer Numbers in your Customer table), click Yes (No Duplicates).

5. **Click the Save toolbar button or choose File⇨Save to make the change permanent.**

   Depending on the size of your table, it may take a few moments of effort to create the index. Don't be surprised if you have to wait a few moments before Access 2002 is done.

To remove an index, follow the preceding steps. In Step 4, choose No on the pull-down menu. Access 2002 wordlessly deletes the field's index.

Chapter 6

New Data, Old Data, and Data in Need of Repair

In This Chapter

▶ Opening databases and tables

▶ Adding new records

▶ Changing an existing record

▶ Deleting the pointless records

▶ What to do after saying, "Oops!"

Maintenance is a substantial cost for anything worth keeping around this planet. No matter what you're talking about — house, car, stereo, television, child, pet, significant other — keeping valuables in good working order usually costs more than we think when we first obtain the item.

Your data is an exception to the rule. Thanks to the tools in Access 2002, data maintenance is easy, relatively painless, and costs less than you expect. In fact, keeping your data up to date is one of the program's main goals.

This chapter covers basic data upkeep: adding new records, deleting old ones, and fixing the broken ones. For table maintenance hints (such as adding new columns, renaming fields, and so on), check out Chapter 9.

Dragging Your Table into the Digital Workshop

Because records cluster together in tables, you need to open a table before worrying about records. Tables prefer company, too. They hang out inside databases. Databases don't care a whit about anything other than themselves, so you may find them lounging in a folder, sulking on a diskette, or holding forth on a network drive.

That background about databases, tables, and records simply means that the first step on the road to record maintenance is opening a database. You have several different ways to open a database, but ultimately they all work the same way.

When you open Access 2002, the program displays the Task Pane (as shown in Figure 6-1), which offers the opportunity to create a new database, reopen one you worked on recently, or wander off into another dialog box to open whichever database strikes your fancy. Each action is presented as a hyperlink. The following list describes things you can do with the Task Pane:

- ✔ To open one of the databases listed, simply click it.

    Access 2002 automatically opens the database.

- ✔ If the database you want isn't on the list, click the More Files option to bring up the Open dialog box.

    This dialog box gives you access to all the table files in a file folder.

- ✔ What? The database you want isn't there either? In that case, check out the nearby sidebar in this chapter for some tips about the fortuitous file-finding features located under the Tools menu of the Open dialog box.

- ✔ If you're in the mood to create a new table, flip to Chapter 4 where all the create-a-table stuff is.

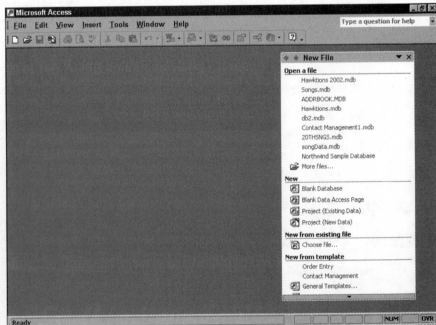

Figure 6-1:
When you open Access, the Task Pane is there to greet you and do your bidding.

These hints are all well and good if Access 2002 just came roaring to life, but what if it's already running? You can simply right-click in the toolbar area and choose Task Pane or you can use the following procedure to open a database the old-fashioned way:

1. **Choose File⇨Open or click the Open Database button on the toolbar.**

   The Open dialog box pops onto the screen (see Figure 6-2).

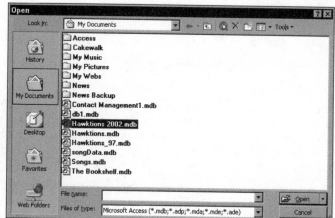

Figure 6-2:
The database I was looking for appears.

2. **Scroll through the list until you find the database you're looking for.**

   If the database you want isn't on this list, it's probably in another folder, on another disk drive, or out on your network. To search for it, click the down arrow in the Look in box (along the top of the Open dialog box) to see a list of your local and network disk drives, then click the drive you want to search. Access 2002 displays a list of all databases and file folders in the current folder.

   To make work *really* easy, add a few shortcuts to your Favorites list. Include your most commonly used network areas, directories on your hard drive, or wherever you (or the data nerds in your company) store Access files.

3. **When you find the database, open it by double-clicking its name.**

   The database file opens with a flourish, as shown in Figure 6-3.

   This window shows how a normal, well-mannered database file acts in polite company. The rest of this chapter assumes that your database behaves this way.

Figure 6-3:
The
database
file opens
and the
Database
window
displays all
of the
tables,
queries, and
so on.

An introductory screen of some kind (known as a *switchboard*) may appear instead of the tabbed dialog box. Access is telling you that your database either contains some custom programming or was created by the Database Wizard. You probably have some special forms that help you interact with the information in your database.

4. **If it's not already selected, click the Tables button under the Objects bar.**

   The Objects bar's Tables button lists the tables in your database.

5. **Double-click the table you want to edit.**

   The screen fills with your data, displayed eloquently in Datasheet view.

Adding Something to the Mix

Few tasks are more frustrating than packing your car for vacation and then suddenly discovering what you forgot to put in (and it's always something big). In the real world, this discovery is a repacking nightmare, but in the digital world of Access 2002, adding one or a hundred extra items to your database is easy.

In fact, adding another record to a table takes only a couple of steps. The following instructions assume that you have opened the database file and selected the table you want to work on. (If you haven't, follow the instructions in the preceding section.) Here's how to add a new record to your table:

1. **Choose Insert⇨New Record or click the New Record button at the bottom of the datasheet window.**

   Access opens a blank record in your table and moves the toothpick cursor into the first field on that record (as shown in Figure 6-4).

Item ID	ItemName	MinimumBid	Description	CustomerID	DateIn
20	Asst men's clothes	$20.00	Box of assorted men's casual clothes	20	2/2/98
1	China setting for 8	$85.00	White pattern edged in light blue. Ful	11	1/10/98
13	HF Radio	$400.00	Ham radio transceiver. Covers 20 to 1	24	1/29/98
12	Mandolin	$125.00	Mandolin, cherry front. Good conditio	7	1/27/98
17	Notebook computer	$780.00	486DX/2 notebook computer. 16mb F	12	2/1/98
7	Painting -- boat on lake	$100.00	16x20 original oil painting	37	1/25/98
8	Painting -- Children	$100.00	16x20 original oil painting	37	1/25/98
9	Painting -- Convertible	$100.00	16x20 original oil painting	37	1/25/98
10	Painting -- Old man	$100.00	16x20 original oil painting	37	1/25/98
11	Painting -- Round Barn	$100.00	16x20 original oil painting	37	1/25/98
18	Portable printer	$100.00	Portable ink-jet printer. Handles both	12	2/1/98
16	SW receiver	$325.00	Continuous tuning shortwave receiver	24	1/30/98
19	Wedding dress	$720.00	White silk and satin wedding dress, s	20	2/2/98

Record: |◄| ◄| | 25 | ►| ►|| ►*| of 25

Figure 6-4:
A new record — denoted by the asterisk — ready to be filled in.

The first field in many databases is an AutoNumber type field, because this field does such a good job of assigning unique customer numbers, part numbers, or whatever kind of number you have in mind. At this point in the process, it's normal for an AutoNumber field to just sit there and stare at you. The AutoNumber field doesn't start working until the next step.

Prior versions of Access displayed "Auto Number" in the first column if the data type was, in fact, Auto Number. Access 2002 doesn't display anything at all. When you begin typing in the next column, the number magically appears.

2. Type your information.

If the first field is an AutoNumber type, press Tab and begin typing in the second field. As soon as you start typing, the AutoNumber field generates a new number and displays it in the field (see Figure 6-5).

Don't panic if the AutoNumber field seems to skip a number when it creates an entry for your new record. When an AutoNumber field skips a number, it means that you probably entered (or at least started to enter) a record and then deleted it.

3. When you're done entering the record, press Tab to add another record if you want.

Because Access 2002 automatically saves the new record while you're typing it, you have nothing more to do. Pretty cool!

If you change your mind and want to kill the new addition, choose Edit⇨ Undo Saved Record or press Ctrl+Z and then click Yes when Access 2002 asks about deleting the record. If the Undo Saved Record menu choice isn't available, click in the record you just added and then choose Edit⇨Delete Record. As before, click Yes when asked whether you're sure about the deletion.

Figure 6-5:
The record
is almost
completely
entered —
Access has
already
generated
the Auto-
Number
entry.

Item ID	ItemName	MinimumBid	Description	CustomerID	DateIn
20	Asst men's clothes	$20.00	Box of assorted men's casual clothes	20	2/2/98
1	China setting for 8	$85.00	White pattern edged in light blue. Ful	11	1/10/98
13	HF Radio	$400.00	Ham radio transceiver. Covers 20 to 1	24	1/29/98
12	Mandolin	$125.00	Mandolin, cherry front. Good conditio	7	1/27/98
17	Notebook computer	$780.00	486DX/2 notebook computer. 16mb R	12	2/1/98
7	Painting -- boat on lake	$100.00	16x20 original oil painting	37	1/25/98
8	Painting -- Children	$100.00	16x20 original oil painting	37	1/25/98
9	Painting -- Convertible	$100.00	16x20 original oil painting	37	1/25/98
10	Painting -- Old man	$100.00	16x20 original oil painting	37	1/25/98
11	Painting -- Round Barn	$100.00	16x20 original oil painting	37	1/25/98
18	Portable printer	$100.00	Portable ink-jet printer. Handles both	12	2/1/98
16	SW receiver	$325.00	Continuous tuning shortwave receiver	24	1/30/98
19	Wedding dress	$720.00	White silk and satin wedding dress, s	20	2/2/98
26	A new item	$13.00	I can't tell WHAT the heck this is	11	3/15/98

Record: 14 4   26 ▶ ▶I ▶* of 26

Finding those files that hide

Finding your database files isn't always such an easy thing to do. Fear not though, because someone at Microsoft has invented a clever way to find those missing files, even if they deliberately hide from you!

In the Open dialog box, a Tools item sits at the top right. Click it and one of the choices is Search. Select Search to see a variety of different ways

to search for your errant databases. In the figure, I clicked the Advanced tab and told Access that I wanted to locate all databases whose file name includes the word *Northwind*. The results are displayed at the bottom. I can simply double-click to open the database or right-click for other options.

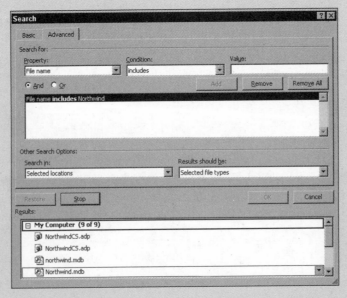

Changing What's Already in a Record

Although your stuff is safely tucked away inside a table, you can reach in and make changes easily. In fact, editing your data is so easy that I'm not sure whether this is a good feature or a bad one.

Whenever you're browsing through a table, please be careful! Access 2002 doesn't warn you before saving changes to a record — even if the changes are accidental. (If I were one of those preachy authors, I'd probably make a big, guilt-laden point about how this "feature" of Access 2002 makes regular backups all the more important.)

To change something inside a record, scroll through the table until you find the record that needs some adjusting. Click in the field you want to change, and the blinking toothpick cursor pops into the field.

If you have the Microsoft IntelliMouse, use the wheel button to quickly spin through the table. For such a small innovation, that wheel is a big time-saver! In Chapter 8, I show you even more about browsing your data with Microsoft's answer to the Big Wheel — the IntelliMouse.

What you do next depends on what change you want to make to the field:

- ✔ To replace the entire field, press F2 to highlight the data and then type the new information. The new entry replaces the old one.

- ✔ To repair a portion of the data in a field, click in the field and then use the right- and left-arrow keys to position the toothpick cursor exactly where you want to make the change. Press Backspace to remove characters to the left of the cursor; press Delete to remove them to the right. Insert new characters by typing.

- ✔ If you're in a time/date field and want to insert the current date, press Ctrl+; (semicolon). To insert the current time, press Ctrl+: (colon).

When you're done with the record, press Enter to save your changes. If you change your mind and want to restore the original data, press Esc or Ctrl+Z to cancel your edits.

Don't press Enter until you're positively sure about the changes you typed. After you save them, the old data is gone — you can't go back.

Kicking Out Unwanted Records

There's no sense mourning unneeded records. When the time comes to bid them adieu, do it quickly and painlessly. Here's how:

1. **With the table open, right-click the button to the left of the record you want to delete.**

   A pop-up menu appears.

   Be sure that you click the correct record before going on to the next step! Discovering the mistake now is much less painful than finding it later.

2. **Choose Delete Record from the pop-up menu.**

   Access 2002 does a truly cool screen effect and visually swallows the old record. But, it's not gone yet! Access now displays the dialog box, shown in Figure 6-6, asking you to confirm the delete.

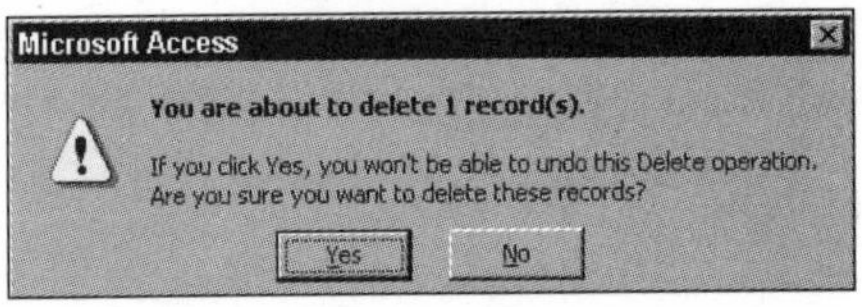

Figure 6-6:
Are you
sure you
want to
delete a
record?

3. **Click Yes to banish the record to oblivion or No if you have changed your mind.**

   If you're the slightest bit unsure, click No and do some more thinking before exercising the Delete Record command on anything else in your table.

Access 2002 may tell you that it can't delete the current record. The reason may be that you're working with a table that's related to another one and the record you're trying to delete contains child records in the other table. If you still want to delete the record, you must first either delete the child records or edit them so that they're no longer related to the record you're trying to delete. If that doesn't make sense, go back and read Chapter 5 about how to make tables relate to one another.

Recovering from a Baaaad Edit

I have only three suggestions for picking up the pieces from a bad edit. Unfortunately, none is a super-cool elixir that magically restores your lost data. I wish I had better news to close the chapter with, but I'm fresh out of headlines.

✔ You can recover from one add or edit with the Undo command.

Unfortunately, there is no undo for deletes.

✔ Double-check any change you make before saving it.

If the change is important, triple-check it. When you're sure that it's right, press Enter and commit the change to the table. If you're not sure about the data, don't save the changes. Instead, get your questions answered first and then feel free to edit the record.

✔ Keep a good backup so that you can quickly recover missing data and get on with your work.

Good backups have no substitute. If you make good backups, the chance of losing data is greatly reduced, your boss promotes you, your significant other unswervingly devotes his or her life to you, and you may even win the lottery.

Chapter 7

Making Your Table Think with Formats, Masks, and Validations

In This Chapter

▶ Finding where the settings live

▶ Better formatting for prettier data

▶ Keeping bad data out with input masks

▶ Performing detailed testing through validations

Scientists have incredibly detailed, long-winded explanations of what it means to think, but my definition is simpler. If you see dragons in the clouds, marvel at a child's playtime adventures, or wonder what makes flowers grow, you're thinking.

Whether you use my definition or one from the experts, one thing is certain: Access 2002 tables *don't* think. If you have nightmarish visions of reading this chapter and then accidentally unleashing The Table That Ate Microsoft's Competitors, have no fear; it's not going to happen. (After all, if such a scenario could happen, don't you think Microsoft would have arranged it by now?)

This chapter explains how to enlist your table's help to spot and prevent bad data from getting into your table. The chapter focuses on three different tools: *formats, masks,* and *validation rules*. These tools may sound technical, but you can handle them.

Each tool has its own section, so if you're looking for specific information, feel free to jump right to the appropriate section.

Finding the Place to Make a Change

The first bit of knowledge you need is *where* to make all these cool changes to your table. Luckily, all three options are in the same place: the Table Design window's General tab.

Use the following steps to put your table into Design view, and then flip to the appropriate section of the chapter for the details on applying a format, input mask, or validation to a field in your table.

1. **Open the database file and click the table you want to adjust. Click the Design button or right-click the table and choose Design view (see Figure 7-1).**

   The table flips into Design view, showing its nerdish underbelly to the world.

   If the table you want is already on-screen in Datasheet view, just click the Design button on the far-left side of the toolbar to get into Design view.

2. **Click the name of the field you want to work on.**

   The General tab in the Field Properties section (the bottom half of the window) displays the details of the current field, as shown in Figure 7-2. You're ready to do your stuff!

3. **Click in the appropriate box in the Field Properties section (along the bottom of the window) and type in your changes.**

   Format, Input Mask, and Validation Rule each have a box. (The Validation Text has a box too, but you have to look in the validations section later in this chapter to find out more about it — it's a secret for now.)

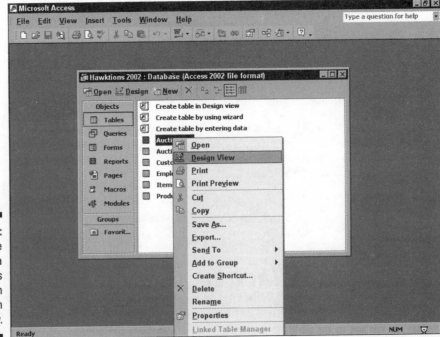

Figure 7-1: You can see and edit a table's structure in Design view.

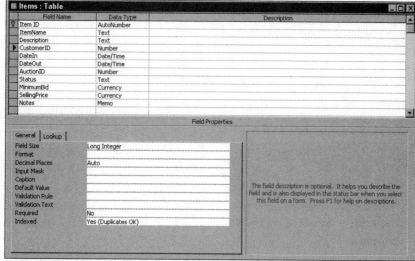

Figure 7-2:
Working on
the
CustomerID
field.

4. **Repeat Step 2 if you want to work on other fields.**

5. **When Access prompts you to save your changes, click Yes and then close the table.**

Granted, using formats, masks, and validations involves many more details, but the steps to get started are the same no matter which tool you apply. The following sections tackle each tool individually.

To Format, Perchance to Better See

Formats only change the way you *see* your data on-screen, not how your data is actually stored in the table. Although formats don't directly catch errors, they *do* make your information look simply marvelous.

Each field type has its own set of formats. Pay close attention to the type of field you're working with. Applying the wrong format to a field is both pointless and frustrating (and goodness knows there are *enough* pointless and frustrating aspects of your computer without actively courting another one) because your data can't look right, regardless of how hard you try.

To prevent that error, I organize the following formatting information by field type. Check the field type you're working with and then refer to the appropriate section for the available formatting options.

If your format command doesn't work the first time, just double-check the field type and then review the format commands. In no time at all, you ferret out the problem.

Text and memo fields

Four ways exist to format text and memo fields. At my editor's insistence, I have listed each of them here:

- The *greater than symbol* (>) makes all the text in that field appear in uppercase, regardless of how the text was entered. To use this option, type a single greater than symbol in the Format text box.

  Although Access 2002 stores the data *just as it was typed,* the data appears in uppercase only.

- The *less than symbol* (<) does just the opposite of the greater than symbol. The less than symbol shows all that field's text in lowercase. Apply this format by typing a single less than symbol in the Format text box.

  If you entered the data in mixed case, Access 2002 displays the data as lowercase. As with the greater than symbol, only the display is changed to protect the innocent, otherwise the data is still stored as mixed case.

- The *at sign* (@) forces Access 2002 to display either a character or a space in the field. If the field data is smaller than the format, Access 2002 adds extra spaces to fill up the format. For example, if a field uses @@@@@@ as its format, but the field's data is only three characters long (such as *Tim* or *now*), Access 2002 displays three spaces and *then* the data. If the field data is four characters long, the format pads the beginning of the entry with two spaces.

- The *ampersand* (&) is the default format. It means "display a character if there's one to display; otherwise don't do anything." You can use this to create special masks. For example, the mask "&&&-&&-&&&&" can be used in a Social Security number field. If the user entered 123456789, the display would be "123-45-6789".

  You include one at sign or ampersand *for each character* in the field, unlike the greater than and less than symbols, which require only one symbol for the whole field.

Number and currency fields

The friendly folks at Microsoft did all the hard work for you on the number and currency field types. They built the six most common formats into a pull-down menu right in the Format text box. To set a number or currency field format, click in the Format text box and then click the down arrow that appears at the right side of the box. Figure 7-3 shows the pull-down menu, complete with your choices.

Hey Access, save my place!

This tip is a certified Nerd Trick, but it's so useful that I have to tell you about it. When entering data, sometimes you need to skip a text field because you don't have that particular information at hand. Wouldn't it be great if Access 2002 automatically marked the field as blank as a reminder for you to come back and fill in the info later?

Access 2002 can create such a custom text format for you, and you don't even have to be a master magician to pull off this trick. Here's how

to do it: Type @;"Unknown"[Red] into the field's Format text box.

This peculiar notation displays the word Unknown in red print if the field doesn't contain a value. You must type the command exactly like the example (quotation marks, square brackets, and all), or it doesn't work. Feel free to substitute your own word for Unknown, though — the command doesn't care what you put between the quotation marks.

Each format's given name is on the left side of the menu. The other side shows a sample of how the format works. Here's a quick rundown of the most common choices:

- ✔ **General Number:** This format is the Access 2002 default. It merely displays whatever you put into the field without making any editorial adjustments to it.

- ✔ **Currency:** This format makes a standard number field look just like a currency field. It shows the data with two decimal places, substituting zeros if decimals aren't present to begin with. Currency format also adds the appropriate currency sign and punctuation, according to the Regional Settings in the Windows Control Panel.

- ✔ **Euro:** Similar to Currency except uses the Euro symbol €.

- ✔ **Fixed:** This format locks the field's data into a specific number of decimal places. By default, this format rounds to two decimal places. To specify a different number of decimal places, use the Decimal Places setting right below the Format setting.

- ✔ **Standard:** This format is like Fixed but adds a thousands separator as well. Adjust the number of decimals by changing the Decimal Places setting.

- ✔ **Percent:** This format turns a simple decimal such as .97 into the much prettier 97%.

  Remember to enter the data as a decimal (.97 instead of 97); otherwise Access 2002 displays some truly awesome percentages! If your percentages display only as 0.00% or 1.00%, see the next paragraph for a solution.

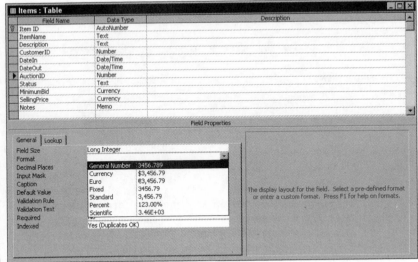

Figure 7-3:
Choose a number format from the list.

If your entries automatically round to the nearest whole number and always display zeros in the decimal places, change the Field Size setting (right above Format) from Long Integer to Single. This setting tells Access 2002 to remember the decimal part of the number. By default, Access 2002 rounds the number to an integer as you enter it.

Date/time fields

Like the Number and Currency format options, date/time fields have a ready-to-use set of formats available in a pull-down menu. Click in the Format text box and then click the down arrow that appears on the box's right side, and the menu in Figure 7-4 dutifully pops down to serve you.

The choices are pretty self-explanatory, but I want to pass along a couple of tips.

✔ When you use one of the larger formats such as General Date or Long Date, make sure that the datasheet column is wide enough to display the whole date. Otherwise, the cool-looking date doesn't make sense because a major portion of it is missing.

✔ If more than one person uses the database, choosing a format that provides *more* information rather than one that provides less is much better.

My favorite is the Medium Date format, because it spells out the month and day. Dates such as 3/7/99 may cause confusion, because people in different countries interpret that format differently.

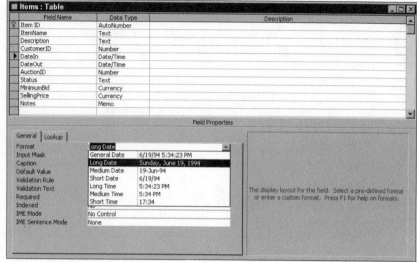

Figure 7-4:
A format for
every date
and a date
for every,
uh, never
mind.

Yes/No fields

You can only say so much about a field with three options. Your preset
formatting choices are somewhat limited (see Figure 7-5). By default, Yes/No
fields are set to the Yes/No formatting. Feel free to experiment with the other
options, particularly if they make more sense in your table than Yes and No.

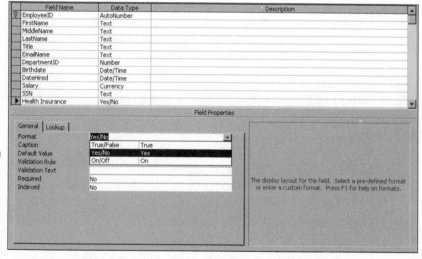

Figure 7-5:
This
format's
cupboard is
pretty bare.

To display your *own* choices instead of a boring Yes and No, you have to type a customized format. This procedure works very much like the custom text format earlier in this chapter. A good example format is something like this: "In stock"[Green];"REORDER"[Red]. If an item is in stock, the text *In stock* appears in green. Otherwise, *REORDER* screams a warning in bright red. Substitute your own words for mine if you like, because Access 2002 displays whatever you put between the quotes without making any editorial decisions about the content. Make certain that the Display Control under the Lookup tab (next to the General tab) is set to Text Box, otherwise you may have check boxes in your field.

What Is That Masked Data?

Although they have a funny name, *input masks* are filters that allow you to enter only certain data into a field. When they're paired with validations (I cover them later in this chapter), the fields in your table are *very* well protected against bad information.

An input mask is just a series of characters that tells Access 2002 what data to expect in a particular field. If you want a field to contain all numbers and no letters, an input mask can do the job. It can also do the reverse (all letters and no numbers) and almost any combination in between. Input masks are stored in the Input Mask area of the field's General tab, along with everything else described in this chapter.

More than half the fields in an Access 2002 table can have their own input mask. Before creating the mask, you have to know *exactly* what the field's data looks like. Creating a mask that allows only letters into a field doesn't do any good if your goal is to store street addresses. Know your data intimately *before* messing around with input masks.

Input masks work best with *short, highly consistent* data. Numbers and number/letter combinations that all look alike are excellent candidates. Part numbers, stock-keeping units, postal codes, phone numbers, and Social Security numbers beg for input masks to ensure that the right data gets into the field.

You create an input mask in one of two ways:

- ✔ Type the mask manually
- ✔ Ask the Input Mask Wizard for help

    As luck has it, the Input Mask Wizard isn't terribly bright — it only knows about text and date fields. And even then, the Input Mask Wizard offers just a few options. To accomplish anything more means cracking your knuckles and working it by hand.

Using the Input Mask Wizard

The Input Mask Wizard gleefully helps if you're making a mask for a phone number, Social Security number, United States zip code, or simple date and time field. Beyond those fields, the Input Mask Wizard is clueless, so don't look for its help with anything other than text or time/date type fields.

To ask for the wizard's help, follow these steps:

1. **With the database file open, click the table you want to work with and then click Design.**

   The table flips into Design view.

2. **Click the name of the field you want to adjust.**

   The General tab in the Field Properties section (the bottom half of the window) displays the details of the current field.

3. **Click the Input Mask box.**

   The cursor hops into the Input Mask box. To the right of the box, a small button with three dots appears. That's the Build button, which comes into play in the next step.

4. **Click the Build button at the right side of the Input Mask text box.**

   The wizard appears, offering a choice of input masks as shown in Figure 7-6.

   You can use the wizard only with text and date fields.

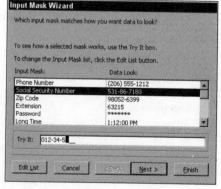

Figure 7-6:
The Input
Mask
Wizard.

5. **Scroll through the list of available input masks to find what you want. Click your choice and then click Next.**

6. **If you want to see whether the mask *really* does what you want, click in the Try It area at the bottom of the dialog box. When you're done, click Finish to use the mask with your field.**

The chosen mask appears in the Input Mask area on the table design screen (see Figure 7-7).

If you click Next instead of Finish, the wizard offers you an arcane choice about storing characters along with your data. The wizard wants to know whether you want the dashes, slashes, and parentheses that the input mask displays to be stored in your table along with the data you typed. The default is No, which I recommend sticking with. Click Finish to complete the process.

Employees : Table

Field Name	Data Type	Description
EmployeeID	AutoNumber	
FirstName	Text	
MiddleName	Text	
LastName	Text	
Title	Text	
EmailName	Text	
DepartmentID	Number	
Birthdate	Date/Time	
DateHired	Date/Time	
Salary	Currency	
SSN	Text	
Health Insurance	Yes/No	

Field Properties

General | Lookup

Field Size	9
Format	&&&-&&-&&&&
Input Mask	000-00-0000;; _
Caption	
Default Value	
Validation Rule	
Validation Text	
Required	No
Allow Zero Length	Yes
Indexed	No
Unicode Compression	Yes
IME Mode	No Control
IME Sentence Mode	None

A pattern for all data to be entered in this field

Figure 7-7: The Input Mask Wizard did all that work for me.

Making a mask by hand

Few projects are more gratifying than making something yourself. Building an input mask with your bare hands, raw nerve, and these instructions *may* give you that same feeling of accomplishment. The stuff that input masks *do* isn't terribly complicated, but a finished mask often *looks* complicated. Don't worry, though. After you get the hang of it, building powerful input masks is easy.

To design and use an input mask, follow these steps:

1. **Write on a piece of paper an example of the data that the mask is supposed to let into the table.**

As I mention earlier in the chapter, knowing your data is the first step in the input mask process.

If the information you're storing has subtle variations (such as part numbers that end in either a letter/number or letter/letter combination), include examples of the various possibilities so that your input mask accepts them all.

2. Write a simple description of the data, including which elements are required and which are optional.

If your sample is a part number that looks like 728816ABC7, write six numbers, three letters, one number; all parts are required. Remember to allow for the variations, if you have any. The difference between *one number* and *one letter or number* can be crucial.

Access 2002 uses different codes for required and optional data, so you need to note the difference:

- *Required* information must be entered into the field (such as a phone number).

- *Optional* elements are just that — optional (such as an area code or extension number).

3. Enter your Input Mask in Access 2002 based on the codes in Table 7-1.

Because you know what data you're storing (numbers, letters, or either one), how many characters you need, and whether each one is required or optional, working through the table and creating the mask is easy.

This mask uses both the backslash and quotation mark to put parentheses around the area code plus a space between the area code and phone number.

- To include a dash, slash, or parenthesis in your mask, put a backslash (\) in front of it.

- To include more than one character, put quotation marks around them. For example, the mask for a phone number with an area code is !\(999") "000\-0000.

See the following sidebar to find out why I included an exclamation point in this example.

4. If your field includes letters and you want them to always be uppercase, add a greater than symbol (>) to the beginning of your mask.

To make the letters lowercase, use a less than symbol (<) instead.

You're ready to tell Access 2002 about your input mask.

5. Click in the Input Mask box.

The blinking toothpick cursor hops into the box, ready for action.

6. Carefully type your finished mask into the Input Mask area of Field Properties (as shown in Figure 7-8).

Products : Table

Field Name	Data Type	Description
ProductID	AutoNumber	Product ID
ProductName	Text	Product Name
Prod Description	Text	Product Description
Quantity	Number	Current Stock Level
Code	Text	Product Code

Field Properties

General | Lookup |

Field Size	50
Format	
Input Mask	>0000000\-LA\-LA;;
Caption	
Default Value	
Validation Rule	
Validation Text	
Required	No
Allow Zero Length	Yes
Indexed	Yes (Duplicates OK)
Unicode Compression	Yes
IME Mode	No Control
IME Sentence Mode	None

A pattern for all data to be entered in this field

Figure 7-8:
Putting a
mask on the
Code field.

Don't worry if the mask looks like a text version of the Frankenstein
monster. Beauty is optional in the world of technology.

**7. At the end of the mask, add ;;_ (two semicolons and an underscore
character).**

These three characters tell Access 2002 to display an underscore where
you want each letter to appear. This step isn't required, but I think that
input masks make more sense with this option. Your mileage may vary.

8. Click the Table View button on the toolbar to check out your handiwork.

Try typing something into the now-masked field. The input mask should
prevent you from entering an incorrect value. If it doesn't work, take the
table back into Design view (click the Design View button on the left side
of the toolbar) and make some repairs.

If you're adding a mask to an existing table, the mask doesn't ferret out
incorrect data that's *already* in the table. You have to click each entry in
the masked field (yes, that means clicking on this field in *every* record of
the table) to check it. If something is wrong, Access 2002 tells you, but
not until you click.

Table 7-1	Codes for the Input Mask	
Kind of Characters	*Required Code*	*Optional Code*
Digits (0 to 9) only	0 (zero)	9
Digits and +/- signs	(not available)	# (U.S. pound sign)
Letters (A to Z) only	L	? (question mark)
Letters or digits only	A	a (must be lowercase)
Any character or space	& (ampersand)	C

The exclamation point: To know it is to love it

Getting to know the exclamation point took me a while. After all, my input masks seemed very happy without it. Even the explanation in the Access 2002 online Help file didn't change my mind. (I suppose that if the Help file's explanation had made sense, it may have had a better chance.)

While playing with the phone number example, I finally realized what the exclamation point does and why it's so useful. The exclamation point tells Access 2002 to fill up the field from the right instead of the left. Although this notion may sound like the unintelligible ramblings of an over-caffeinated nerd, it really is an important point. Let me tell you why.

In the phone number example, the area code is optional, but the number itself is required. If I leave the exclamation point out of the input mask, Access 2002 lets me skip the area code

and type a phone number into the phone number spaces. Everything looks fine until I press Enter. Then my seven-digit phone number displays as (555) 121-2. Eeeeewwww — not exactly what I had in mind. That's because Access 2002 filled the mask from the left, starting with the optional numbers in the area code (the numbers I didn't enter).

By adding the exclamation point to the input mask, Access 2002 takes my data and fills the mask from the right. This time, the phone number appears on-screen as ( ) 555-1212, which is what I wanted all along.

The exclamation point can go anywhere in the input mask, but try to get into the habit of putting it either at the beginning or the end. I suggest making the exclamation point the first character in the mask, simply because you won't overlook it in that position.

Validations: The Digital Breathalyzer Test

Your third (and, arguably, most powerful) tool in the War Against Bad Data is the *validation*. With a validation, Access 2002 actually tests the incoming data to make sure that it's what you want in the table. If the data isn't right, the validation displays an error message (you get to choose what it says!) and makes you try the entry again.

Like the other options in this chapter, validations are stored in the General tab of the Field Properties area. Two spaces relate to validations:

- **Validation Rule:** The rule is the actual validation itself.
- **Validation Text:** The text is the error message you want Access 2002 to display when some data that violates the validation rule wanders in.

Validations work best with number, currency, and date fields. Creating a validation for a text field is possible, but the validations usually get *very* complicated *very* fast. In the name of protecting your sanity and hairline, Table 7-2 contains some ready-to-use validations that cover the most common needs. They're organized by field type, so finding the validation rule that suits your purpose is easy.

I include different kinds of examples to show off the power of the logical operators that validations use. Feel free to mix and match with the operators. Play around and see what you can come up with! Watch out for these gotchas:

- ✔ When using AND, remember that both sides of the validation rule must be true before the rule is met.

- ✔ With OR, only one side of the rule needs to be true for the whole rule to be true.

- ✔ Be careful when combining >= and <= examples.

    Accidentally coming up with one that can't be true (such as <= 0 AND >= 100) is too easy!

Table 7-2	Validations for Many Occasions	
Field Type	*Validation Rule*	*Definition*
Number	> 0	Must be greater than zero
Number	<> 0	Cannot be zero
Number	> 0 AND < 100	Must be between 0 and 100 (noninclusive)
Number (inclusive)	>= 0 AND <= 100	Must be between 0 and 100
Number	<= 0 OR >= 100	Must be less than 0 or greater than 100 (inclusive)
Date	>= Date ()	Must be today's date or later
Date	>= Date () OR Is Null	Must be today's date, later, or blank
Date	< Date ()	Must be earlier than today's date
Date	>= #1/1/90# AND <= Date ()	Must be between January 1, 1990, and today (inclusive)

Chapter 8

Making Your Datasheets Dance

In This Chapter

▶ Wandering around your datasheet

▶ Adjusting column width, row height, and more

▶ Seeing the datasheet in a whole new font

▶ Changing the background

*H*aving your new datasheet look and act just like every *other* datasheet is pretty boring. Where's the creativity in that? Where's the individuality? Where's the life, liberty, and pursuit of ultimate coolness?

Granted, Access 2002 *is* a database program, and databases aren't generally known for being the life of the party, but that doesn't mean you're trapped in a monotonous world of lookalike datasheets. This chapter explores the tools at your disposal to turn even the most dreary datasheet into a slick-looking, easy-to-navigate presentation of your data.

The following pages focus on datasheet tricks — what to do when you're working with information in a datasheet. These tricks work with datasheets from both tables and dynasets, so use them to amble through and spruce up every datasheet in sight. If you haven't heard about dynasets, don't worry. I cover them in Part III.

Wandering Here, There, and Everywhere

When a table appears in Datasheet view, Access 2002 presents a window to your data. That window displays a certain number of rows and columns, but (unless you have a really small table) what's shown certainly isn't the whole enchilada. To see more, you need to move through the table, which means moving your window around to see what else is out there.

Access 2002 offers several ways to hike through a datasheet. Which method you choose depends on how far you want to go:

- ✔ **To move from field to field:** Use the right- and left-arrow keys. Clicking on the arrows on either end of the horizontal scroll bar does the same with the mouse.

- ✔ **To move between records:** Try the up- and down-arrow keys. If you're a mouse-oriented person, click in the arrows at the ends of the vertical scroll bar.

- ✔ **To display a new page of data:** The PgUp and PgDn keys come in handy (depending on your keyboard, these may be called Page Up and Page Down, instead).

  - PgUp and PgDn scroll vertically through the datasheet.
  - Ctrl+PgUp and Ctrl+PgDn scroll horizontally.

  Clicking in either scroll bar does the same.

Table 8-1 outlines the process from a keystroke-by-keystroke point of view. Between the preceding movement tips and the following table, you now know just about every possible way to move through an Access 2002 datasheet.

Table 8-1	**Moving through a Table**
Keystroke or Control	*What It Does*
Ctrl+End	Jumps to the last field in the last record of the table
Ctrl+Home	Jumps to the first field in the first record of the table
Ctrl+PgDn	Scrolls one screen to the right
Ctrl+PgUp	Scrolls one screen to the left
↓	Moves down one record in the table
End	Goes to the last field in the current record
Home	Goes to the first field in the current record
Horizontal scroll bar	Scrolls right or left one window at a time through the table
IntelliMouse wheel	Turn the wheel to scroll up or down three records at a time through the table (only available with IntelliPoint mouse and driver software)

Keystroke or Control	What It Does
IntelliMouse wheel button	Press the wheel like a button and it becomes a super-arrow key; scroll one row or column at a time through the table (only available with IntelliPoint mouse and driver software)
←	Moves one field to the left in the current record
PgDn	Scrolls one screen down
PgUp	Scrolls one screen up
→	Moves one field to the right in the current record
↑	Moves up one record in the table
Vertical scroll bar	Scrolls up or down one window at a time through the table

Seeing More (Or Less) of Your Data

First on the datasheet tune-up list is fiddling with the look of your datasheet. You have plenty to fiddle with, too. At first blush, your datasheet looks pretty mundane, much like Figure 8-1. To perk it up a bit, you can change the column width, row height, and column order, and you can lock a column in place while the others scroll around it. Heck, you can even make columns disappear temporarily.

The following sections explore techniques for changing the way your data looks. You can use one option (such as changing the column width) or a number of options — you make the call. Each adjustment is independent of the others. Plus, these changes don't affect your actual data — they just present the data differently on-screen.

Most of the commands work from the mouse, but some of them send you back to the menu bar. If a command is in both places, it works the same either way.

After you make any of these adjustments to your table, be sure to tell Access 2002 to save the table's formatting changes, or all your hard work is lost forever. To notify Access 2002, either choose File⇨Save or simply close the window. If any unsaved changes are in the table when you try to close the window, Access 2002 automatically prompts you to save the new formatting.

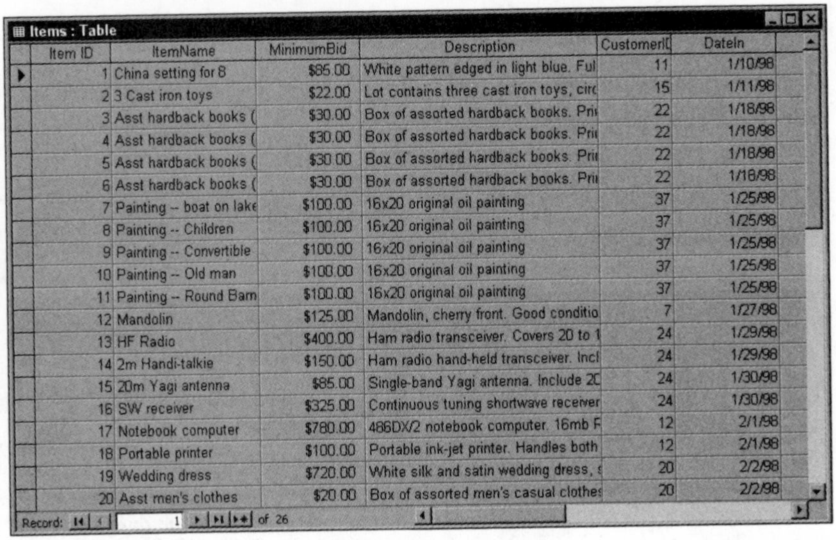

Items : Table					
Item ID	ItemName	MinimumBid	Description	CustomerID	DateIn
1	China setting for 8	$85.00	White pattern edged in light blue. Full	11	1/10/98
2	3 Cast iron toys	$22.00	Lot contains three cast iron toys, circ	15	1/11/98
3	Asst hardback books (	$30.00	Box of assorted hardback books. Pri	22	1/18/98
4	Asst hardback books (	$30.00	Box of assorted hardback books. Pri	22	1/18/98
5	Asst hardback books (	$30.00	Box of assorted hardback books. Pri	22	1/18/98
6	Asst hardback books (	$30.00	Box of assorted hardback books. Pri	22	1/18/98
7	Painting -- boat on lake	$100.00	16x20 original oil painting	37	1/25/98
8	Painting -- Children	$100.00	16x20 original oil painting	37	1/25/98
9	Painting -- Convertible	$100.00	16x20 original oil painting	37	1/25/98
10	Painting -- Old man	$100.00	16x20 original oil painting	37	1/25/98
11	Painting -- Round Barn	$100.00	16x20 original oil painting	37	1/25/98
12	Mandolin	$125.00	Mandolin, cherry front. Good conditio	7	1/27/98
13	HF Radio	$400.00	Ham radio transceiver. Covers 20 to 1	24	1/29/98
14	2m Handi-talkie	$150.00	Ham radio hand-held transceiver. Incl	24	1/29/98
15	20m Yagi antenna	$85.00	Single-band Yagi antenna. Include 20	24	1/30/98
16	SW receiver	$325.00	Continuous tuning shortwave receiver	24	1/30/98
17	Notebook computer	$780.00	486DX/2 notebook computer. 16mb F	12	2/1/98
18	Portable printer	$100.00	Portable ink-jet printer. Handles both	12	2/1/98
19	Wedding dress	$720.00	White silk and satin wedding dress, ‹	20	2/2/98
20	Asst men's clothes	$20.00	Box of assorted men's casual clothes	20	2/2/98

Record: 14 ‹ | 1 | › | ›I | ›* | of 26

Figure 8-1: Access presents your data in rows (records) and columns (fields).

Changing the column width

Although Access 2002 is pretty smart, it has trouble figuring out how wide to make a column. In fact, it usually just gives up and sets all the column widths identically, leaving some far too wide and others way too narrow. Pretty wimpy solution for a powerful program, if you ask me.

Setting a new column width is a quick operation. Here's what to do:

1. **With your table in Datasheet view, put the mouse pointer on the vertical bar to the right of the field name (as shown in Figure 8-2).**

   The mouse pointer changes into a bar with arrows sticking out of each side.

2. **Click and hold the left mouse button while moving the mouse appropriately.**

   Changing the field width is intuitive:

   • To make the column wider, move the mouse to the right.

   • To make it smaller, move the mouse to the left.

3. **Release the mouse button when the width is just right.**

   The column is locked into its new size, as shown in Figure 8-3.

Alternative ways of getting around

If you're blessed with a Microsoft IntelliMouse and its IntelliPoint driver software, you have an extra tool for moving through your Access 2002 datasheets. Between the two regular mouse buttons, the IntelliMouse sports a wheel that acts as a third button.

✔ Rolling the wheel scrolls up and down through your datasheet three lines at a time.

✔ Clicking and dragging with the wheel button moves the window around the datasheet in whichever direction you move the mouse. (This maneuver works just like a normal click and drag, except that you're using the wheel button instead of the left mouse button.)

If you spend a great deal of time with Access 2002 or jumping among the Office XP applications, I suggest you take the new mouse for a test drive. Each program applies the wheel button a little differently, but *all* the programs (and even Windows itself) use it to make your life a little easier.

But wait, there's more!

Office XP introduces new ways of interacting with your computer (at least with Office programs) beyond the traditional keyboard and mouse that we've all grown to know and hate. Specifically, Office XP now supports handwriting recognition and voice recognition. Although handwriting recognition could certainly be incorporated into an Access project, doing so is beyond the scope of this book. You may, however, find voice recognition useful. Voice recognition enables you to dictate to your computer and give it commands. Chapter 25 covers voice recognition in full detail.

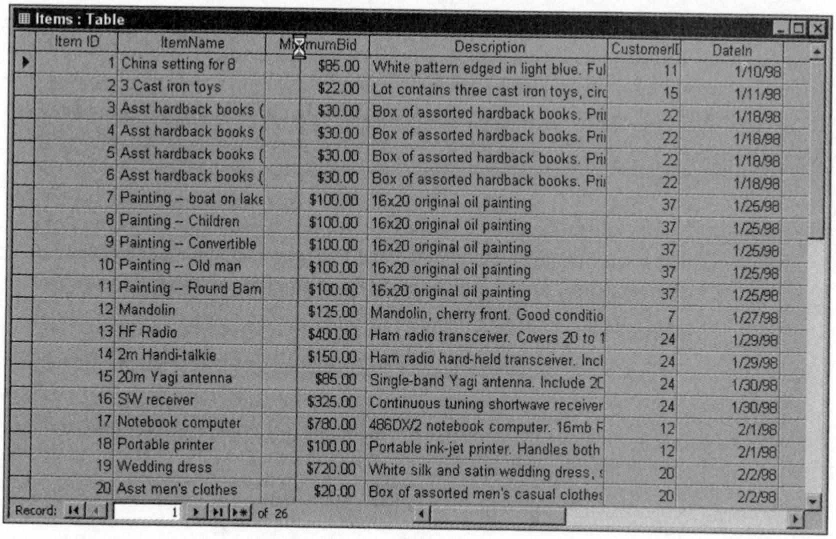

Figure 8-2:
You can resize any column to suit your needs.

Item ID	ItemName	MaximumBid	Description	CustomerID	DateIn
1	China setting for 8	$85.00	White pattern edged in light blue. Ful	11	1/10/98
2	3 Cast iron toys	$22.00	Lot contains three cast iron toys, circ	15	1/11/98
3	Asst hardback books (	$30.00	Box of assorted hardback books. Prir	22	1/18/98
4	Asst hardback books (	$30.00	Box of assorted hardback books. Prir	22	1/18/98
5	Asst hardback books (	$30.00	Box of assorted hardback books. Prir	22	1/18/98
6	Asst hardback books (	$30.00	Box of assorted hardback books. Prir	22	1/18/98
7	Painting – boat on lake	$100.00	16x20 original oil painting	37	1/25/98
8	Painting -- Children	$100.00	16x20 original oil painting	37	1/25/98
9	Painting -- Convertible	$100.00	16x20 original oil painting	37	1/25/98
10	Painting -- Old man	$100.00	16x20 original oil painting	37	1/25/98
11	Painting -- Round Barn	$100.00	16x20 original oil painting	37	1/25/98
12	Mandolin	$125.00	Mandolin, cherry front. Good conditio	7	1/27/98
13	HF Radio	$400.00	Ham radio transceiver. Covers 20 to 1	24	1/29/98
14	2m Handi-talkie	$150.00	Ham radio hand-held transceiver. Incl	24	1/29/98
15	20m Yagi antenna	$85.00	Single-band Yagi antenna. Include 20	24	1/30/98
16	SW receiver	$325.00	Continuous tuning shortwave receiver	24	1/30/98
17	Notebook computer	$780.00	486DX/2 notebook computer. 16mb F	12	2/1/98
18	Portable printer	$100.00	Portable ink-jet printer. Handles both	12	2/1/98
19	Wedding dress	$720.00	White silk and satin wedding dress,	20	2/2/98
20	Asst men's clothes	$20.00	Box of assorted men's casual clothes	20	2/2/98

Record: 1 of 26

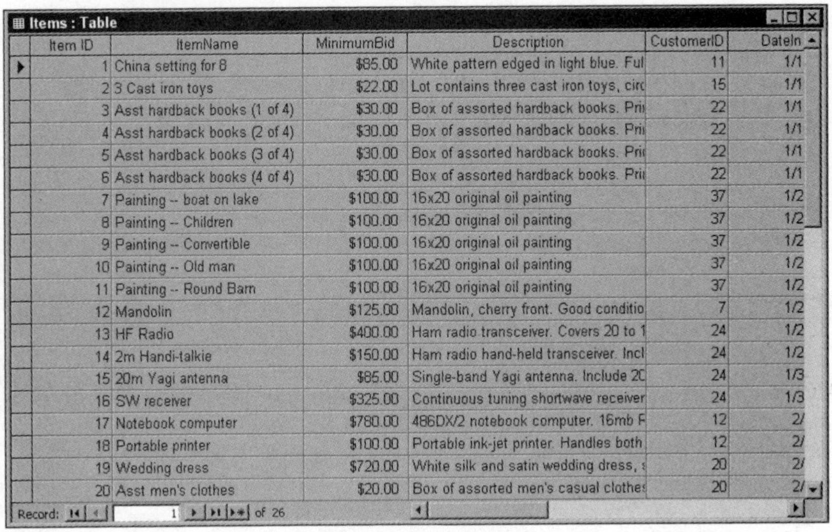

Figure 8-3:
The
ItemName
column has
been
resized to
show all of
its contents.

Changing the row height

Access 2002 does a little better in the row height department than it does with column widths. It automatically leaves enough room to separate the rows while displaying plenty of information on-screen.

Access 2002 still has room for improvement, because you can't see all the data in your table's longest fields. Changing the row height fixes this problem by showing more data in each field while displaying the same number of columns on-screen.

Like changing column width, adjusting the row height takes only a couple of mouse clicks:

1. **While in Datasheet view, put the mouse pointer in the far-left side of the window on the line between any two rows in your spreadsheet (as shown in Figure 8-4).**

   The mouse pointer changes into a horizontal bar with arrows sticking out vertically.

2. **Click and hold the left mouse button; then move the mouse to change the row height.**

   Change the row height like this:

   • Move the mouse down to make the row higher.

   • Move the mouse up to squash the row and put the squeeze on your data.

Items : Table

Item ID	ItemName	MinimumBid	Description	CustomerID	DateIn
1	China setting for 8	$85.00	White pattern edged in light blue. Ful	11	1/1
2	3 Cast iron toys	$22.00	Lot contains three cast iron toys, circ	15	1/1
3	Asst hardback books (1 of 4)	$30.00	Box of assorted hardback books. Prir	22	1/1
4	Asst hardback books (2 of 4)	$30.00	Box of assorted hardback books. Prir	22	1/1
5	Asst hardback books (3 of 4)	$30.00	Box of assorted hardback books. Prir	22	1/1
6	Asst hardback books (4 of 4)	$30.00	Box of assorted hardback books. Prir	22	1/1
7	Painting -- boat on lake	$100.00	16x20 original oil painting	37	1/2
8	Painting -- Children	$100.00	16x20 original oil painting	37	1/2
9	Painting -- Convertible	$100.00	16x20 original oil painting	37	1/2
10	Painting -- Old man	$100.00	16x20 original oil painting	37	1/2
11	Painting -- Round Barn	$100.00	16x20 original oil painting	37	1/2
12	Mandolin	$125.00	Mandolin, cherry front. Good conditio	7	1/2
13	HF Radio	$400.00	Ham radio transceiver. Covers 20 to 1	24	1/2
14	2m Handi-talkie	$150.00	Ham radio hand-held transceiver. Incl	24	1/2
15	20m Yagi antenna	$85.00	Single-band Yagi antenna. Include 20	24	1/3
16	SW receiver	$325.00	Continuous tuning shortwave receiver	24	1/3
17	Notebook computer	$780.00	486DX/2 notebook computer. 16mb F	12	2/
18	Portable printer	$100.00	Portable ink-jet printer. Handles both	12	2/
19	Wedding dress	$720.00	White silk and satin wedding dress, ε	20	2/
20	Asst men's clothes	$20.00	Box of assorted men's casual clothes	20	2/

Record: I◄ ◄ 1 ► ►I ►* of 26

Figure 8-4:
You can
modify the
height of
datasheet
rows.

3. Release the mouse button when the row height is where you want it.

Access 2002 redisplays the table with its new row height (as shown in
Figure 8-5).

Reorganizing the columns

When you laid out the table, you put quite a bit of thought into which field
came after which other field. Most of the time, your data looks just the way
you want it on-screen, but occasionally you need to stir up your system.

To move a field to a different place on the datasheet, use these steps:

**1. Click the field name of the column you want to move; then click and
hold the left mouse button.**

The whole column darkens, and the mouse pointer changes to an arrow
with a smaller box at the base of the mouse pointer (as shown in Figure 8-6).

2. Drag the column to its new destination.

As you move the mouse, a dark bar moves between the columns, showing you where the column lands when you release the mouse button.

If you accidentally let go of the button before the dark bar appears,
Access 2002 doesn't move the column. In that case, start again with
Step 1 (and keep a tight grip on that mouse).

3. When the column is in place, release the mouse button.

The column, data and all, moves to the new spot (as shown in Figure 8-7).

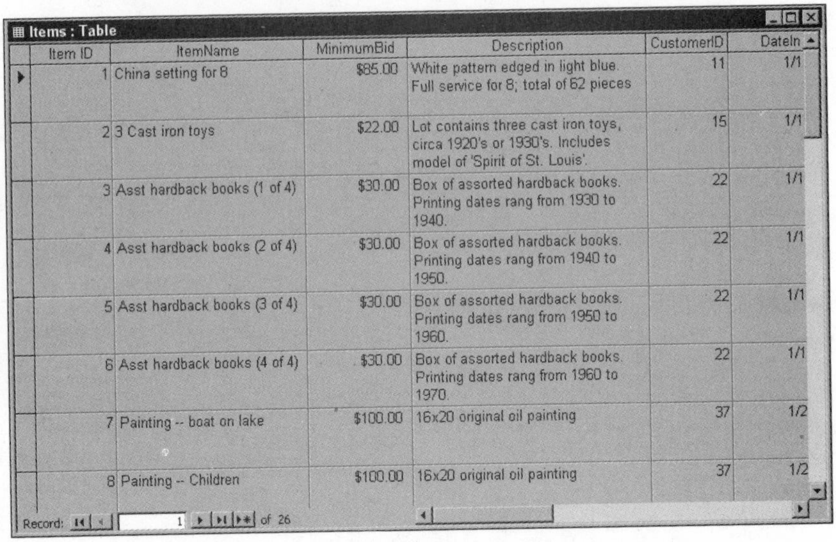

Figure 8-5:
Description
now has
room to
wrap.

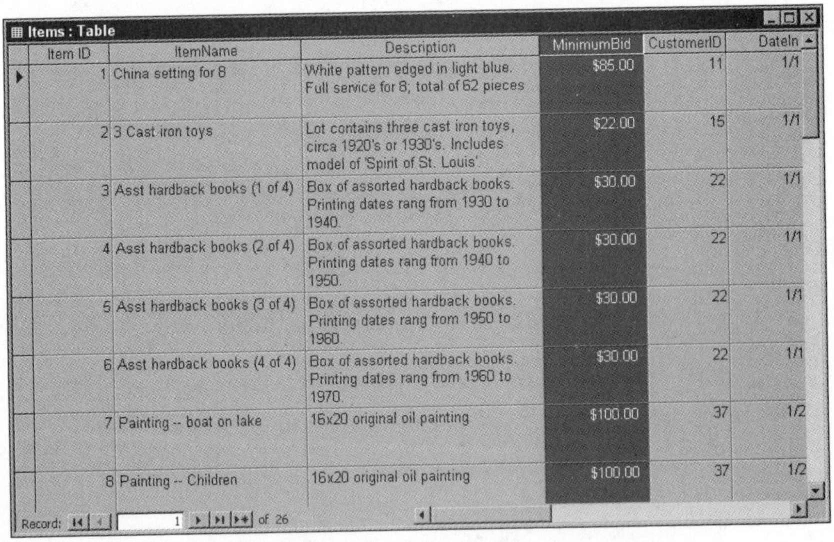

Figure 8-6:
Preparing
to move
MinimumBid
to its new
location.

Hiding a column

Hiding a column is one of those features that seems totally unimportant until the moment you need it. Then it's worth its weight in gold. If you want to temporarily conceal a particular column, just hide the little fellow. The data is still in the table, but it doesn't appear on-screen. Too cool, eh?

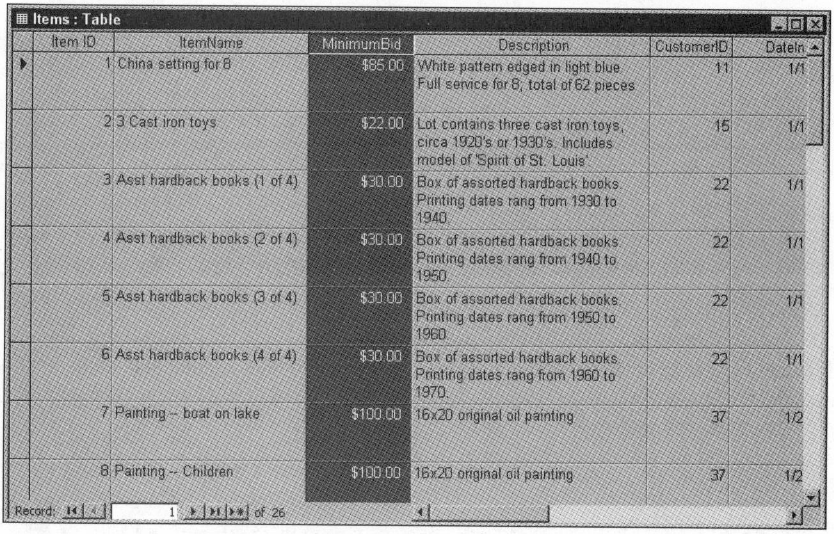

Figure 8-7: The MinimumBid field now resides between ItemName and Description.

To hide a column, follow these steps:

1. **With your table in Datasheet view, right-click the name of the column to hide.**

   The whole column goes dark, and a pop-up menu appears.

2. **Choose Hide Columns from the menu (as shown in Figure 8-8).**

   Poof! The column vanishes.

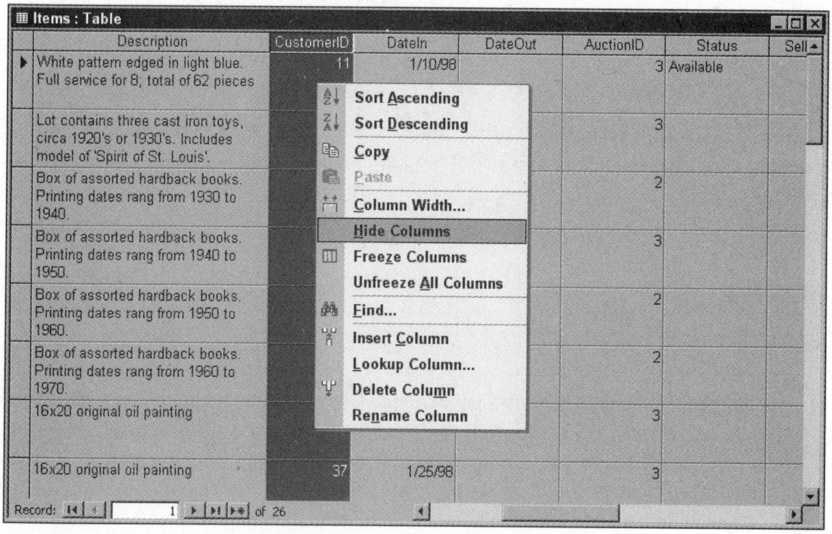

Figure 8-8: I don't want to see the CustomerID.

Making design changes in Datasheet view — danger, Will Robinson!

Moving or hiding columns, changing column widths, adjusting row heights — all these are innocuous settings that simply make your digital world a prettier place.

The story changes with the Rename Column, Insert Column, Lookup Column, and Delete Column options that appear on the right-click pop-up menu. These choices actually change the structure of your table, so go slow and treat them carefully!

✔ Rename Column changes the field name.

✔ Insert Column adds a new column on the datasheet, which translates into a new field in the table.

✔ Lookup Column starts the Lookup Wizard and helps you insert a column for data pulled in from another table.

✔ Delete Column is pretty self-explanatory (remember that Access 2002 undoes only the last action you took, so don't delete anything until you're sure that it's the right column to kill).

You alter the table's structure with these options. Have a look through Chapter 9 for more about these options and how to use them safely. (It's that important.)

To hide more than one column at a time, click and drag across the names of the columns you want to squirrel away and then choose Format➪Hide Columns.

When you're ready to bring back the temporarily indisposed column, do this:

1. **Choose Format➪Unhide Columns.**

   Up pops a small dialog box listing all the fields in the current table. The fields with a check mark in the box next to them are displayed.

2. **Click any of the unchecked check boxes next to the respective column that you want to see on-screen again (see Figure 8-9) and then click Close.**

   Depending on the number of fields in the list, you may have to scroll around to find all the fields.

Freezing a column

If you have many fields in a table, they don't all fit in the window. As you scroll from one side of the table to the other, fields are constantly appearing on one side of the window and disappearing from the other. What if you want to keep looking at a column way over on one side of the table *while* looking at fields from the other side?

Figure 8-9:
I can use
Unhide
Columns to
hide *and*
unhide
columns by
checking
only those I
want to see.

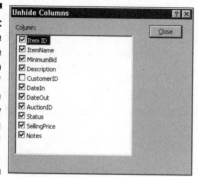

The secret is to *freeze* the column in place. This action locks a column into the left side of the window so that it just sits there while you scroll merrily back and forth through the table. Of course, an *unfreeze* step goes along with it — you don't want your tables catching cold, do you?

Here's how to freeze a column:

1. **Right-click the name of the column you want to freeze.**

    The column turns dark, and the ever-anticipated pop-up menu appears.

2. **Select Freeze Columns from the pop-up menu.**

    The column is now locked in place. You can scroll back and forth through your table with impunity (and you don't have any restrictions, either).

If you want to freeze more than one column, follow these steps:

1. **Select the columns by holding down the Shift key and clicking the column names.**

    The boundary of the columns that you want to freeze forms.

2. **Click the first column's name, hold down the Shift key, and then click the second column's name to highlight all the columns in between.**

3. **After you highlight all the columns you want to freeze, choose Format⇨Freeze Columns from the menu bar.**

    All highlighted columns are immediately frozen in place.

When you want to thaw out the columns, choose Format⇨Unfreeze All Columns.

Fonting around with Your Table

Access 2002 displays your table in a basic, business-oriented font. You're not stuck with that font choice forever. You control the font, style, and the color of your data.

These settings apply to the *entire table,* not just a particular row or column.

To change the font, style, or color of your table, follow these steps:

1. **With the table in Datasheet view, choose Format⇨Font.**

   The Font dialog box elbows its way onto the screen.

2. **Click your choice from the Font list on the left side of the dialog box.**

   Access 2002 shows the font in the Sample box on the right side of the dialog box.

   Picking a TrueType font is best. TrueType fonts have the double-T symbol.

3. **Click the preferred style in the Font style list.**

   Some fonts may not have all the common style options (normal, bold, italic, and bold italic).

4. **To select a different size, click a number in the Size list.**

   If you use a printer font (the ones with a picture of a printer next to them), you may be limited to just a few size options.

5. **If you want a new color, click the arrow next to the Color box and pick your favorite from the drop-down menu.**

6. **Click OK to apply your font selections.**

Giving Your Data the 3-D Look

This final change is purely cosmetic, but even tables like to feel good about how they look. Access 2002 gives you a couple of cool-looking, three-dimensional options for your datasheet. To turn your datasheet into a cool work of art, follow these steps:

1. **Choose Format⇨Datasheet from the menu bar.**

   The Datasheet Formatting dialog box pops onto the screen.

2. **For 3-D, click the Raised or Sunken radio buttons in the Cell Effect area.**

   The Sample box previews your selection. (I prefer Raised.)

If you don't want the *gridlines* cluttering up your datasheet, leave Cell Effect set to Flat and uncheck the Gridlines Shown check boxes.

3. **Click OK when you're done.**

The datasheet changes according to your selections.

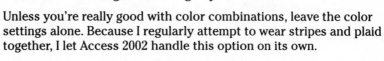 Unless you're really good with color combinations, leave the color settings alone. Because I regularly attempt to wear stripes and plaid together, I let Access 2002 handle this option on its own.

Chapter 9

Table Remodeling Tips for the Do-It-Yourselfer

In This Chapter

▶ The standard "worried author" disclaimer

▶ Adding a field to your table

▶ Removing a field you don't need

▶ Changing a field's name

*R*emodeling is a part of life — at least it is if you're a homeowner. A touch of paint here, a new wall there, and pretty soon your entire house is a mess, because the jobs never *quite* get finished. For example, my wife has given up hope on updating the electrical outlets in our old house. I worked on the job for three years or so, and I ended with eight outlets done, eight outlets to go, and nobody left on base. I fixed about one outlet per quarter, usually spurred to action because I needed to plug in something that didn't work with the old outlet.

My databases, on the other hand, are a completely different story. There, I'm a digital Bob Vila, with everything organized and up-to-date. When I start changing a table, I finish the job right then and there. My wife says the difference has to do with my aversion to physical labor, but the real reason is the tools that Access 2002 provides for the job. (That and the fact that hammers simply don't like me.)

Whether you're adding a new field, removing an old one, or making some other subtle changes to your table and the data therein, this chapter guides you through the process. Be sure to read the chapter's first section before attempting any serious surgery on your tables. Some grim pitfalls await you out there, and I want you to miss them cleanly.

Make your changes through Design view, where you're in full control of the process. The steps in this chapter walk you through making such changes in Design view. Although you can do some of the tasks in this chapter in Datasheet view (specifically, add and delete whole columns in your table), I don't recommend that approach. One change in Datasheet view quickly turns into a full-fledged data disaster if anything goes wrong.

This Chapter Can Be Hazardous to Your Table's Design

I'm all for starting on a pleasant note, but *now* isn't the time.

To properly set this chapter's mood, I wanted to begin with big, full-color pictures of items that have a natural *don't touch* sign on them — such as snapping alligators, roaring lions, and the *I dare you to audit me* box on your income tax form. My editor suggested that I use a warning icon instead. In the name of compromise (and because finding good editors is so hard these days), I agreed.

Tread lightly in this chapter. You're tinkering with the infrastructure of your entire database system. A mistake (particularly of the *delete* kind) can cause massive hair loss, intense frustration, and large-scale data corruption. Put simply, it's bad.

Putting a New Field Next to the Piano

No matter how well you plan, sometimes you just forget to include a field in your table design. Or, after using the table for a while, you discover some unforeseen data that needs a home. Regardless of the circumstances, Access 2002 doesn't make a big deal out of adding a new field.

Dropping a new field into your table takes only a moment. Before starting this project, make sure that you know the following bits of information. This makes a good paper and pencil project, so grab your tools and figure out the following items:

- ✔ Typical examples of the data that the field holds
- ✔ The field type (text, number, yes/no, and so on)
- ✔ The size the field needs to be to hold the data, if applicable
- ✔ What you plan to call the field
- ✔ Where the field fits in the table design

Is it a column or a field?

The answer to this lyrical question — is it a column or a field — is *yes.* In Access 2002 lingo, *columns* and *fields* are really the same critters. When you insert a column into a table in Datasheet view, you actually add a new field to every record. If you build a field in Design view, you create a new column for the datasheet. Either way you say (or do) it, you get the same result.

So when is a field different from a column? It's different when you edit the data in a particular

record. If you change one person's postal code in an address table, you aren't changing the whole column. Instead, you're changing the value of the field in that record.

Here's how to keep the two terms straight:

✔ When Access 2002 talks about columns, it means a certain field in every record of the table.

✔ When the program refers to a field, it means the data in one part of a particular record.

With that information in hand, you're ready to make a new field. To add the field in Design view, follow these steps:

1. **With the database file open, right-click the table you want to work with and then choose Design View from the pop-up menu.**

   The table structure appears in Design view.

2. **Highlight the row where you want to insert your new field by clicking on the row button to the left of the Field Name column.**

   Some tasks are easy when you see them, but confusing to explain — and this step is one of them. On that note, take a gander at Figure 9-1 to make sense of this maneuver.

3. **Choose Insert⇨Rows from the main menu.**

   Access 2002 inserts a nice, blank row right where you clicked. Everything below that row moves down one row to make room for the new arrival.

   Don't worry about your data — Access 2002 takes good care of your work. Inserting a new row doesn't hurt anything in the table. *Deleting* a row (see the following section) is another story.

4. **Click in the Field Name area of the new row and then type the name of your new field.**

   The field name flows smoothly into the text area.

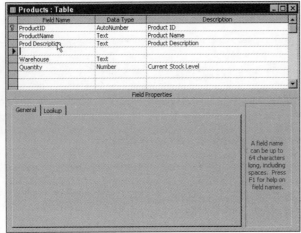

Figure 9-1:
Click the
button on
the left
(where the
little
arrowhead
is) to select
an entire
row.

5. **Press Tab to move into the Data Type column. Click the down arrow and select the field's data type from the pull-down list (see Figure 9-2).**

   If you're uncertain which data type works best for this field, flip back to Chapter 4.

Figure 9-2:
Pick a data
type from
the list.

6. **Press Tab to hop into the Description area. Type a short description of the stuff that this field contains.**

   Although this step is optional, I *highly* recommend adding a description. Trust me on this one!

 7. **Save your changes by choosing File⇨Save or by clicking the Save button on the toolbar.**

Saying Good-bye to a Field (And All Its Data)

Times change, and so do your data storage needs. When one of your fields is past its prime, send it to that Great Table in the Sky by deleting it from your design. Getting rid of the field *also* throws out all the data *in* the field. You probably know that already, but the point is important enough that I want to make sure you keep these suggestions in mind:

✔ Killing a field *erases all data* in the field. Proceed with caution!

✔ If the data in a table is important, make a backup copy before you delete any of the fields. Backing up the data *before* you delete it is always easier. When it's gone, it's gone.

Here's how to delete a field from your table:

1. **With the database file open, right-click the table you plan to change and then choose <u>D</u>esign View from the pop-up menu.**

   The Design window pops onto the screen, filled to overflowing with your table design.

2. **Click the gray button on the left side of the Field Name that you want to delete.**

   The doomed field appears highlighted.

3. **Choose <u>E</u>dit⇨Delete <u>R</u>ows from the main menu.**

   A dialog box appears, asking whether you really want to do the deed (see Figure 9-3). If the Office Assistant is busily assisting you with Access 2002, it offers a slightly friendlier version of the dialog box, but the question remains the same.

4. **Click <u>Y</u>es to delete the field; click <u>N</u>o if you're having second thoughts.**

   If you delete the field and immediately wish you hadn't, press Ctrl+Z or choose Edit⇨Undo Delete (as shown in Figure 9-4). Your field instantly comes back from beyond.

Figure 9-3:
Access
warns that
the delete
involves
more than
just the
field.

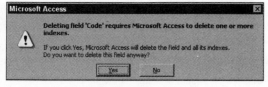

Figure 9-4:
If you get
carried
away
deleting
fields, Undo
Delete can
bring them
back.

5. Make the deletion permanent by choosing File⇨Save or by clicking the Save button on the toolbar.

The key word in this step is *permanent,* as in *never to be seen or heard from again.* You can't undo this step — when it's gone, it's gone.

A Field by Any Other Name Still Holds the Same Stuff

Access 2002 really doesn't care what you name the fields in a table. Granted, it has some technical rules for what a legal field name looks like, but editorially speaking, it leaves all the choices up to you. Field names are really a human element, after all (silly humans, we're always running around naming stuff).

Access 2002 offers two ways to change the name of a field:

- ✔ Retyping the name of the field in Design view (the *official* way, according to Nerds That Know)
- ✔ Right-clicking the field name in Datasheet view (the intuitive way)

Which method you use is entirely up to you — I show you both methods in the next two sections.

Changing a field name in Design view

Here's how to change a field name in Design view, the Access 2002 version of a digital tune-up bay for your tables:

1. **Right-click the table you want to change and then choose <u>D</u>esign View from the pop-up menu.**

   The table appears.

2. **Click the field you plan to rename and then press F2 to highlight it (see Figure 9-5).**

   The name of the field quivers in anticipation at the prospect of your next step.

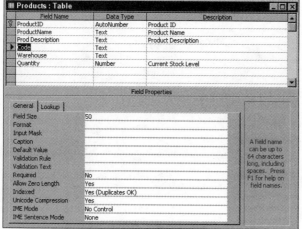

Figure 9-5:
The field
name is
highlighted
and ready
for the
change.

3. **Type a new name for the field.**

   Because you highlighted the field name before typing, Access 2002 automatically overwrites the old name with the new one.

4. **To save the change, choose <u>F</u>ile⇨<u>S</u>ave or click the Save button on the toolbar.**

   The process is complete!

Changing a field name in Datasheet view

Renaming a field in Datasheet view takes about the same number of steps, but some people think that this method is easier. In the name of diversity, here's how to change a field name in Datasheet view:

1. **With your database file open, double-click the table you want to change.**

   Surprise — the first step here is *different* than all the other steps!

   The table appears on-screen in Datasheet view.

2. **Right-click the field name (at the top of the datasheet window) you want to change.**

   The column is highlighted and a pop-up menu appears.

3. **Select Rename Column from the pop-up menu (as shown in Figure 9-6).**

   The name of the column lights up, bracing for the impending change.

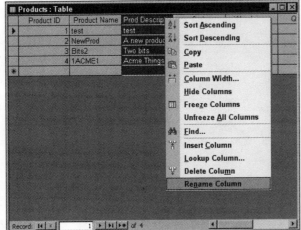

Figure 9-6: Right-click a column heading and choose Rename Column.

4. **Type the new name and then press Enter.**

   Although you made the change in Datasheet view, Access 2002 actually changes the table's design.

 5. **To make the change permanent, click Save on the toolbar or choose File⇨Save.**

   And another field finds happiness and meaning in a stylish new name. Congratulations — you're done!

Part III
Finding the Ultimate Answer to Everything (Well, Not Everything)

The 5th Wave   By Rich Tennant

"I've been in hardware all of my life, and all of a sudden it's software that'll make me rich."

In this part . . .

*E*lectronically collecting the data together in one place
is nice, but if you're just stacking it on the hard disk
instead of piling it around your office, what did you gain
(apart from a less cluttered office)?

At the risk of sounding like a marketing brochure, your
ability to interact with your data is one of the truly cool
features of Access 2002. Because this is a computer product, you can't just say that you're interacting with or ques-
tioning the data. No — that would be too easy. In database
lingo, you're *querying* the tables.

Although saying you're going to query something sounds
a lot cooler than saying you're going to ask a quick question, the basic concept is the same. This part digs into the
whole query concept, starting out with simple questions
and leading you into progressively more complex prog-
nostications. This is juicy stuff, so work up a good
appetite before digging in.

Chapter 10

Quick Searches:
Find, Filter, and Sort

• •

In This Chapter

▶ Using the Find command

▶ Sorting your database

▶ Filter by selection

▶ Filter by form

• •

*Y*ou probably don't need me to tell you what databases do: They help you store and organize the information that's important to your world. That's hardly a new concept, though — that's what 3 x 5 index cards do (and I bet you never spent $600 upgrading your index card box). To justify all the time, trauma, and accelerated hair loss associated with them, databases have to do something that a simple stack of paper products just can't match. Something like sifting through an imposing mound of data in the merest blink of an eye and immediately finding that one elusive piece of data.

Thanks to the magic of the Find, Sort, and Filter commands, Access 2002 tracks and reorganizes the stuff in your tables faster than ever. When you need a quick answer to a simple question, these three commands are ready to help. This chapter covers the commands in order, starting with the speedy Find, moving along to the organizational Sort, and ending with the flexible Filter.

Find, Sort, and Filter do a great job with *small* questions (like "Who's that customer in Tucumcari?"). Answering big, hairy questions (such as "How many people from Seattle bought wool sweaters on weekends last year?") still takes a full-fledged Access 2002 query. Don't let that threat worry you, because Chapter 11 explains queries in light and winsome detail.

Finding Stuff in Your Tables

When you want to track down a particular record *right now,* creating a whole query for the job is overkill. Fortunately, Access 2002 has a quick-and-dirty way to find one specific piece of data within your project's tables and forms — the Find command.

Find is available both on the toolbar and through the main menu (choose Edit⇨Find or, for the keyboard-oriented folks out there, press Ctrl+F). Access 2002 doesn't care which way you fire up the Find command — it works the same from either avenue.

Although the Find command is pretty easy to use on its own, knowing a couple of tricks makes it do its best work. After you know the Find basics (covered in the next section), check the tips for fine-tuning the Find command in the section, "Tuning a search for speed and accuracy." That section tweaks the Find settings for more detailed search missions.

Finding first things first (and next things after that)

Using the Find command is a pretty straightforward task. Here's how it works:

1. **Open the table or form you want to search.**

   Yes, Find works in both Datasheet view and with Access forms. If you really want to dive into forms right now, flip ahead to Chapter 22.

2. **Click in the field that you want to search.**

   The Find command searches the *current* field in all the records of the table, so make sure that you click in the right field before starting the Find process. Access 2002 doesn't care which record you click — as long as you hit the right field, Access is happy (and it's important to keep your software happy!).

3. **Start the Find command either by clicking the Find toolbar button (the one with the binoculars on it) or choosing Edit⇨Find.**

   The Find and Replace dialog box pops into action.

4. **Type the text you're looking for into the Find What box, as shown in Figure 10-1.**

   Take a moment to check your spelling before starting the search. Access 2002 isn't bright enough to figure out that you actually mean *hero* when you type *zero.*

Figure 10-1:
The Find
and Replace
dialog box
gets ready
to do its
stuff.

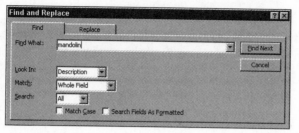

5. Click Find Next to begin your search.

Before you can count to one by eighths, the Find command tracks down the record you want, moves the cursor there, and highlights the matching text.

If Find doesn't locate anything, it laments its failure in a small dialog box. In that case:

- Click OK to make the dialog box go away.

- Make sure that you clicked in the correct field and spelled everything correctly in the Find What box.

You may also want to check the special Find options covered in the next section to see whether one of them is messing up your search.

What if the first record that Access finds isn't exactly the one you're looking for? Suppose that you wanted the second, third, or the fourteenth *John Smith* in the table? No problem — that's why the Find and Replace dialog box has a Find Next button. Keep clicking Find Next until Access 2002 either works its way down to the record you want or tells you that it's giving up the search.

Tuning a search for speed and accuracy

Sometimes, just providing the information in the Find What box isn't enough. Either you find too many records or the ones that you match aren't really the ones that you want. The best way to reduce the number of wrong matches is to add more details to your search.

Precise adjustment makes the pursuit faster, too.

Access 2002 offers several tools for fine-tuning a Find. Open the Find dialog box by clicking the Find button on the toolbar or by choosing Edit⇨Find. The following list describes how to use the various options:

✔ **Look In:** By default, Access 2002 looks for matches only in the *current* field — whichever field you clicked in before starting the Find command. To tell Access 2002 to search the entire table instead, change the Look In setting from *field* to *table,* as shown in Figure 10-2.

✔ **Match:** Access 2002 makes a few silly assumptions, and this setting is a good example. By default, Match is set to Whole Field, which assumes that you want to find only fields that *completely match* your search text. The Whole Field setting means that searching for *Sam* doesn't find fields containing *Samuel, Samantha,* or *Mosam.* Not too bright for such an expensive program, is it? Change this behavior by adjusting the Match setting to Any Part of Field, which allows a match anywhere in a field (finding both *Samuel* and *new sample product*), or to Start of Field, which recognizes only a match that starts from the beginning of the field. To change this setting, click the down arrow next to the field (see Figure 10-3) and then pick your choice from the drop-down menu that appears.

✔ **Search:** If you're finding too many matches, try limiting your search to one particular portion of the table with the Search option. Search tells the Find command to look either

- At all the records in the table (the default setting)

- Up or Down from the current record

Clicking on a record halfway through the table and then telling Access 2002 to search Down from there confines your search to the bottom part of the table.

Tune your Search settings by clicking the down arrow next to the Search box and picking the appropriate choice from the drop-down menu.

✔ **Match Case:** Match Case requires that the term you search for be exactly the same as the value stored in the database including the case of the characters. In other words, if the database is storing "SmItH," Match Case finds that value only if you enter SmItH. A good use for Match Case is when searching for names.

✔ **Search Fields As Formatted:** Search Fields As Formatted instructs Access 2002 to look at the formatted version of the field *instead* of the actual data you typed. Limiting the search in this way is handy when searching dates, stock-keeping unit IDs, or any other field with quite a bit of specialized formatting. Turn on Search Fields As Formatted by clicking the check box next to it. This setting doesn't work with Match Case, so if Match Case is checked, Search Fields As Formatted is grayed out. In that case, uncheck Match Case to bring back Search Fields As Formatted.

Most of the time, this option doesn't make much difference in your life. In fact, the only time you probably care about this Find option is when (or if) you search many highly formatted fields.

If your Find command isn't working the way you think it should, check the options in the preceding list. Odds are that one or more of these options aren't set quite right!

Figure 10-2:
To search the entire table, change the Look In setting.

Figure 10-3:
Look *inside* all those little fields by using the Match option.

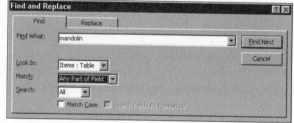

Sorting Out Life on the Planet

Very few databases are already organized into nice, convenient alphabetical lists. So what do you do when your boss wants the world neatly sorted and on her desk within the hour?

The solution is the Sort command, which is *really* easy to use! The Sort command is on the Records menu, plus two buttons on the toolbar (Sort Ascending and Sort Descending) do the job as well.

 ✔ Sort Ascending sorts your records alphabetically from top to bottom, so records that begin with A are at the beginning, and records that begin with Z are at the end.

 ✔ Sort Descending does just the opposite; records that begin with Z are at the top, and records that begin with A are at the bottom of the list.

You can sort by more than one column at a time like this:

1. **Click on the heading of the first column to sort by.**

   The entire column is highlighted.

2. **Hold down the Shift key and click on the heading of the last column to sort by.**

   All columns from the first one to the last one are highlighted.

3. **Choose either Sort Ascending or Sort Descending.**

   The sort is always done from left to right. In other words, you can't sort by the contents of the fourth column and, within that, by the contents of the third column.

   The columns chosen must be contiguous (they must be all together).

Anything that's *this* useful simply must exhibit an odd behavior or two to keep life interesting. True to form, Sort has its own peculiarity when working with numbers inside a text field. When sorting a field that has numbers mixed in with spaces and letters (such as street addresses), Access 2002 ranks the numbers as if they were *letters,* not actual numbers. Unfortunately, this behavior means that Access 2002 puts "10608 W. Vermont" before "119 Spring Mill." (The 0 in the second position comes before the 1 in the second position.)

Filtering Records with Something in Common

Sometimes, you need to see a group of records that share a common value in one field — they all list a particular city, a certain job title, or the same genre of books. Ever the willing helper, Access 2002 includes a special tool for this very purpose — the Filter command.

Filter uses your criteria and displays all the matching records, creating a little minitable of only the records that meet your requirements. It's like an instant query without all the extra work, hassle, and overhead (and without a *lot* of the power).

The Filter commands live on the Records menu and the toolbar. Access 2002 offers five unique filter commands:

- ✔ Filter For
- ✔ Filter by Selection
- ✔ Filter by Form
- ✔ Filter Excluding Selection
- ✔ Advanced Filter/Sort

Each command performs the same basic function, but in a different way and with different bells and whistles attached. The following sections cover the first four options. For details of the Advanced Filter/Sort, flip to Chapter 11.

Filters work in tables, forms, and queries. Although you *can* apply a filter to a report, filtering reports is really a different beast (and not a very friendly beast, at that). The following sections apply filters to tables, but the same concepts apply when you're working with queries and forms.

Filter For

Filter For enables you to filter your records so that you view only records meeting very specific criteria. Suppose, for example, that you wanted to see all records where the minimum bid was less than $30. Here's how to do it:

1. **Right-click in the MinimumBid column.**

   Access 2002 displays a pop-up menu like the one in Figure 10-4.

2. **Enter the Filter For search condition.**

   In this case, "<30". If you entered simply 30 (without the less than symbol), Access 2002 would assume you mean "=30".

3. **Press Enter.**

   Access searches the column in which you clicked and displays only those records that meet your Filter For criteria.

If you right-click on another column and perform another Filter For, Access 2002 applies the filter only to the current records.

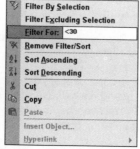

Figure 10-4: Filter For in action.

Filter by Selection

The Filter by Selection command is the easiest of the filter commands to use. It assumes that you have found one record that matches your criteria. Using Filter by Selection is much like grabbing someone in a crowd and shouting: "Okay, everybody who's like him, line up over there."

Suppose, for example, that you want to find all the items for sale at an auction with a minimum bid of exactly $30. You can use Filter by Selection in this manner:

1. **Click in the field that has the information you want to match.**

   In this case, the MinimumBid field.

2. **Scroll through the list until you find an item whose minimum bid is $30.**

3. **Click on the value you're searching for and click the Filter by Selection button. Or, you can right-click and choose Filter by Selection.**

   Access 2002 immediately displays a table containing only the items with a minimum bid of exactly $30 (as shown in Figure 10-5).

Figure 10-5:
Access shows only those records matching the Filter by Selection criteria.

Item ID	ItemName	MinimumBid	Description	CustomerIt	Date
3	Asst hardback books (1 of 4)	$30.00	Box of assorted hardback books. Printing dates rang from 1930 to 1940.	22	1
4	Asst hardback books (2 of 4)	$30.00	Box of assorted hardback books. Printing dates rang from 1940 to 1950.	22	1
5	Asst hardback books (3 of 4)	$30.00	Box of assorted hardback books. Printing dates rang from 1950 to 1960.	22	1
6	Asst hardback books (4 of 4)	$30.00	Box of assorted hardback books. Printing dates rang from 1960 to 1970.	22	1

Items : Table

Record: 14 4 [1] ▶ ▶I ▶* of 4 (Filtered)

4. **Click the Remove Filter button on the toolbar after you finish using the filter.**

   Your table or form returns to its regular display.

 At this stage of the game, you may want to save a list of everything that matches your filter. Unfortunately, the Filter's simplicity and ease of use now comes back to haunt you. To permanently record your filtered search, you need to create a query (see Chapter 11 for more details about creating queries).

Filter by Form

You can tighten a search by using additional filters to weed out undesirable matches, but that takes a ton of extra effort. For an easier way to isolate a group of records based on the values in more than one field, turn to the Filter by Form feature (try saying that three times fast!).

Filter by Form uses more than one criterion to sift through records. (In some ways, it's like a simple query. It's so similar that you can even save your Filter by Form criteria *as* a full-fledged query!) Suppose, for example, that you need a list of all the customers at your auction who came from Illinois or Indiana. You can perform two Filter by Selection searches and write down the results of each to get your list, or you can do just *one* search with Filter by Form and see all the records in a single step.

To use Filter by Form, follow these steps:

1. **Choose Records➪Filter➪Filter by Form or click the Filter by Form button on the toolbar.**

   An empty replica of your table fills the screen, like the one shown in Figure 10-6.

TIP

   (Figure 10-6 shows an arrow button next to the table's CustomerID field. The arrow button appears because that field was active when the Filter by Form command was selected. The arrow is helpful if you want to filter by customer ID number, but you're looking at states of residence. Scroll right and click in the State/Province column. The arrow jumps to that column. You can then click the arrow to open a list box showing all the entries for that field in your open database, as shown in Figure 10-7.)

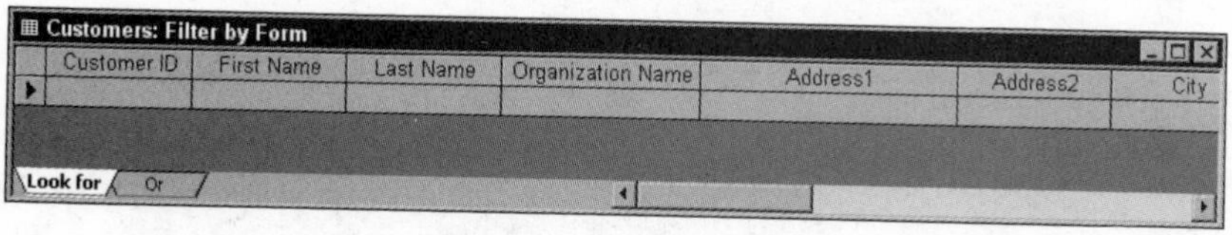

Figure 10-6:
Filter by Form lets you provide very explicit guidance as to what records you want to see.

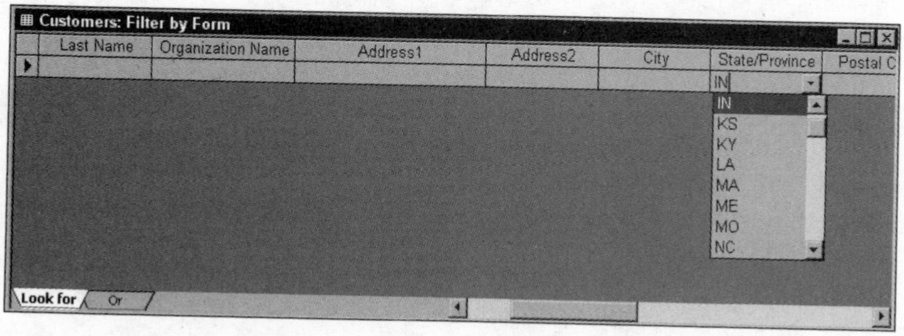

Figure 10-7:
The drop-down list shows all unique values in this field.

2. **Click the Look For tab in the lower-left corner of the table, and then click an entry in the State/Province column to designate it as your primary search criterion.**

   If you select IL from the drop-down list of the State/Province list box, IL moves into the State/Province column.

3. **Click the Or tab in the lower-left corner of the table.**

   A second Filter by Form window appears, letting you add an alternate search condition.

4. **Click the State/Province list box to open it.**

   The list box reopens.

5. **Click another entry (such as IN or MA).**

   Access 2002 searches for that entry as well as for "IL." Filter by Form enables you to look for multiple values if, for example, records have the state entered as "IN."

   Repeat this step as many times as you need and in any field you need. Every time you click the Or tab, another Or tab appears so that you can add still more criteria to your search. Figure 10-8 shows how the Filter by Form table looks with an extra Or tab in place.

6. **When you finish entering all the criteria for the filter, click the Apply Filter button.**

   Figure 10-9 shows the results.

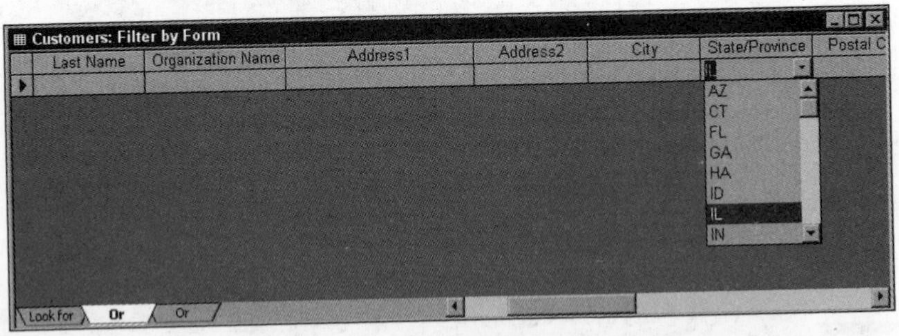

Figure 10-8:
You can use as many Or statements as you need to define the criteria.

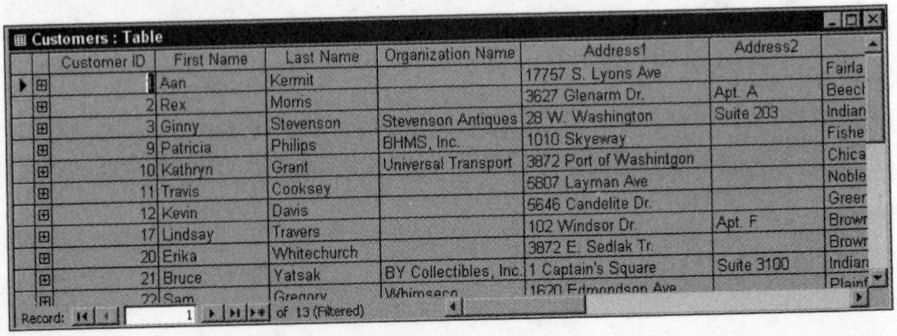

Figure 10-9:
Access finds all customers from either IL or IN.

Here are a couple of final thoughts about Filter by Form:

✔ Although you can get fancy by adding Or searches to your heart's content, keeping track of your creation gets tough in no time at all. Before creating *The Filter That Identified Incredibly Detailed Sub-Sets of Manhattan*, remind yourself that queries work better than filters when the questions get complex. Flip to Chapter 11 for the lowdown on queries.

✔ Convert your cool Filter by Form creation into a full-fledged query by clicking the Save As Query button on the toolbar. Access 2002 dutifully remakes your work into a query and then adds it to the Query list in your database.

When you finish fiddling with your filter, click the Remove Filter by Form toolbar button. At that point, your table returns to normal (or at least as normal as data tables ever get).

Removing your mistakes (or when good criteria go bad)

What do you do when you enter criteria by mistake? Or when you decide that you really don't want to include Ohio in your filter right after you click OH? No problem — the Clear Grid button comes to the rescue!

When you click the Clear Grid button, Access 2002 dumps all the entries in the Filter by Form grid and gives you a nice, clean place to start over again.

If you want to get rid of just a single Or tab instead of clearing the whole grid, click that tab and then choose Edit⇨Delete Tab.

Filter by exclusion

Filter Excluding Selection is the inverse of Filter by Selection: It allows you to select everything *except* a certain value. For example, if you want to display all items whose DateIn is other than 1/18/98, here's what you do:

1. **Find the appropriate value (1/18/98) in the field you are examining (DateIn).**

2. **Right-click on the value and choose Filter Excluding Selection (see Figure 10-10).**

3. **Press Enter.**

    Access 2002 shows everything *except* the records where DateIn is 1/18/98.

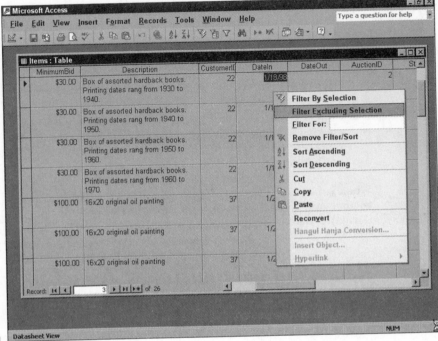

Figure 10-10:
I want
to see
everything
except
1/18/98.

Chapter 11

Pose a Simple Query, Get 10,000 Answers

· ·

In This Chapter

▶ Defining a query

▶ Answering easy questions with Advanced Filter/Sort

▶ Digging deeper with queries

▶ Calling the Simple Query Wizard

· ·

Someone infinitely smarter than me once observed that the most interesting insights in life spring not from the answers that life gives us, but instead from the questions that we pose along the way. One way or another, *everything* that we know — every shred of information in our minds — springs from questions that we either asked aloud, pondered silently, or whispered furtively to the student at the next desk in hopes that he would take the risk of broaching the subject in class for us.

Databases follow this rule of life pretty well. Gathering your information into a database isn't easy, nor does the simple act of *gathering* really make the data easier to use. (After all, when you're done, all you have is an electronic pile of the same stuff that previously lived in file cabinets.) The real power of a database flows from the questions you ask of it and the answers that it provides.

Access 2002 (and all databases in general) uses its own terminology for questions posed to your database. Access calls these questions *queries* — and they're the wily technological animals that this chapter covers.

The chapter starts with an introduction to the gentle (and frequently arcane) art of asking questions about the information in your database. Next, the chapter explores the basics of the simplest query in Access 2002, which is *so* simple that the programmers gave this query the confusing name *Advanced Filter/Sort* just to keep it murky. From there, the chapter guides you deeper into the data jungle where you find the true power of Access 2002, the Select Query.

Don't worry if your first few queries produce odd results. That's how queries start for everybody (myself included). Queries aren't easy to master, but the payoff at the end is huge. Go slowly, be patient with yourself, and take comfort in the fact that others before you trod the same path you now walk — the path called "Hmm, that's not the answer to the question I thought I asked."

Database Interrogation for Fun and Profit

Of all the cool features in Access 2002, queries take the medals as the true heroes in the ongoing Battle to Enhance Your On-The-Job Performance. Queries help you make sense of all the data that you, your co-workers, and a cast of a thousand others have slavishly typed over the course of too many hours, days, months, years, biannual bird migrations, and deep space satellite voyages.

Just as tables prepare your data for work by lining up all the information in neat rows and columns, queries make the data work for you by culling out the irrelevant details and shining light on murky mysteries. When you use queries, your data starts paying a return on all of your labor.

All of this querying sounds great, but it leaves open a simple question: *What the heck is a query?* Simply put, a *query* is a question about the data in one or more of the tables in your database. Queries make lists, count records, and even do calculations based on the data lurking in your database.

Queries discover useful information like how many spools of purple silk thread sit in your warehouse, which customers bought the most organic cactus face cream (in both non-prickly and extra prickly varieties), and how weather affects carry-out pizza sales. In short, queries put the power behind your Access 2002 data.

Query magic doesn't stop with just answering questions. More advanced queries can add or delete records in your tables, calculate summary figures, perform statistical analyses, and, with the right add-ons from Microsoft, probably even wash your dog.

On Your Way with a Simple Query — Advanced Filter/Sort

At first glance, you may wonder why I just spent all this time talking about queries if the first technical issue in the chapter is a *filter*. Trust me — there's a method to my madness (nice for a change, isn't it?).

The folks who created Access 2002 know that different searches require different techniques. For different searches, they include *two* search tools in the software: filters and queries.

Filters, the simpler tool of the two, quickly scan a single table for whatever data you seek. Filters are fast but not terribly smart or flexible. For example, if you want to quickly see a list of all records for people living in Nevada, then a filter works wonderfully. If you want to do *more* than merely *see* the list, then the filter falls short. Chapter 10 covers filters in their limited but useful glory.

Queries go far beyond filters. But to get there, queries add more complexity. After all, a bicycle may be easy to ride, but a bike won't go as far or as fast as a jumbo jetliner. For all of its power, the jet is a tad more complex to operate than your average two-wheeler. And so it goes with queries. Queries work with one or more tables, let you search one or more fields, and even offer the option to save your results for further analysis.

For all of the differences, the most advanced filter is, in reality, a simple query, which makes some perverse sense. Your first step into the world of queries is also your last step from the domain of filters. Welcome to the Advanced Filter/Sort, the super filter of Access 2002, masquerading as a mild-mannered query.

As its name implies, Advanced Filter/Sort is more powerful than a run-of-the-mill filter. The filter is *so* powerful that it's really a simple query. You use exactly the same steps to build an Advanced Filter/Sort that you use to create a query — and the results look quite a bit alike, too.

Even though it looks, acts, and behaves like a query, Advanced Filter/Sort is still a filter at heart, while being constrained by a filter's limits. The Advanced Filter/Sort limitations include the following:

- ✔ Advanced Filter/Sort only works with one table or form in your database at a time, so you can't use it on a bunch of linked tables.

- ✔ You can only ask simple questions with the filter.

    Real, honest-to-goodness queries do a lot more than that (which is why a whole part in this book is about queries).

- ✔ The filter displays all of the columns for every matching record in your table. With a query, *you* pick the columns that you want to appear in the results. If you don't want a particular column, leave it out of the query. Filters aren't bright enough to do that.

Even with those limitations, Advanced Filter/Sort makes a great training ground to practice your query building skills.

Although this section only talks about applying filters to tables, you can also filter a query. You might wonder why you'd want to apply a filter to a query . . . well, so would I! Actually, it's pretty simple: As you will see in your new career as Query Master, some queries can take a long time to run. Suppose, for example, that you run a complicated Sales Report query, you look at the results, and you notice that it includes data from every state, but you only wanted to see sales from Wisconsin. Rather than modify the query and run it again, you can simply apply a filter.

Peering into the Filter window

The Filter window is split into two distinct sections:

- ✔ The upper half of the window holds the *field list,* which displays all the fields in the current table or form.

    For now, don't worry about this portion of the window — the upper half comes more into play when you start working with full queries.

- ✔ The lower half of the screen contains a blank query grid where the details of your filter go. Even though you're building a *filter,* Access 2002 calls the area at the bottom of the screen a *query* grid. You see almost the exact grid later in the chapter in the section about building real queries.

To build the filter, you simply fill in the spaces of the query grid at the bottom of the window, as shown in Figure 11-1. Access 2002 even helps you along the way, with pull-down menus and rows that do specific tasks. The following sections cover each portion of the query grid in more detail.

Building a simple query — er, filter

Start your filter adventure by firing up the basic query tool of Access 2002, the Advanced Filter/Sort. Here's what to do:

1. **Open the table that you want to interrogate.**

    With good luck and wind from the east, your table hops into view.

    The Advance Filter/Sort tool also works on forms. If you feel particularly adventuresome (or if you mainly work with your data through some ready-made forms), give the filter a try. Filtering a form works just like filtering a table, so just follow the other steps below.

2. **Decide what question you need to ask and which fields the question involves.**

    You may want a list of products in inventory more than 60 days, customers who live in Munich or Amsterdam, books by your favorite author, or recipes that take less than an hour to cook *and* also contain spinach. Whatever you want, figure out which field in your table contains the answer to your question, and exactly what your question is.

Don't worry if your question includes more than one field (such as the recipe problem above) or multiple options (such as the customer city example). Filters — and queries — can handle multiple-field and multiple-option questions.

3. **Choose Records➪Filter➪Advanced Filter/Sort.**

The Filter window appears on-screen, ready to accept your command (see Figure 11-1).

Figure 11-1:
The
Advanced
Filter/Sort
window
looks a lot
like a
regular
query
window.

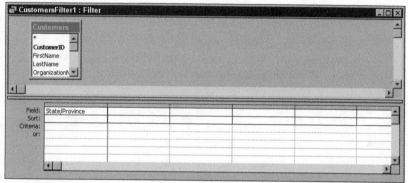

The Filter window is nothing but a simplified query window. The filter looks, acts, and behaves a lot like a real query. To simplify the process, the Filter window offers fewer bells and whistles than the full query window. More about full queries comes later in the chapter, so flip ahead to the next section if that's what you need.

4. **Click in the first box on the Field row and then click the down arrow that appears on the right side of the Field box.**

The drop-down menu lists all of the fields in your table.

5. **Click the first field you identified in Step 2.**

Access 2002 helpfully puts the field name into the Field box on the query grid. So far, so good.

6. **To sort your filter results by this particular field, click the Sort box, and then click the down arrow that appears. Select either Ascending or Descending from the drop-down menu.**

If you want to see the results in the same order that your data always appears in, just skip this step entirely.

Ascending order means lowest to highest (for example, A, B, C . . .); *descending* is highest to lowest (for example, Z, Y, X . . .).

7. **Click in the Criteria box under your field. Type the question for your filter to answer.**

Setting the criteria is the most complex part of building a query — it's the make or break item in the whole process. The criteria is your actual question, formatted in a way that Access 2002 understands. Building a query with the right criteria can involve a lot, but Table 11-1 gives you a quick introduction to the process.

Flip to Chapter 13 for a deeper look into the world of Boolean logic, the language of Access criteria.

8. **If your question includes more than one possible value for this field, click in the Or box and type your next criteria.**

Feel free to include as many Or options as you need. Just keep scrolling down to open up a new row for your criteria.

Table 11-1		Basic Comparison Operators	
Name	*Symbol*	*What It Means*	*Example*
Equals	(none)	Displays all records that exactly match whatever you type.	To find all items from customer 37, put 37 into the Criteria row.
Less Than	<	Lists all values that are Less Than your criteria.	<30 in the MinimumBid field finds all bids from $29.99 to negative infinity.
Greater Than	>	Lists all values in the field that are Greater Than the criteria.	>30 in the MinimumBid field finds all bids that are more than $30 (starting with $30.01).
Greater Than or Equal To	>=	Works just like Greater Than, except it also includes all entries that exactly match the criteria.	>=30 finds all values from 30 to infinity.
Less Than or Equal To	<=	If you add the = sign to Less Than, your query includes all records that have values below and equal to the criteria value.	<=30 includes not only those records with values less than 30, but also those with a value of 30.
Not Equal To	<>	Finds all entries that don't match the criteria.	If you want a list of all records except ones with a value of 30, enter <>30.

If you type a bunch of Or lines, your first entries seem to disappear. Don't worry — you didn't mess up anything. Access 2002 just scrolled the table up a bit to make room for the new criteria. Click the up arrow on the scroll bar to see your original entries again.

9. **Repeat Steps 4 through 8 if your question involves more than one field.**

    With all the criteria in place, it's time to take your filter for a test drive.

10. **To turn on the filter, choose Filter⇨Apply Filter/Sort or click the Apply Filter button on the toolbar.**

    After a moment of thinking (or whatever Access 2002 does when it's figuring out something), your table view changes and only the records that match your filter are left on display (as shown in Figure 11-2). Pretty cool, eh?

    To see all the data again, click the Apply Filter button one more time. The filtered records join their unfiltered brethren in a touching moment of digital homecoming.

Figure 11-2:
Ta-dah!
Your filtered
data
appears as
if by magic!

Customer ID	First Name	Last Name	Organization Name	Address1	Address2	Cit
24	Gretchen	Hankla	Daisyfield Shops	227 Daisyfield Dr.		Noblesvi
4	Gary	Holko		2557 Fisher Drive		Anderso
37	Gerald	Hollingsly	Victorian Properties	2769 Roundtable Ct.		Indianap

Record: ◄◄ ◄ 1 ► ►► of 3 (Filtered)

If you really love this particular filter, save it like this:

1. **Click the Save As Query button on the toolbar (the picture of a disk with a funnel over it).**

    Access 2002 displays a dialog box asking what you want to call the query.

2. **Type a name and then click OK.**

    Access carefully saves your filter as a query, including this query with the others of its kind on the Queries page in your database window.

Plagued by Tough Questions? Try an Industrial Strength Query!

Sometimes, quick and easy information is all that you need — ask the question, get the answer, and then go on with life. At other moments though, you need introspection, analysis, and concerted thought — in other words, your information calls for work. Thanks to the Access 2002 query tools, that work just got easier.

The basic query tool, created to make your life easier, is the Select query. Because developers use all their creativity writing programs, they tend to name their creations according to what the software actually does — hence, a Select query. These queries *select* matching records from your database and display the results according to your instructions.

Unlike its simplified predecessor in this chapter, a Select query offers all kinds of helpful and powerful options. These options include:

✔ More than one table in a query.

Because Select queries understand the relational side of Access 2002, this query can pull together data from more than one table.

✔ Show only the fields that you want in your results.

Select queries include the ever-popular *Show* setting, which tells Access which fields you really care about seeing.

✔ Put the fields into any order you want in the results.

Organize your answers with fields where *you* want them, without changing anything in your original table.

✔ List only as many matching entries as you need, thanks to the Select query's Top Value option.

If you only need the top 5, 25, or 100 records, or even a percentage like 5% or 25%, Access meets your need through the Top Value's setting.

The following section covers the basics of building a single-table Select query, but the other chapters in this part dig into detail on the goodies mentioned in the preceding list.

Build a Better Query and the Answers Beat a Path to Your Monitor

Creating a Select query is a lot like putting together one of those Advanced Filter/Sort thingies, but the Select query includes a few extra interesting buttons and levers. The following steps run through the process and toss out some tips about advanced stuff that you don't want to miss:

1. **Open the database that you want to interrogate and then click the Queries button on the left side of the screen.**

   Access lists all of your existing queries (assuming that you have some in there), plus a couple options for query creation.

2. **Decide what question you're asking with the query, which fields you need to answer the question, and which fields you want in your results.**

   Because Select queries let you pick and choose with more detail, you need to think through more options than you did with the Advanced Filter/Sort. The basic step remains the same, though. Which fields contain the data you want to know about? Which fields do you need in the solution? Think it through carefully, because these decisions form the major groundwork of your query.

3. **Double-click Create query in Design view.**

   The screen does a quick change, and you get two new windows:

   • Blank Select Query screen

   • Show Table dialog box

4. **In the Show Table dialog box, click the table you want to use and then click <u>A</u>dd. Click <u>C</u>lose to get rid of the Show Table dialog box.**

   Access puts a little window listing the table's fields into the top of the Select Query window.

5. **Select the first field for your query by clicking the down arrow in the Field box and then click the name of the field in the drop-down menu.**

   Access automatically puts the name of the table in the Table box and assumes that you want to include the field in your results by putting a checkmark in the Show box.

   You can also scroll through the field list in the small table window (the one that's in the upper part of the query window) and double-click each field that you want in the query. As you double-click, Access fills the field names into the query grid. I prefer this way, particularly when you start using multiple-table queries (which I cover in the next chapter).

6. **Repeat Step 5 until all of the fields you want are in the query grid.**

   Now, you're ready to adjust the sorting options.

7. **To sort the query results by a particular field, click in that field's Sort box, click the down arrow, and select Ascending or Descending from the drop-down menu.**

   Just like Advanced Filter/Sort, Access gives you the little-to-big and big-to-little options you know and love.

   If you tell Access to sort with more than one field, Access starts with the field closest to the left of the query grid, and then sorts the other fields when it runs into identical records in the first field. See the sidebar "Putting everything in *your* order," later in this chapter for more information about sorting your data.

8. **If you don't want a field to appear in the results, uncheck the Show box for that field.**

9. **Enter the criteria for each field that's part of the question.**

   Select queries use the same rules as the Advanced Filter/Sort, including all of the operators shown in Table 11-1. If you need some *Or* criteria (such as customers in Indiana or Illinois), use the Or lines in the query grid (see Figure 11-3).

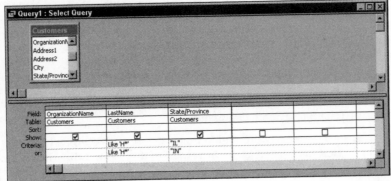

Figure 11-3: I want to see Customers whose last names begin with H and who live in IL or IN.

Thanks to their extra power, Select queries support some special operators in the Criteria section in addition to the ones in the table. Flip ahead to Chapter 13 to see the super-duper cool operators from Mr. Boole's bag of tricks.

10. **Take one last look at everything, take a deep breath, and click the Run button.**

    After a few (or perhaps *many*) moments of chunking and thunking, your query results pop onto the screen, looking like Figure 11-4.

Figure 11-4: Here's the result of your Select query!

If what you see *isn't* exactly what you thought you asked for (isn't that just like a computer?), double-check your query instructions. Common problems include mixing up the greater than (>) and less than (<) signs, leaving out an equals sign (=) in your greater-than-or-equal-to statements, or simply misspelling a region name, state, or postal code.

If you love this Select query (in a friendly and useful way), be sure to save it!

TIP

Putting everything in *your* order

Access has a nice tool for sorting the results from a query. After all, queries don't get much easier than clicking a little box labeled *Sort,* and then telling the program whether Ascending or Descending is your pick for sort-flavor-of-the-moment.

The only problem with this little arrangement is that Access automatically sorts the results from *left* to *right.* If you only request one sort, this order is no big deal. But if you request *two* sorts (for example, organize the results by both Customer ID *and* Item ID), the column that's closest to the *left* side of the query automatically becomes the primary sort, with any other field playing second (or third) fiddle.

Taking control of the sort order isn't hard, but it also isn't very obvious. Because Access looks at the query grid and performs the sorts from left to right, the trick is to *move the column* for the main sorting instruction to the left side of the grid. (Only a computer jockey can come up with a solution like this.)

To move a column in the grid, put the tip of the mouse pointer in the thin gray box just above the field name on the query grid. When the mouse turns into a down-pointing arrow, click once. All of a sudden, the chosen field highlights for you. (Fear not — highlighting the field was the hard part of the process.)

With the mouse pointer aimed at the same little gray area right above the field name, click and drag the field to its new position on the grid. As you move the mouse, a black bar moves through the grid, showing you where the field lands when you let up on the mouse button. When the black bar is in the right place, release the mouse button. The field information pops into view again, safe and happy in its new home.

In addition to changing the sort order of your query, this moving trick *also* changes the order that the fields display in your query results. Feel free to move fields here, there, or anywhere, depending on your needs. Is this some great flexibility or what?

Toto, Can the Wizard Help?

Besides the Advanced Filter/Sort query and the Select query, you can rely on the Simple Query Wizard. Also, if you know how to build queries by hand with the New Query function, the Simple Query Wizard is a breeze. Like all of the other wizards in the land of Access 2002, the Simple Query Wizard takes care of the behind-the-scenes work for you, but you have to enter the sorting and criteria information on your own. If you want to use the Simple Query Wizard instead of New Query, follow these steps:

1. **Click the New command on the Query tab and then choose the Simple Query Wizard.**

   The Simple Query Wizard dialog box appears, asking which fields you want in your query (see Figure 11-5).

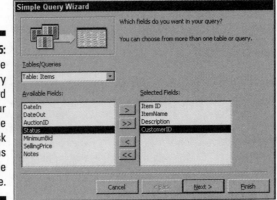

Figure 11-5:
The Simple
Query
Wizard
holds your
hand while
you ask
questions
of the
database.

2. **Click the down arrow and select the tables/queries you want to use in your query from the list that appears.**

3. **Select an option from Available Fields.**

   • To move a field into the Selected Fields box, highlight the field by clicking it and then click the > button.

   • To transfer all of the fields in the database to the Selected Fields box, click the > button.

   • If you decide that you don't want a field that you've transferred, highlight that field in the Selected Fields box and click the < button.

   • If you want to remove all of the selected fields, click the << button.

4. **Click Next after you tell the wizard which fields to use.**

   The wizard thinks for a moment, and then asks if you want a lot of Detail (to see every field of every record) or if you merely want a Summary (which automatically totals the numeric fields in your table).

5. **Pick an option and then click Next.**

   The wizard asks you to name your query (see Figure 11-6).

6. **Type a name for your query.**

   If you want to dress up the query by adding some cool extras, select the Modify the Query Design radio button, which tells the wizard to send your newly-created query directly into the shop for more work such as sorting and totals.

   If you're satisfied with your options at this point, select the Open the Query to View Information button to see the Datasheet view.

The check box at the bottom of the screen automatically opens a Help file that explains how you can customize your query.

7. Click Finish after you make your selections to see your handiwork.

Figure 11-6:
Every good
query
deserves a
name.

Chapter 12

Searching a Slew of Tables

In This Chapter

▶ Setting up queries with more than one table

▶ Enlisting the Query Wizard's help

▶ Building multiple-table queries in Design view

Questioning just one table at a time kind of defeats the purpose of a relational database program. After all, relational database programs, which Access 2002 proudly claims to be, spend all of their time and energy encouraging you to organize your data into *multiple* tables. Why do that without including *some* way to link the various tables together and ask intelligent questions? (Yes, they *may* do it just to be annoying, but assume that's not a possibility here.)

In keeping with its membership in the Relational Database Application Club of America, Access 2002 does indeed include tools for querying multiple tables. Because the process is on the arcane side, this chapter focuses on enlisting the Query Wizard to help you through the process. For the more technically inclined out there, this chapter explains how to build a multiple-table query by hand, too.

There's no shame in using the wizard's help when building a multiple-table query. The process isn't easy — remember, some people go to college to *study* databases — but the Query Wizard covers the hard parts for you.

Some General Thoughts about Multiple-Table Queries

You may need to look at information from a variety of tables to get full use of your data. (In fact, if you're in the corporate world, it's almost a foregone conclusion that you need to blend data from multiple tables.) Fortunately, Access is specifically called a *relational database* because it enables you to establish *relationships* among the different tables you work with. This feature means that Access queries can look at two or more tables and (with your help and guidance) recognize information that goes together.

In most cases, a multiple-table query works the same as a single-table query. You merely need to let Access 2002 know that you are drawing on information from different tables, and the software does the rest.

Access 2002 maintains links between the tables in your database. Usually you (or your Information Systems department) create this link when you first design the database. When you build the tables and organize them with special *key fields,* you actually prepare the tables to work with a query.

Key fields are the glue that links Access tables together. Queries use these links to match records in one table with their mates in another. For example, in Figure 12-1, the auction house considers the people who sell items to its customers. The auction house, which sells the items for its customers, wants to keep track of the sold items, so it records each sold item in the Items table. The auction house also must keep track of its customers (the sellers) so the auction house knows where to send the money for each item sold. To keep track of the customers, the auction house creates a Customers table. Because each item also has a seller (or auction house customer), the Items table has a CustomerID field which stores a value corresponding to a unique record in the Customers table. The CustomerID field in the Items table tells Access 2002 who the customer of the item is.

Figure 12-1:
In a
multiple-
table query,
the tables
are linked to
share their
data.

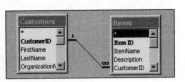

The CustomerID field is not a key field in the Items table because the main goal of the Items table is to keep track of the items that are sold. For the Items table, a key field called ItemID is created. This key field is unique and necessary because, after all, the auction house can't sell the same item twice. If more information is needed about the customer, the auction house has the Customers table with the CustomerID that matches the CustomerID, found in the Items table. The CustomerID field is a key field in the Customers table, which is unique because the auction house doesn't want a customer's information placed in their Customers table more than once.

Before building a bunch of multiple-table queries, you *must* understand how the tables in your database work. More specifically, you need to know which fields the tables use to link the data together. If you don't know, then you're begging for trouble (which arrives in the form of queries that don't tell you anything useful). To find out more about relationships in general and how to use the relationship-building tools of Access 2002, flip back to Chapter 5.

Calling on the Query Wizard

The Query Wizard isn't much of a wizard if all it does is create single-table queries. Luckily, it's one *heckuva* wizard because it comprehends the multiple-table query details as well.

To create a multiple-table query, follow these steps:

1. **In the database window, click the Queries button below the Objects bar on the left side of the window.**

    The window lists all of the queries currently living in the database.

2. **Double-click Create Query by Using Wizard to start the Simple Query Wizard.**

    The Simple Query Wizard window appears. Don't be surprised if the window looks familiar — it's the same one you use to make single-table queries. With a twist of the wrist (and a click of the mouse), it *also* builds multiple-table queries!

3. **Click the down arrow next to the Tables/Queries box (as shown in Figure 12-2), and then click the name of the first table to include in this query.**

    The Available Fields list changes and displays the fields available in the table (but you probably guessed that).

4. **Double-click each field you want to include in the query.**

    If you click the wrong field, just double-click it in the Selected Fields list. The field promptly jumps back to the Available Fields side of the window.

5. **When you finish adding fields from this table, repeat Steps 3 and 4 for the next table you want to use in the query.**

    After you list all of the fields you want in the Selected Fields area, go to Step 6.

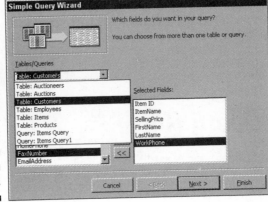

Figure 12-2:
Use the
Simple
Query
Wizard to
select from
more than
one table.

6. Click Next to continue building the query.

A screen amazingly similar to Figure 12-3 *may* hop into action, but don't
panic if it doesn't. If Access 2002 wants you to name the query instead,
skip ahead to Step 8.

If you include fields from two tables that aren't related, the Access 2002
Office Assistant leaps into action when you click Next. Office Assistant
reminds you that the tables must be related and suggests that you fix the
problem before continuing. Actually, *suggests* isn't quite correct — it
politely *demands* that you fix the relationship before trying to create the
query. If this error appears, click the OK button in the Office Assistant's
message to go directly to the Relationships window. Repair the relationship and then restart the Query Wizard to try again. I tell you about table
relationships in Chapters 4 and 5.

Figure 12-3:
Depending
on the
types of
information
in your
query, the
Query
Wizard may
offer to
summarize
the data
for you.

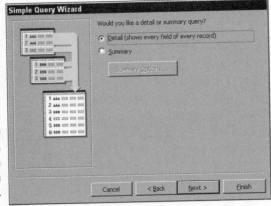

7. **If the wizard asks you to choose between a <u>D</u>etail and a <u>S</u>ummary query, click the radio button next to your choice:**

    • Detail creates a datasheet that lists all the records that match the query. As the name implies, you get all the details.

    • Summary tells the wizard that you aren't interested in seeing every single record; you want to see a summary of the information, instead.

    If you want to make any special adjustments to the summary, click Summary Options to display the Summary Options dialog box shown in Figure 12-4. Select your summary options from the list and then click OK.

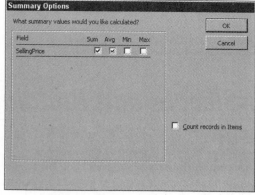

Figure 12-4:
Access
offers
different
ways of
summarizing
the data.

8. **Click Next after you choose how (and whether) to summarize your data.**

9. **Type a title for your query into the text box and then click <u>F</u>inish.**

    The query does its thing and Access 2002 displays the results on-screen, as shown in Figure 12-5. Congratulations!

Figure 12-5:
The
Datasheet
view of the
multiple-
table
summarized
query.

First Name	Last Name	Work Phone	Sum Of SellingPrice	Avg Of SellingP
Anistasia	Kimmerly	(317) 687-0819	$44.60	$44.60
Edward	Anderson	(317) 388-1842	$5.00	$5.00
Erika	Whitechurch	(317) 388-2727	$58.86	$8.41
Gerald	Hollingsly	(317) 237-7965	$265.36	$53.07
Gretchen	Hankla	(317) 779-4773	$147.94	$36.99
Kevin	Davis	(317) 367-2827	$12.10	$6.05
Sam	Gregory	(317) 292-8367	$47.00	$11.75
Travis	Cooksey		$14.12	$14.12

Items Query2 : Select Query

Record: 1 of 8

A gaggle of geese, a waggle of wizards

Is there a collective noun for a group of wizards? If not, there should be, because Access 2002 is loaded down with a whole plethora of wizardly assistants. Chapter 11 introduces the Simple Query Wizard, the most useful wizard for your general Access 2002 query needs.

But the wizard corps doesn't stop there. Access 2002 includes three other Query wizards that await your call: the Crosstab Query Wizard, the Find Duplicates Query Wizard, and the Find Unmatched Query Wizard.

Unfortunately, not all of the wizards are as straightforward as the Simple Query Wizard. Of the remaining three, the Crosstab Query Wizard is the only one that normal humans are likely to use. To find out about the Crosstab Query Wizard, check out Chapter 14. The remaining two wizards (Find Duplicates Query Wizard and Find Unmatched Query Wizard) are so weird that you don't need to worry about them.

Rolling Up Your Sleeves and Building the Query by Hand

Using a wizard to build your multiple-table queries isn't always the best solution. Maybe the query is too complex or requires some special summaries (or perhaps you just don't feel up to tangling with the Query Wizard at the moment). For those times when creating a query by hand is the best choice, use Design view instead.

Although it sometimes looks a bit complicated, Design view is nothing to be afraid of. After you get the hang of it, you may discover that you *prefer* building queries this way. (What a scary thought!)

Here are a couple of quick starting thoughts about building queries before you get into the details of Design view:

✔ Building database relationships between your tables before the design and construction of your database is complete is a bad idea. Building your relationships within the queries is typically a much better approach because you can change your table designs in the future without deleting your database relationships. When your database design and construction is complete, building relationships for the database can be very useful for automating updates between tables. For the scoop about relating tables together, see Chapter 5.

✔ If you know how to build single-table queries, you're well on your way to creating multiple-table queries, because the process is almost exactly the same.

Before starting a new multiple-table query, make sure that the tables are related! If you aren't sure about the table relationships, get back to the database window and click the Relationships button on the toolbar. (See Chapter 5 for more about table relationships.)

To build a multiple-table query by hand in Design view, follow these steps:

1. **Click the Queries button below the Objects bar on the left side of the database window.**

   The database window lists all of your queries, ready for action.

2. **Double-click Create a Query in Design View.**

   After a moment, the Show Table dialog box appears. Behind it, you see the blank query window where your query takes shape.

3. **Double-click the name of the first table you want to include in the query.**

   A small window for the table appears in the query window (see Figure 12-6).

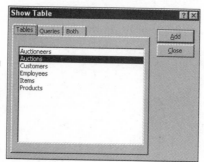

Figure 12-6:
The first table takes its place in the query.

4. **Repeat Step 3 for each table you want to add to the query. When you're done, click Close to make the Show Table dialog box go away.**

   Don't worry if lines appear between your tables in the query window (as shown in Figure 12-7). That's good — it shows that Access 2002 knows how to link the two tables.

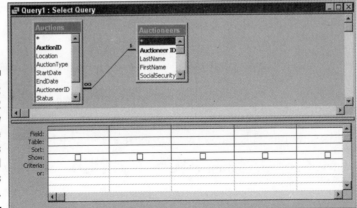

Figure 12-7:
Access 2002 knows how to link the Auctions and Auctioneers tables.

What happens if you create a query but there is no line between the tables? Access is telling you that it doesn't have a clue how to link the tables together but you can easily fix that. One solution is to cancel the query by closing the query window, and then use the Relationships button to build some relationships. Another solution is to simply create the relationship right in the Query designer by dragging a field from the first table and dropping it onto the related field in the second table.

5. **Add fields to the query grid by double-clicking on them in the table dialog boxes (as shown in Figure 12-8). Repeat this step for all of the fields you want to include in the query.**

Figure 12-8:
You can mix and match the fields from different tables in a single query.

Pick your fields in the order you want them to appear in the query results. Feel free to include fields from any or all of the tables at the top of the query window. After all, that's why you included the tables in the query to begin with.

If you accidentally choose the wrong field, you can easily fix your mistake. Click the field name's entry in the query grid and then select the oddly named Edit⊏>Delete Columns option from the menu bar. The incorrect field's entry (its column) is gone.

6. **If you want to sort by a particular field, click in the Sort box under the field name and then click the down arrow that appears at the edge of the Sort box. Click either Ascending or Descending (as shown in Figure 12-9).**

If you want to sort by more than one field, repeat this step. Remember, though, that sorts are performed from left to right. If you want to sort by the second field and then by the first, you should first rearrange your columns.

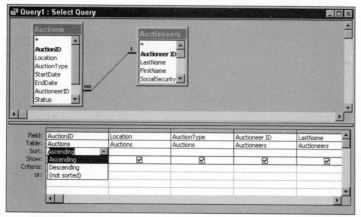

Figure 12-9:
A sorting we
will go . . .
ascending,
that is.

7. **In the Criteria box for each field, set up the selection information for the query.**

Even though this is a multiple-table query, you build criteria in the same way you do for single-table queries. Refer to Chapter 11 for help.

8. **If you want to include a field in the query but you don't want that field to appear in the final results, uncheck the Show entry for that field.**

9. **Review your work one more time. When you're sure it looks good, save the query by choosing File⇨Save.**

10. **In the Save As dialog box, type a name for the query and then click OK.**

    You don't want to lose all that hard work by not saving your query!

11. **Cross your fingers and then choose Query⇨Run (or click the Run button) to run your query.**

    How did it work? Did you get the answer you hoped for? If not, take your query back into Design view for some more work.

 12. **Choose View⇨Design View (or click the Design button).**

Chapter 13

The Ands and Ors of Dr. Boole

In This Chapter

▶ The difference between AND and OR

▶ Using the AND operator

▶ Using the OR operator

▶ Using AND and OR in the same query

*I*t's a fact of life: The longer you work with Access 2002, the more complex are the questions that you ask of your data. Sorting your stuff up, down, right, and left, and filtering it through and through is not enough — now you want it to march in formation while doing animal impressions. (Well, you always did set high goals.)

Access 2002 queries may make your data do tricks, but even queries need some help to complete the most advanced prestidigitation. That's where Dr. Boole and his magic operators enter the picture. By enlisting the unique capabilities of Boolean operators, your queries can scale new heights, perform amazing acrobatics, and generally amuse and astound both you and your coworkers. They may even surprise your boss!

This chapter looks at AND and OR, the two main operators in the world of Access 2002. It explains what the operators do, how they do it, and (most importantly) why you care. Get ready for a wild ride through the world of logic — strap your data in tight!

Comparing AND to OR

AND and OR are the stars of the Boolean sky. In spoken and written language, AND sticks phrases together into a complex whole, while OR describes a bunch of options from which to choose. In the world of databases, they perform much the same duties.

For example, if the woods are full of *lions AND tigers,* you can expect to find both types of animals anticipating your arrival. On the other hand, if the woods are full of *lions OR tigers,* then you know that *one or the other* is out there, but you don't expect to see both. In database terminology, AND means *both,* whereas OR means *either* (egad — this sounds like a grammar class).

Here's an easy rule to keep the two operators straight:

- ✔ AND narrows your query, making it more restrictive.
- ✔ OR opens up your query, so more records match.

If you start looking for an individual with blue eyes AND red hair AND over six feet tall AND male, you have a relatively small group of candidates (and I'm not among them). On the other hand, if you look for people with blue eyes OR red hair OR over six feet tall OR male, the matching group is much, much bigger. In fact, half of the people who worked on the book — including my spitz dog — meet the criteria.

Finding Things between Kansas AND Oz

One of the most common queries involves listing items that fall between two particular values. For example, you may want to find all the records that were entered after January 1, 1999, and before January 1, 2000. To ask this type of question, you use an AND criteria.

Using an AND criteria is pretty easy:

- ✔ Put the two conditions together on the same line.
- ✔ Separate the conditions with an AND.

Figure 13-1 shows the query screen restricting DateIn in the Items table of the Auction database to sometime during the year 1999.

Don't worry about the pound signs — Access puts those in automatically to feel like it contributes to your query. Wait a minute! Since when do we put pound signs around a date? Call it a condition of the drinking water in Redmond, Washington, that caused the engineers there to come up with this one, but for some reason, dates are surrounded by pound signs . . . if you forget, Access 2002 inserts them for you.

Take a close look at the formula in the query. Access 2002 begins processing the query by sifting through the records in the table and asking the first question in the criteria, "Was the record entered *on or after* January 1, 1999?" If the record was entered before this date, Access 2002 ignores it and goes on to the next one. If the record was entered after January 1, 1999, Access 2002 asks the second question, "Was the record entered before January 1, 2000?" If yes, Access 2002 includes the record in the results. If not, the record gets rejected and Access 2002 moves on to the next one.

Figure 13-1: The AND operator finds all dates from Jan 1, 1999, to Jan 1, 2000.

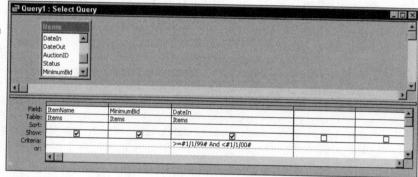

The comparison uses greater than or equal for the first date (January 1, 1999) to include records written on the first day of the year as well.

This type of "between" instruction works for any type of data. You can list numeric values that fall between two other numbers, names that fall within a range of letters, or dates that fall within a given area of the calendar. Access 2002 doesn't care *what* data you test.

Another way to have searched for dates in 1999 would have been with the BETWEEN operator (see Figure 13-2 for an example of BETWEEN in action). The criteria BETWEEN #1/1/99# AND #12/31/00# causes records to be selected if the dates are within that range (January 1, 1999, to December 31, 2000) *inclusive*.

Figure 13-2: An even better BETWEEN!

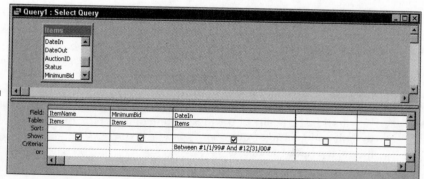

Multiple ANDs: AND Then What Happened?

One of the best features of Access 2002 is its flexibility. Overall, Access lets you do whatever you want in a query. For example, Access doesn't limit you to just *one* criteria in each line of a query. You can include as many criteria as you want. Access 2002 treats the criteria as if you typed an AND between each one.

Multiple criteria queries are tricky, though. Each AND criteria that you add must sit together on the same row. When you run the query, Access 2002 checks each record to make sure that it matches all of the expressions in the given criteria row of the query before putting that record into the result table. Figure 13-3 shows a query that uses three criteria. Because all of the criteria sit together on a single row, Access treats the three criteria as if they were part of a big AND statement. This query only returns records for auctions held at "The Ranch" that included items from customer "Donati" that had a minimum bid of less than $25.

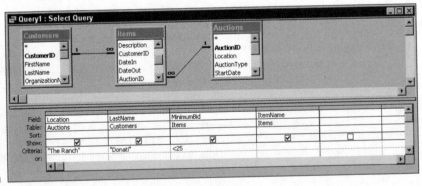

Figure 13-3: Show me only records that meet all of my requirements, please.

When you have a very large database and you want to restrict your results down to a minimum of records, combining a few criteria together is the most useful way to go.

Need to narrow your results even more? (Wow, your boss *is* demanding!) Because Access 2002 displays the query results in Datasheet view, all of the cool Datasheet view tools work with the query — tools like your old friend, the filter! Just use any of the filter commands (on the Records➪Filter menu) to limit and massage your query results. If you need a quick refresher about filters, flip back to Chapter 10.

Are You a Good Witch OR a Bad Witch?

Often, you want to find a group of records that match one of several different possibilities, (such as people who live in France OR Belgium OR the United States). This search calls for the OR criteria, the master of multiple options.

Access 2002 makes using an OR criteria almost too easy for words. There's nothing special to type, nothing to buy, and no salesman will call. In fact, the OR option is built right into the Access query dialog box, ready and waiting for your call.

To make a group of criteria work together as a big OR statement, list each criteria on its own line at the bottom of the query. Each line can include criteria for whichever fields you want, even if another line in the query *already* has a criteria in that field. (Trust me, this is easier than it sounds.) Figure 13-4 shows a query asking to see all records where the last name is Donati or Anderson or Smith.

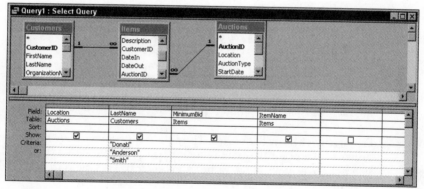

Figure 13-4: Looking for auctions by these three families.

Of course, you can list the criteria in different columns, too. For example, Figure 13-5 shows the Items table of the Auction database with a request for items that were entered by the Donati, Anderson, or Smith families OR which have a MinimumBid of $30 or less. So, all items entered by Donati (or Anderson or Smith) will appear in my report as will any item with a minimum bid of $30 regardless of the last name.

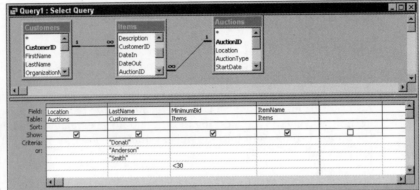

Figure 13-5:
Create OR
criteria from
different
fields.

Each of the criteria is on a separate line. If the criteria are on the same line, you are performing an AND operation — only records that match both rules appear.

AND and OR? AND or OR?

Sometimes, using the AND and OR operators by themselves isn't enough. You need to ask a question about several different groups. Part of the question involves restricting the groups (with an AND), and other parts require including records based on a different criteria (with an OR).

Be careful with these queries. They get *really* fancy *really* fast. If a query grows to the point that you're losing track of which AND the last OR affected, you're in over your head. Either start over or seek help from a qualified database nerd.

The most important point to remember is that each OR line (each line within the criteria) is evaluated separately. If you want to combine several different criteria, you need to make sure that each OR line represents one aspect of what you are searching.

For example, in the Auctions database, knowing which items sell for less than $30 or more than $100 at a single auction site may be useful. Finding the items in those price ranges requires the use of an OR condition. (To find items with a MinimumBid *between* $30 and $100, use an AND criteria instead.) Using an OR condition means that the criteria go on separate lines.

However, that restriction isn't enough. You only want the items that are for sale at one site (in this example, it's The Ranch). For this query to work, you need to repeat the site information on each OR line. Congratulations — you have a bouncing baby AND/OR combination query.

To set up this query, you need a two-criteria line. One criteria asks for those items that are less than $30 AND are for sale at site one; the other criteria calls out items that are over $100 AND are for sale at site one. Because the criteria are on two lines, Access treats them as a big OR statement. Figure 13-6 shows the two ANDs with an OR.

Figure 13-6:
Any criteria on the same line are AND operators and restrict the search. Any criteria on separate lines are OR operators and expand the search.

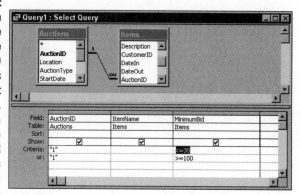

When reviewing your criteria, look at each line separately to make sure that line represents a group that you want included in the final answer. Then check to see that the individual lines work together to distill the answer you're seeking:

- ✔ AND criteria all go on the same line and are evaluated together.

- ✔ OR criteria go on separate lines, and each line is evaluated separately.

- ✔ Criteria that you want to use in each OR statement must be repeated on each of the separate lines.

Chapter 14

Teaching Queries to Think and Count

In This Chapter

▶ Using the Totals row

▶ Grouping entries together

▶ Understanding the Count and Sum functions

▶ Asking crosstab queries

▶ Choosing the top values

▶ Applying more functions

*G*etting quick answers to simple questions about the stuff in your database is nice, but there's more to life than finding out precisely how many folks from Montreal or Bombay bought pastel-colored back-scratchers between January and May of last year. What if you needed to know the total amount of money they spent on back-scratchers? Or the number of orders people placed? Or which 25 cities purchased the most?

In what's rapidly becoming a recurring theme of the book, Access 2002 comes to the rescue. Well, technically speaking, it's Access 2002 *query calculations* and *counting tools* to the rescue.

Query calculations do simple math, count matching entries, and perform several other tricks, provided you know how to ask for their help. The program's Top Values tool quickly and easily helps you focus on the records that *best* match your criteria. This chapter explains the inner-workings of these helpful functions. Read on and put those queries to work!

Totaling Everything in Sight

In addition to just answering questions, Select queries can also perform simple calculations on the data in your tables. For example, if you tell Access to list all the customers from Germany, it can count them at no extra charge. What a deal!

The first step in adding a total to your query is to turn on the Total row in the query grid. (For the sake of keeping queries as simple as possible, Access doesn't display this row by default.) With your query on-screen, choose View⇨Totals from the main menu or click the Totals button. Figure 14-1 shows the Select Query screen with the Total row added.

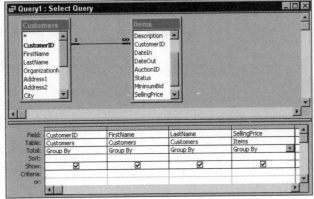

Figure 14-1:
The Total row appears between the Table and the Sort rows.

 The symbol on the face of the Totals button is the Greek letter *sigma,* meaning *to add everything up.* Mathematicians, engineers, and others with interpersonal communication difficulties use this symbol when they want a total.

Assume you need to see a total of sales for each customer — follow these steps:

1. **Set up an average, normal Select query, just as you usually do. Select those tables and fields that you want to see on the report.**

   In this case, you probably want to see CustomerID, FirstName, LastName, and SellingPrice.

2. **Click the Totals button to add a Total row to the query.**

   The Total row fills in with the Group By entry automatically. The Group By entry tells Access to organize the query results into groups based on that particular field. In addition, the Group By entry eliminates duplicate entries in your results. If you have more than one field showing with the Group By instruction, the query results show each unique combination of those fields.

3. **Click the Total row and choose the calculation type for each field on which you want to perform a calculation.**

   You're telling Access 2002 that you want to sum the SellingPrice field by choosing the Sum function (see Figure 14-2).

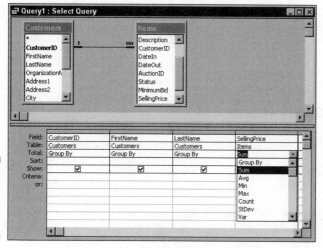

Figure 14-2: Choose yer weapon, er, function.

4. **Click the Run button to run the query.**

Access groups the data by customer showing a total of sales for each, as shown in Figure 14-3. Too cool!

Figure 14-3: Access 2002 is even better than a calculator!

Counting the Good Count

Although computing sums is useful, the Total row can do much more. Another useful option is the *Count* function, which (as the name implies) counts matching records in your table and displays the total in your query results.

The Count instruction requires at least two entries in your query:

- ✔ An entry that creates the groups (with Group By in the Totals row)
- ✔ An entry that counts (with Count in the Totals row)

Select the Count function by clicking on the cell in the Total row for the field that you want to count. After you click, a down arrow appears. Click the down arrow to see a drop-down list of functions, one of which is Count.

The most difficult part of the whole operation is deciding which field to use for counting. If you want to count each record that matches, you must be certain that the field you use has a unique entry for each and every record. For example, Figure 14-4 shows a query that displays a count of all customers in each state. The query is grouped by State/Province and a count is calculated for CustomerID.

Figure 14-5 shows the results of a Count query.

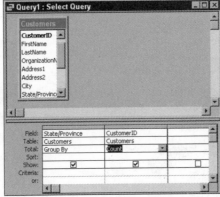

Figure 14-4:
I try to
obtain a
count of
how many
customers
are in each
state or
province.

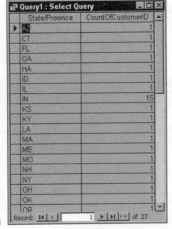

Figure 14-5:
The results
of the query
show how
many
customers
are in
each state.

When you do a grouping query, the default for Access 2002 is to sort your data in the same way that you group it; if you group by State/Province, then Access 2002 sorts the data that way as well. You don't have to stand for that behavior, however. Instead, you can force Access 2002 to accede to your will by creating you own sort. You can even sort the query by the results of a computed field; in Figure 14-6, I sort the query by the count of customers in ascending order (so that the state with the most customers appears first).

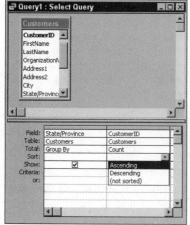

Figure 14-6:
Access 2002 allows you to sort your query by the result of a function.

Counting with Crosstab

Some types of information naturally lend themselves to being grouped by two categories. For example, polls often use gender (which is traditionally a two-option category) to break down their results for each question. You can do the same breakdown in Access with a crosstab (or *cross tabulation*) query.

Figure 14-7 shows what crosstab query results look like. Even though you may not know the name *crosstab,* you more than likely recognize how it works. This crosstab query shows average sales price for each auction location broken down by the customer's home state.

Crosstab queries always involve three fields:

　✔ *Row Heading* is used for the row categories.

　✔ *Column Heading* tells Access 2002 where to find the column category.

　✔ The third field explains where the values for the crosstab come from.

Figure 14-7:
The
Datasheet
view of a
simple
crosstab
query.

State/Province	Avg Selling Price	Fairgrounds Bld	The Ranch
IN	$9.43	$9.30	$9.56
MA	$36.99		$36.99
NC	$53.07	$53.07	
OR	$5.00	$5.00	
WA	$44.60	$44.60	

Avg Selling Price By State and Location : Crosstab Query

Record: 1 of 5

You can also use one or many criteria to limit which records are included in the summary. As with other queries in this chapter, you do so by adding criteria to one of the fields being used. The easiest way to do this is by adding another field to the query, using the Where instruction (so that the field doesn't show up in the results), and then adding the criteria to that field.

To create a crosstab query, follow these steps:

1. **Open your database and then click the Queries Options Bar button (no surprises there).**

2. **Click the New button in the database window and then double-click Crosstab Query Wizard.**

   Follow the wizard's carefully presented path to find crosstab success by selecting a report source, column headings, row headings, and record details.

There's More to Life Than Sum and Count

Don't get the idea that the world of queries begins and ends with Sum and Count. Access 2002 includes many other functions to organize, evaluate, and generally figure out what your data is saying. Table 14-1 lists some of the more popular and useful functions.

Each entry in the table includes the name of the function and a brief description of what it does. Each function can be selected from the drop-down list on the Total line.

Table 14-1	Access Functions and What They Do
Function	*Purpose*
Group By	Organizes the query results in this field
Sum	Adds up all the values from this field in the query results
Avg	Calculates the average of the values in this field
Min	Tells you the lowest value the query finds
Max	Gives you the highest value the query finds
Count	Tells you the number of records that match the query criteria
First	Returns the first record that Access 2002 stumbles across that meets the query criteria
Last	Returns the last matching record Access 2002 finds, or the opposite of First
Expression	Tells Access that you want a calculated field (see Chapter 15 to see some of the different calculations you can perform)
Where	Tells Access to use this field as part of the query criteria

Chapter 15

Calculating Your Way to Fame and Fortune

In This Chapter

▶ Developing an expression

▶ Performing more complex calculations

▶ Calculating text fields

▶ Using the Expression Builder

*O*ne of the big rules in database creation is the decree that a table should contain as few fields as possible. Smaller tables load faster, are easier to document and maintain, and take up less disk space. One extra field isn't much by itself, but it adds up when your table contains several hundred thousand records!

So how do the pros keep their tables small? By storing only what they *really* need and using *calculations* to figure out whatever else they require. For example, if your table contains the wholesale cost and the retail price of an item, why bother storing the markup percentage? When you need that information, use a *calculated field* to create it on the fly!

A calculated field takes information from another field in the database and performs some arithmetic to come up with new information. In fact, a calculated field can take data from more than one field and combine information to create an entirely new field, if that's what you want.

This chapter shows you how to build all kinds of calculations into queries. From simple sums to complex equations, the information you need is right here.

Although the examples in this chapter deal with calculated fields within queries, the same concept applies to calculated fields within reports. For a few tips about calculating fields and reports, flip ahead to Chapter 20.

A Simple Calculation

When you want to create a calculated field within a query, first figure out which fields you need for the calculation and then find out which tables contain those fields. The query must include all of the tables on your list. If the fields live in one table, include only that table in the query (see Figure 15-1). If the fields are split among several tables, make sure to include all of the tables containing fields that you want to use in the calculation at the top of the query screen. Otherwise, Access can't do the calculations. (Even with its sometimes-amazing antics, Access is *still* merely software — it's not terribly bright, and it gets confused easily.)

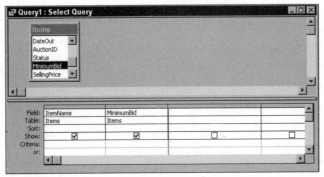

Figure 15-1: To display the expected price for an item, select the Item Name and Minimum Bid fields.

Start building the calculated field by clicking in the empty field name box of the column where you want the results to appear. Instead of selecting an existing field, type the calculation that you want Access 2002 to perform.

As you may suspect, Access uses a special syntax for building calculated fields. You can't just type *add these together and display the result* — that's *way* too simple and understandable. Surprisingly, calculating is not much tougher than that.

Basically, you type the calculation just like you enter it into a pocket calculator, except that you substitute field names for at least some of the numbers. The key to the whole process is the square bracket symbol ([ ]). To make Access understand which parts of the calculation are fields, you put square brackets around the field names themselves. Access miraculously recognizes that those entries refer to fields in your table. Anything else Access finds in the calculation (such as numbers, for example), Access treats as constants (which is the math nerd term for *it means whatever it says*).

Using the auction example, suppose that research says that most items sell for 47 percent more than the minimum bid price. To calculate the expected price, you need to add 47 percent to the MinimumBid. The formula to do this is

```
[MinimumBid] * 1.47
```

The square brackets around MinimumBid tell Access that MinimumBid is a field in the table, not just a bunch of text in the calculation. Because the 1.47 on the end doesn't have any brackets around it, Access assumes that you mean the numeric value 1.47.

Because Access 2002 isn't smart enough to recognize the percent sign, you need to convert percentages to decimals (thus 147% turns into 1.47).

Calculations go into the Field line anywhere in your query. Figure 15-2 shows the finished formula. Here are some general guidelines to keep in mind when creating formulas:

Figure 15-2: I add a third column displaying the minimum bid marked up by 47 percent.

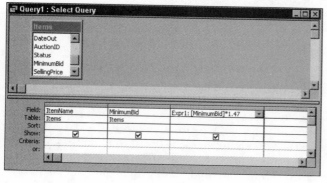

✔ You have to manually type each field name into your formula — you can't just drag the field name down from the table list.

Dragging the field name adds it as a field itself (which isn't *quite* what you had in mind).

✔ Don't worry if your query grows past the edge of the Field box. Access still remembers everything, even if it doesn't appear on-screen. For a quick tip about adjusting the query grid to make some extra room, see the sidebar later in this chapter.

✔ To include fields from more than one table in a single calculation, tell Access the table name for each field in the query. Hang onto your hat — the details get kinda weird. To include the table name with the field in the calculation, type the table name in square brackets, type an exclamation point, and then type the field name in square brackets. Your finished entry looks something like this: `[table]![field]`. Yes, it *does* sound like an odd fraternity ritual.

When you run a query containing a calculation, Access produces a datasheet showing the fields you specified, plus it adds a new column for the calculated field. In Figure 15-3, the datasheet shows the item name, the minimum bid, and the calculated field containing the expected price for each item.

ItemName	MinimumBid	Expr1
China setting for 8	$85.00	124.95
3 Cast iron toys	$22.00	32.34
Asst hardback books (1 of 4)	$30.00	44.1
Asst hardback books (2 of 4)	$30.00	44.1
Asst hardback books (3 of 4)	$30.00	44.1

Record: 1 of 26

Figure 15-3: The calculation actually worked!

The column for the expected price is labeled a little strangely. Left to its own devices, Access came up with the clever moniker Expr1, which stands for Expression 1. Expr1 is the default name for the first expression (or formula) in a calculation. Changing the expression heading is easy. If you look back at the query grid after creating an expression, you find that Access 2002 inserted the Expr1 default field name and a colon in front of the calculation. To give the field a different name, simply highlight Expr1 and type your replacement (as shown in Figure 15-4).

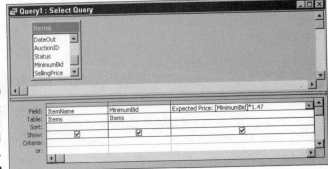

Figure 15-4: Changing the field name.

In addition to changing the field name, you may want to change its format. Follow these steps:

1. **Right-click the field in the query grid and select Properties from the pop-up menu.**

   The Field Properties dialog box appears (see Figure 15-5).

2. **Click in the Format line and then click the button that appears on the right end of the field (the one with the downward-pointing arrow).**

   A drop-down list appears.

3. **Select the type of format that you want to use for the field.**

   For this example, select Currency, as shown in Figure 15-5.

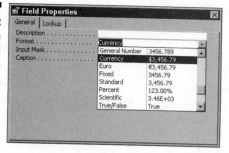

Figure 15-5:
Use the
Field
Properties
dialog box
to select an
appropriate
data format.

4. **Run the query.**

   Figure 15-6 shows the new query results after changing the field name and adding the Currency format.

ItemName	MinimumBid	Expected Price
China setting for 8	$85.00	$124.95
3 Cast iron toys	$22.00	$32.34
Asst hardback books (1 of 4)	$30.00	$44.10
Asst hardback books (2 of 4)	$30.00	$44.10
Asst hardback books (3 of 4)	$30.00	$44.10

Record: 1 of 26

Figure 15-6:
What a
beautiful
report —
Mom will be
so pleased!

Isn't that box a little small?

Because the field box in the query grid is kind of small, the grid may not display your entire calculation at a time. Isn't that just like a computer? Although the query *stores* your whole calculation, Access may or may not be able to show it all to you. If you want to make the column wider to see your entire formula, you can widen it while you test the query. When the query is working the way that you want it to, simply restore the column size. See Chapter 8 for more information about changing column widths.

Bigger, Better (And More Complicated) Calculations

After getting the hang of simple calculations, you can easily expand your repertoire into more powerful operations, such as using multiple calculations and building expressions that use the values from *other* calculations in the same query. This stuff really adds to the flexibility and power of queries.

Add another calculation — go ahead, add two!

Access makes it easy to put multiple calculations into a single query. After building the first calculation, just repeat the process in the next empty Field box. Keep inserting calculations across the query grid until you just don't care anymore — Access gleefully lets you keep right on going.

You can use the same field in several calculations. Access doesn't mind at all.

Using one expression to solve a different question

One of the most powerful calculated field tricks involves using the solution from one calculated field as part of *another* calculation in the same query. Not only does the calculation create a new field in the query results, but the handy calculation also supplies data to other calculations in the same query, just like it's a real field in the table.

Although the details are simple, the technique borders on the realm of true techno-magic. Tread carefully because a small error in one calculation quickly compounds into a huge mistake when other calculations use an accuracy-challenged number.

Each calculation gets a name (the text that sits in front of the calculation in the query grid), whether the name's the default Expr1 or something more colorful, like DaysInStock. To use the results from one calculation as part of another, just include the name of the first calculation in square brackets. In short, treat the first calculation as if it is a field in your table.

The query in Figure 15-7 shows this technique in action. The answer to the first calculation (Expected Price) is used in the second calculation (Profit).

It looks just like any other field in the query — Access doesn't see the field any differently.

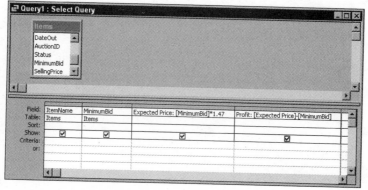

Figure 15-7:
Use the result of one calculated field in another.

Figure 15-8 shows the results of the query using these formulas.

Making Access 2002 ask

At times, you may want a value that's not in your database included in a formula. If you know the value, you can simply type it into the formula, just as you type 1.47 for 147 percent. But if you'd rather enter that value as you run the query, that's easy to do, too.

Simply create a field name to use within your formula. For example, you may choose to calculate an ExpectedPrice field by using a percentage value that you plan to enter when you run the query. Imagine that this field is called PercentIncrease. You then create your calculated field by using this formula:

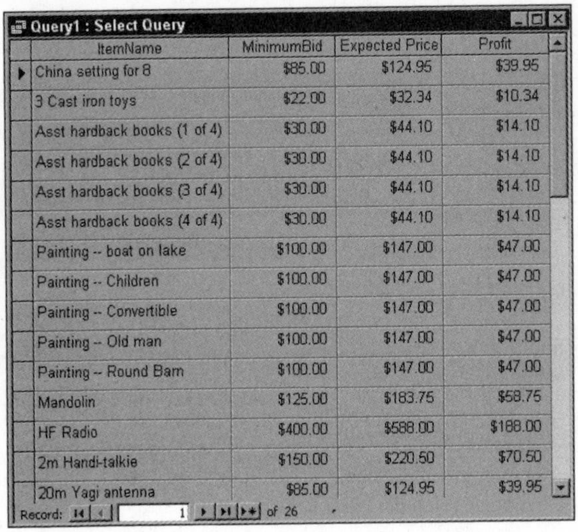

ItemName	MinimumBid	Expected Price	Profit
China setting for 8	$85.00	$124.95	$39.95
3 Cast iron toys	$22.00	$32.34	$10.34
Asst hardback books (1 of 4)	$30.00	$44.10	$14.10
Asst hardback books (2 of 4)	$30.00	$44.10	$14.10
Asst hardback books (3 of 4)	$30.00	$44.10	$14.10
Asst hardback books (4 of 4)	$30.00	$44.10	$14.10
Painting -- boat on lake	$100.00	$147.00	$47.00
Painting -- Children	$100.00	$147.00	$47.00
Painting -- Convertible	$100.00	$147.00	$47.00
Painting -- Old man	$100.00	$147.00	$47.00
Painting -- Round Barn	$100.00	$147.00	$47.00
Mandolin	$125.00	$183.75	$58.75
HF Radio	$400.00	$588.00	$188.00
2m Handi-talkie	$150.00	$220.50	$70.50
20m Yagi antenna	$85.00	$124.95	$39.95

Figure 15-8: The Expected Price and Profit on items from the auction.

```
[MinimumBid] * (1 + [PercentIncrease])
```

When you run the query, Access displays a dialog box like the one shown in Figure 15-9. This dialog box lets you enter a value for the increase that you're expecting.

Figure 15-9: Access asks for a profit margin.

When the dialog box appears, just enter the value of your expected increase (as a decimal value), and then Access 2002 does the rest. This option means that you can use the same query with different values to see how changing that value affects your results.

Working with words

Number fields aren't the only fields you can use for calculations. In fact, performing the calculation by using a text field is often more useful. Figure 15-10 shows one of the most common database formulas, which is used to combine the FirstName and LastName fields to provide the full name.

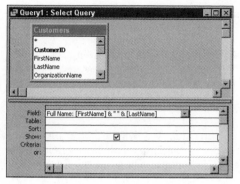

Figure 15-10:
Turning a
name into a
calculated
field.

This formula consists of the FirstName field, an ampersand, then a single space inside quotation marks, followed by another ampersand, and then the LastName field:

```
[FirstName]&" "&[LastName]
```

When you run this query, Access 2002 takes the information from the two fields and puts them together, inserting a space between them. Figure 15-11 shows the results of this query.

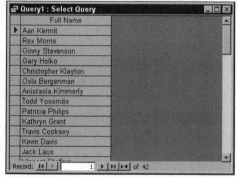

Figure 15-11:
First and
last names
combine for
a more
aesthetically
pleasing
single field
"Full
Name."

Each individual's name appears as it does on a mailing list label. This text calculation makes taking information from your database and turning it into a more readable format easy.

Expression Builder to the Rescue

Creating calculated fields gives you two basic challenges:

- ✔ Figure out what the formula should say.
- ✔ Enter the formula so that Access 2002 can recognize it.

 Unfortunately, Access 2002 can't help you with the first problem — but it can help with the second. To get help creating a calculated field the way Access 2002 wants it, click the Build button and bring out the Expression Builder.

The Expression Builder has several parts, as you can see in Figure 15-12. The top part is the area where you actually create the expression, and immediately below that are the operators you can use to work with the information in your expression.

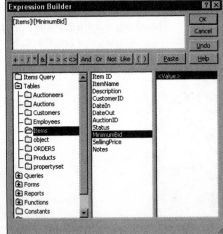

Figure 15-12:
The Expression Builder in action.

The first group of these operators does simple mathematical operations: addition, subtraction, division, and multiplication. The next operator, the ampersand (&), is similar in that you use it to combine two text fields.

The next two groups of operators do logical comparisons. These operators create expressions similar to formulas used in the Criteria field and return a response of True or False. The final two buttons in this collection enable you to enter parentheses. (You can also simply type these symbols directly from your keyboard, which is often easier.)

The lower half of the dialog box has three windows. The left window contains folders of the various parts of your Access 2002 environment, including all the information in your tables.

To add a field from one of your tables, simply open the Tables folder and then open the folder for the table that you want to use. A list of all the fields in that table appears in the middle window. To add a field to the expression, simply double-click (refer to Figure 15-12).

When you use the Expression Builder to add a field, it includes the table name in front of the field name with an exclamation mark between the two. The format for this is

```
[Table Name]![Field Name]
```

The other folders listed in the left window often contain more information. In some cases, this information is organized into categories within the folder. For example, the Functions folder contains a variety of built-in functions, as well as some functions that you or others may have defined in your database. You can use these functions to perform calculations using the information in your database.

To use one of the built-in functions, simply open the Functions folder, select a category of functions from those in the middle window, and then look through the list in the right window until you find the function you want to use. Figure 15-13 shows the Built-In Functions folder open, with the Financial functions displayed in the right window. To select a category of functions, simply click the category name in the middle window. To select a function, double-click it in the right window.

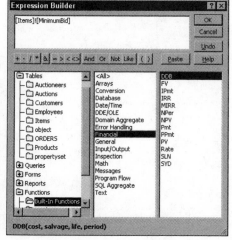

Figure 15-13: The lower-left corner of the screen gives a brief synopsis of how the function works.

The other folders contain useful goodies as well. The Constants folder contains constants that are defined for use in comparisons, including True, False, and some that can represent empty fields. The Operators folder contains symbols used for creating expressions.

The Arithmetic category (inside the Operators folder) includes the same four operators that are available as buttons. It also includes the caret (^), which is used for exponents (raising a number to a higher power); MOD, which is used to return the remainder of a division operation; and the backslash, which is used for integer division. With integer division, dividing 5 by 2 (5/2) gives you the answer 2, and 5 MOD 2 gives you the result of 1, the remainder.

Finally, Common Expressions enable you to include various common entries. These entries are most useful for creating a report and are discussed in Chapter 20.

For intimate details about the operations and other sundry doohickeys in the Expression Builder, fire up the Office Assistant by clicking Help in the Expression Builder window. The Office Assistant offers thoughts, explanations, and samples of most everything the Expression Builder knows how to do.

One of the advantages of using the Expression Builder is that it helps remind you what you need to do. For example, when you create an expression, the Expression Builder won't let you just place two fields side by side. In Figure 15-14, I doubled-clicked the DateOut and DateIn fields, one after the other.

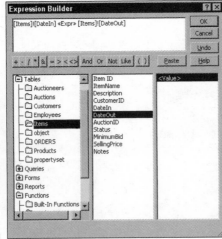

Figure 15-14: Access places <<Expr>> in the formula, prompting you to tell it what action to perform.

Between the two fields, Access 2002 inserts <<Expr>> to remind me that I need to tell Access 2002 what calculation to perform, perhaps inserting a minus sign to subtract the second date from the first.

Chapter 16

Automated Editing for Big Changes

In This Chapter

▶ Anguishing over the process

▶ Replacing data

▶ Deleting data

▶ Updating data

Fixing an incorrect entry in an Access 2002 table is pretty easy. A couple of clicks, some typing, and {poof!} the problem is gone.

But what if you need to fix 26,281 records? Suddenly, you're talking about a whole bunch of clicking and typing and clicking and typing. Editing an entire table by hand doesn't sound like a *poof!* experience to me. It sounds more like a clean-the-elephant-herd-with-a-toothbrush experience.

Fortunately, Access 2002 has a variety of large-scale housekeeping and editing tools. These tools enable you to make widespread changes to your database without wearing down your fingers in the process. This chapter explores the tools available within Access 2002 and gives you examples of how to use them to make quick work of the elephant herd in your life.

First, This Word from Our Paranoid Sponsor

Please, oh *please* read this chapter carefully. The queries I explain here are wonderful tools, but they're also incredibly dangerous double-edged swords.

Used correctly, these automated editing queries save incredible amounts of time. Unfortunately, if something goes wrong, they can inflict incredible amounts of damage to your table with a single click. Any time you plan to remove, change, or add to the data in your tables with one of these queries, take a moment and make a backup copy of at least the table, if not the entire database.

To back up a table, follow these steps:

1. **Open the database file and click the Tables button on the left side.**

   Access displays a list of all the tables in the database.

2. **Right-click the table you plan to edit and then select Copy from the pop-up menu that appears.**

   Access places a copy of the table onto the Windows clipboard.

3. **Right-click anywhere on the open space of the database window and select Paste from the pop-up menu that appears.**

   The Paste Table As dialog box appears.

4. **Type a name for the new table (such as Customer table backup), and then click OK.**

   (Don't worry about the other radio buttons in the dialog box. The default settings work just fine.)

   The dialog box closes and you now have a copy of the original table.

Quick and Easy Fixes: Replacing Your Mistakes

Automated editing queries have a lot of power. Before hauling out the *really* big guns, here's a technique for small-scale editing. The technique may seem simplistic, but don't be fooled; it's quite handy.

You can practice small-scale editing by using the Replace command as follows:

1. **Open a table in Datasheet view.**

2. **Click the column in which you want to change data and choose Edit⇨Replace.**

   The Find and Replace dialog box opens, as shown in Figure 16-1.

3. **Type the value you want to change in the Find What box. Type a new value in the Replace With box.**

   When you enter text in both fields, the buttons on the right side become available; you can use these buttons to move through your data, making changes as you go.

Figure 16-1:
The Find
and Replace
dialog box
enables you
to change
information
throughout
your table.

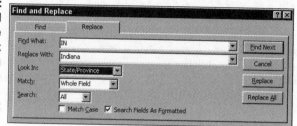

4. **Click Cancel or the "X" button at the top right of the dialog box when you're done.**

The Find and Replace dialog box closes and your data has been changed.

If you misspell "munchkin" throughout your data (I *hate* it when I do that) and need to change all its occurrences to the proper spelling, you can simply put the incorrect spelling in Find What, the proper spelling in Replace With, and click the Replace All button. Your computer goes off and does your bidding, changing each and every instance of the word in the Find What box to the word in the Replace With box.

Access gives you a lot of control over the process. In addition to the options you know and love from the Find command (I discuss these options in Chapter 10), Replace offers additional options:

✔ **Match Whole Field:** Activates when you click the drop-down arrow. It tells Access to look only for cases where the information in the Find What box *completely matches* an entry in the table. (If the data in your table includes any additional characters in the field — even a single letter — Match Whole Field tells Access to skip it.)

✔ **Find Next:** Highlights the next matching item in your table *without* changing the current selection. Find Next is handy if you need to selectively change some data without bothering anything else.

✔ **Replace:** Tells Access to change the current selection and *then* move on to the next match.

✔ **Replace All:** Gives Access a free hand to implement your changes without asking anything else from you. This is the Big Kahuna button in the dialog box.

If your editing goes awry, remember the wonderful Undo option. Just choose Edit➪Undo from the main menu or press Ctrl+Z.

Different Queries for Different Jobs

Although Select queries do most of the work within Access, they aren't alone in the Access universe. Select queries are just one of several types of queries available to you. You can change the type of query you use by selecting a new query type from the Query menu (found in Query Design view) or by clicking the Query Type button on the Query Design View toolbar. Click the downward-pointing arrow at the ride side of the Query Type button and a list of query types drops down, as shown in Figure 16-2.

The last four types of queries (Make-Table, Update, Append, and Delete) contain exclamation points to remind you that these types of queries actually change the way your information is organized. When you work with these four types of queries, you can click the Query View button to preview which records the query affects. I strongly recommend that you do a preview before running any of these queries, because previewing is the only way to make sure that the changes you're making are really the ones you intend.

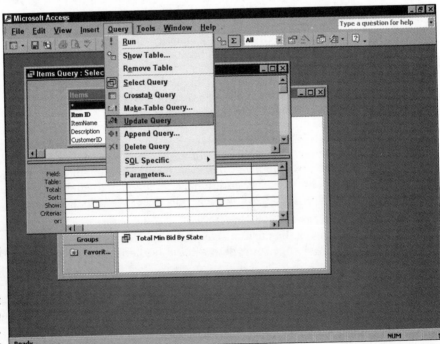

Figure 16-2:
Pick a
different
query type
from the list.

With most types of queries, the difference between using the Run button and the Query View button is minor. But when you use either the Delete query or the Update query, whether you use the Run or the Query View button makes a big difference. When you use the Query View button with these two functions, you see the results without changing your database. If you use the Run button instead, your information changes for all time and eternity (well, unless you have a backup — which you *made,* right?).

You're Outta Here: The Delete Query

The easiest of the editing queries is the Delete query. Unfortunately, the Delete query is also one of the most dangerous. (Why do *easy* and *dangerous* always go together in computer programs?)

Creating a Delete query works just like creating a Select query. In fact, they're identical, except for the query type setting. Before you create a Delete query, create a Select query to test your criteria and make sure that the query finds the records you want. After you know that the criteria work correctly, change the Select query to a Delete query with the preceding Query Type setting.

Here's how to build a Delete query:

1. **Create a normal Select query.**

2. **Set up criteria to identify the records you want to delete.**

3. **Run the Select query to make sure that it finds *only* the records that you want to work with.**

   If the Select query finds *other* records as well, adjust the criteria so that the extras don't match.

4. **Return to Design view.**

5. **Click the Query Type button and choose Delete from the drop-down list that appears (or choose Delete from the Query menu).**

   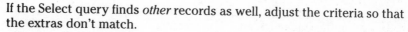

   The name in the Title bar changes and the Sort line changes to a Delete line (see Figure 16-3). Clicking the Run Query button removes all records from the Customers table where the last name starts with an "H." (Information for locating records is in this query — the information was converted from the original Select query that I used to list out these records.)

6. **Start the query.**

   Access displays a message asking whether you want to delete the records. It reminds you that after you delete records, you can't get the data back.

7. **Click Yes if you want to delete the records.**

   The query runs; Access finds the records that match the criteria, and removes those records from the table.

That's all you need to do.

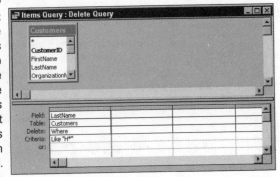

Figure 16-3:
The Delete
query is
about to
eliminate
all the
customers
whose last
names
begin
with H.

You can't undo changes you make by using the Delete query. After you delete these records, they're gone for good, never to be seen again.

You can create Delete queries that use more than one table to locate information. However, be careful when you use multiple tables because the number of changes you make can increase dramatically if your queries don't work quite right. Again, I suggest backing up your database and running a Select query first to list the records that you want to delete.

Making changes gets a bit more complicated when you delete records from more than one table. Access can do this only if records to be deleted in one table are linked one-to-one — in other words, with each record linked to only one record in the other table.

One-to-one links appear with a point symbol in the relationship grid at the top of the Query screen. One-to-many relationships are denoted by the infinity symbol "∞". To delete records from tables with a one-to-many relationship, you must run two separate queries — one to delete from the first table and then another to delete from the second table.

Depending on the database settings, Access may not even *let* you delete the records. One-to-many deletions involve the touchy technical issue of *referential integrity*. Loosely translated, this means that records *must* exist in one table because *matching* records depend on them in some other table. Life gets weird with referential integrity, but many corporate databases use referential integrity because it ensures that huge mistakes don't happen by accident. If you work in a big company and think that you need to delete data but keep running into a referential integrity error, contact your Information Systems folks. After they stop hyperventilating, they can help you.

Making Big Changes

There comes a time in every database's life when it needs to change. Fortunately, you can make radical changes to a database automatically by using the Update query. The Update query enables you to use a query to select records and then use instructions to change the information.

 As with other types of queries that modify your data (particularly the Delete query I discuss earlier in this chapter), making sure that your query works only with the records that you want to change is vital. Setting up and testing your criteria with a Select query before running the query for real is always a good idea.

 When you select the Update query, either by choosing Update Query from the Query menu or by choosing Update Query from the Query Type list, your query grid changes to resemble the one shown in Figure 16-4.

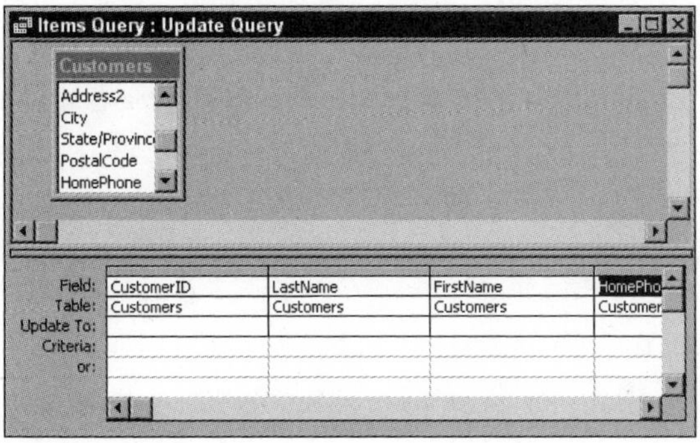

Figure 16-4:
An Update
query has a
new row
called
"Update To."

Although the query looks normal overall, this grid includes a new line labeled Update To. You can use any criteria to select your records, just as in a normal Select query. For example, you may want to select all the records where the customer's last name is Harrison. To do so, set up your criteria with the LastName field and the entry "Harrison" on the Criteria line.

For some reason, the Harrison family has decided to avoid confusion by adopting the same first name: Ralph. You can simply go through and change each record by hand, but using an Update query is easier: simply enter Ralph on the Update To line underneath FirstName. Your Update Query screen looks like the one shown in Figure 16-5.

When you run the query, you get a warning message that you're about to update records. Click Yes to go ahead and make your changes.

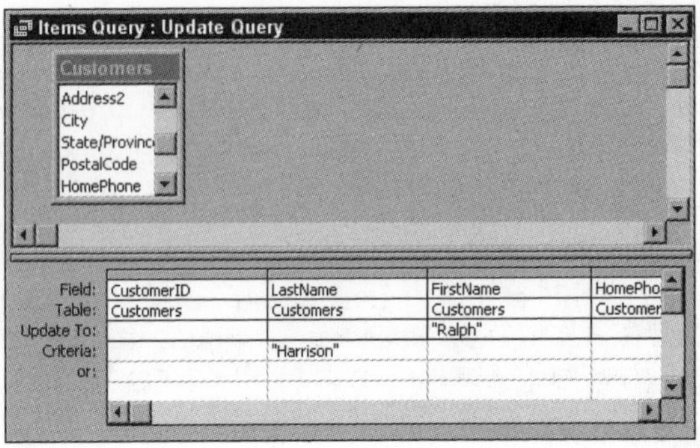

Figure 16-5:
The Update query finds all customers whose last name is "Harrison" and changes their first name to "Ralph."

Your Update query can involve more than one table. Suppose, for example, that you want to add a notation for each customer who has an auction item with a minimum bid of more than $100. Here's how to involve multiple tables:

1. **In the Query Design window, select the tables you need to find the records that you want to update.**

   In this case, you need the Customers and the Items tables.

2. **Join the tables if necessary. (Refer to Chapter 12 if you want a refresher about joining tables.)**

   In this example, the tables are joined by the CustomerID field.

3. **Select the fields that you need to create the Select query.**

   For this query, you need the Notes column from the Customers table (because you're updating it) and the MinimumBid column from the Items table.

4. **Click the Update Query button to change the query type.**

   Access 2002 adds the UpdateTo row to the Query Designer.

5. **Enter the search (select) criteria to locate the records that you want to update.**

   In this example, I typed > **100** in the Criteria row under MinimumBid (see Figure 16-6).

6. **Enter the new value(s) for the field(s) to be updated.**

   In Figure 16-6, I entered **Big Bucks!** in the Update To row in the Notes column of the Query Designer.

7. **Run the query.**

   Access 2002 dutifully tells you how many rows will be updated and offers you a chance to change your mind (click Cancel). Too cool!

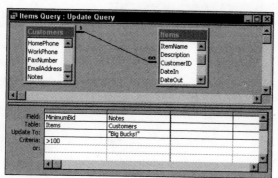

Figure 16-6:
This query finds all customers who bought items for more than $100 and gives them a "Note" of "Big Bucks!"

You can also make changes based upon the existing value in a field. To do that, you use a calculation like the ones I describe in Chapter 15. Suppose, for example, that you want to add 10 percent to the MinimumBid of all items from customers in Ohio. To make changes based on an existing value in a field, follow these steps:

1. **In the Update Query window, select the field that you want to search with and enter an appropriate search condition.**

   In this example, I chose the State/Province field and entered a criteria of "OH."

2. **Select the field that you want to update and enter the new value in the Update To row.**

   In this example, I entered the formula **[Items]![MinimumBid] * 1.1** under MinimumBid (see Figure 16-7).

   The square brackets tell Access 2002 that you're talking about a table or a field. When you see something like [Items]![MinimumBid], the first set of square brackets contains the table name and the second set contains the field name. An exclamation point separates them.

3. **Run the Update Query to make the changes to your data.**

I know I've said it already, but I'll say it again: *Be careful.* These queries (Update and Delete) can affect a lot of data and they cannot be undone. If you run a query without entering any criteria, the update (or delete) is performed on *every* record in the table! At a minimum, you should run the query as a Select query first to make sure that you're selecting the right records; then change the query to an Update or Delete query. Better still, have a good backup in place.

Figure 16-7:
This query
finds all
Ohio
customers
and
increases
their
minimum
bids by
10 percent.

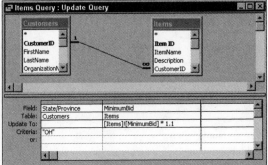

Part IV
Turning Your Table into a Book

The 5th Wave   By Rich Tennant

Now maybe these folks got a decent disaster recovery plan and maybe they don't...

DANGER
WILD RHINOCEROS

In this part . . .

Someone said that the computer revolution would do away with paper. Needless to say, that person was wrong. (Last I heard, that person is now compiling the annual psychic predictions page for one of the national tabloids.)

So far, this book has shown you how to put the data in and then mixed it up a little. Now it's time to pull the data out, clean it up a bit, and record it for posterity on the printed page. Access 2002 has some strong reporting tools to make your multi-thousand-page reports look truly cool. Better still, it offers some great summary tools to make those multi-thousand page reports a thing of the past. Stick your head into this part and see what you can see!

Chapter 17

AutoReport: Like the Model-T, It's Clunky but It Runs

In This Chapter

▶ Choosing between Columnar and Tabular AutoReports
▶ Creating an AutoReport
▶ Perusing your report in Print Preview
▶ Customizing your report with Page Layout

*W*hat do you do if someone (for example, your boss) wants to see all the revelations you made using your datasheets, tables, and queries? And then, what if your boss wants to share the aforementioned revelations with the rest of the company? The odds are good that the whole management team doesn't want to crowd around your monitor and study thousands of records and dozens of queries (besides, your cubicle isn't *that* big).

Lucky for you, Access 2002 includes tools for creating and printing reports. In fact, Access sees report-making as just another part of the whole database experience. Reports take information from your database (specifically, reports can draw from either tables or queries) and organize that information according to your instructions. Access 2002 even includes report wizards to walk you through the steps of designing a report to meet your needs.

You probably found this chapter because the boss wants a report *right now,* so the following pages take you to the AutoReport factory, where a cadre of digital elves wait to create a quick report for you. If your boss gives you the time, the last section in this chapter (plus the other chapters in this part) helps you spruce up the finished report a bit, making it a thing of beauty in addition to an object of truth.

AutoReport Basics for High-Speed Information

Think of AutoReport as your very own information assembly line. The AutoReport tools excel at one task. AutoReport builds a single-table report according to your specifications. Fire up the software, tell it what you want, and your report is as good as done.

Although AutoReport works with only one table at a time, it still offers some choices. AutoReport builds two kinds of reports: Columnar and Tabular. Both reports organize the same data, but in different ways:

- *Tabular AutoReports* place all information for each record on one row, with a separate column for each field. The tabular format puts the field names above each column (often trimming the names until you can't make heads or tails of what they are) and squashes the columns themselves together in the name of fitting everything horizontally on a single page.

- *Columnar AutoReports* organize each record vertically on the page, in two columns — one for the names of the fields and one for the contents of the fields. If the table has more than 15 or so fields, each record generally starts on a new page.

I don't have a profound answer for when to use one AutoReport layout or the other. The choice is more a matter of personal taste and aesthetics than anything else. The only advice I can offer is that the Tabular format is generally more useful if your report has lots of records with small fields, whereas the Columnar format is often better for reports with large fields but fewer records.

Whether you choose the Tabular or Columnar format, feel free to change AutoReport's creation however you want. Use the report that is built as an easy starting point, and then add titles, headers, footers, cool formatting, and more. Because AutoReport builds a normal Access 2002 report, a quick trip into Design mode puts all of the report development and formatting tools at your command. Check out Chapters 19 and 20 for more information about formatting, headers, and the other cool tricks available in the report system.

Putting the Wheels of Informational Progress into Motion

Although AutoReport includes separate tools for building Columnar and Tabular reports, the *good* news is that both systems work exactly the same way. The only difference between these two styles is in how they organize the data in the finished report. From a *how this works* standpoint, they're the same.

The query advantage

The fact that Access 2002 lets you base a report on a query is wonderful. When you build a report on a table, you get a report containing each and every record in the table. But what if you only want a few of the records? Access makes it easy. Create a query and then base the report upon that query.

The advantages don't stop there. If you create a query based on multiple tables, Access neatly organizes your results into a single datasheet. If your query produces the information that you want in its datasheet, then a report, based on that query's results, organizes and presents the information in the way you want. (In Chapter 12, I show you how to create queries using more than one table.)

Follow these steps to create either a Columnar or Tabular AutoReport:

1. **Click the Reports button below the Objects bar of your main database window and then click New.**

   The New Report dialog box appears, showing all the report types from which you can choose.

2. **Click AutoReport: Columnar or AutoReport: Tabular depending on your informational needs.**

   After you click the AutoReport entry in the list, the graphic in the New Report window changes into a tiny image of the report layout (see Figure 17-1).

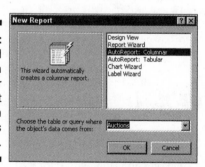

Figure 17-1: The Wizard creates a Columnar report based on the Auctions table.

3. **Click the drop-down list at the bottom of the dialog box to select which table or query you want to use.**

   Scroll through the options until you find the table or query on which you want to base your report. Remember that each AutoReport covers only one query or table.

4. Click OK.

After a bit of clunking and thunking, Access displays your finished report on-screen in Print Preview mode (as shown in Figure 17-2), which is programmerese for "This is what the report looks like if you print it." I show you some neat Print Preview tools in the next section, "Previewing Your Informational Masterpiece."

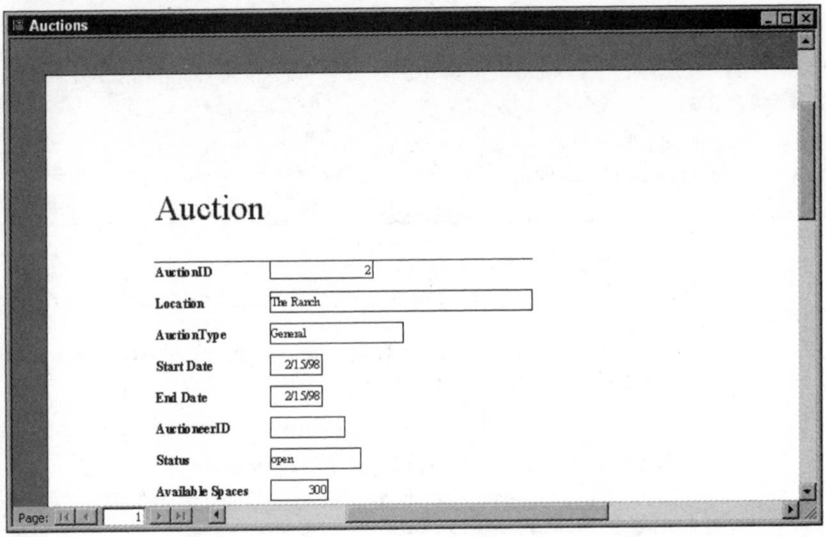

Figure 17-2:
Use the
Print
Preview
window to,
well,
preview
what your
report will
look like
when it's
printed.

Auctions

Auction

AuctionID	2
Location	The Ranch
AuctionType	General
Start Date	2/15/98
End Date	2/15/98
AuctioneerID	
Status	open
Available Spaces	300

Page: 1

Although Access thinks quite a lot of the report (it's having one of those proud parent moments), usually the report has a look that only a digital parent can love. Before sending the report out into the cold, cruel world, you probably should take it into Design view and dress it up a bit. See the section, "Truth Is Beauty, So Make Your Reports Look Great," later in this chapter for the basics of spiffing up a dull AutoReport.

Previewing Your Informational Masterpiece

When you're in Print Preview mode, you can't do a whole lot with your report except print it. But Print Preview does enable you to check out exactly what your document looks like. Table 17-1 shows the tools Print Preview provides to help with your inspection.

Table 17-1	Print Preview Tools	
Tool	**What It Is**	**What It Does**
	View	Allows you to flip back and forth from Design View to Print Preview.
	Print	Sends your report to the you-know-what.
	Zoom	Alternates zooming levels (between fit to screen and 100%).
	One Page	Displays one page at a time.
	Two Pages	Displays two pages at a time.
	Multiple Pages	Displays up to six pages at a time.
100%	Zoom	Unlike the other Zoom button, selects one of ten zoom levels.
Close	Close	Closes the Print Preview window.
Setup	Setup	Page and printer setup.
W	Office Links	Sends the report to Microsoft Word or Excel (assuming that Word or Excel are installed on your computer).

Zooming around your report

In Figure 17-2, the entire page is not visible. The parts that show look pretty good, but you can't see the whole record, let alone the whole page. In Figure 17-3, Access displays the report full-size, just like it looks on the printed page.

- Need to see what the whole page looks like? Click the Zoom button and change the setting to Fit. This displays the full-page view shown in Figure 17-3. Access calls the full-page view the Fit view because it *fits* the whole page on your screen.

- Alternatively, you can use the Zoom control (the one with the text in it, not the one that looks like a magnifying glass) and choose other zooming levels from 10% all the way to 1000%. If, for some reason, you wanted 82%, you can also type a value directly into the box and press Enter to see the results.

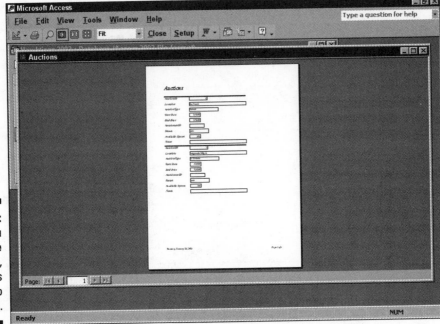

Figure 17-3:
When you view the whole page, the report is too tiny to read.

When you move your mouse pointer over the preview of your report, your pointer changes to look like a magnifying glass. Use this to zoom in closer to the report and check individual sections. Just click what you want to see and Access swoops down, enlarging that portion of the report so you can see it clearly. Click again, and your view changes back to the previous setting.

Note that clicking any of the page-number buttons (one page, two page, multiple pages) sets the Zoom view to the Fit view setting. When you have two pages showing, the odd-numbered page is always on the left, unlike book publishing, which puts the odd-numbered page on the right — unless the production department is having a very, very bad day.

If you choose View⇨Pages from the main menu, Access 2002 offers quite the selection of page view options, as you see in Figure 17-4. Set your system to show one page, two pages, or a mind-numbing (and eye-squinting) twelve pages on a single screen.

Calling on the pop-up menu

You can right-click anywhere on the Print Preview screen to see a pop-up menu that gives you the choice of switching the Zoom or viewing a specific number of pages. When you select the Zoom command, a submenu appears with the same choices that appear on the Zoom Control. Two other commands are available when you right-click the Print Preview screen:

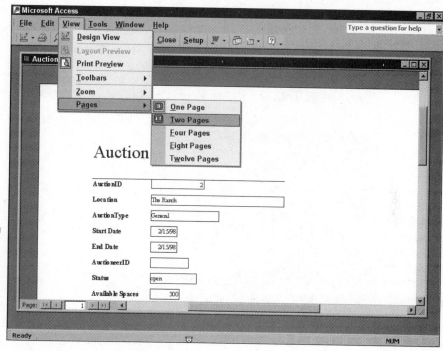

Figure 17-4:
Preview up
to 12 pages
of your
report at
a time.

✔ **Save As/Export:** Choose this command to save your Access 2002 report in a format used by another program.

A very cool feature of Access 2002 is its capability of exporting to HTML. That's right — you can create a report and then save it as a Web page by exporting to HTML.

✔ **Send:** Choose this command to take a copy of your Access 2002 report and send it as a mail message.

Truth Is Beauty, So Make Your Reports Look Great

After looking at your report in the Print Preview window, you have a decision to make. If you're happy with how your report looks, great! Go ahead and print the document. However, a few minutes of extra work does wonders for even the simplest reports.

Start with the basics in the Page Setup dialog box of Access 2002. To get there, choose File⇨Page Setup from any Report view in Access 2002 or simply click the Setup button on the toolbar. This dialog box provides three tabs of options to ensure that your report is as effective and attractive as it can be.

The Margins tab

No surprises here — the Margins tab of the Page Setup dialog box controls the width of the margins in your report. Figure 17-5 displays your options. The page has four margins, so the dialog box includes a setting for each one (Top, Bottom, Left, and Right). Here is how to set or change margins:

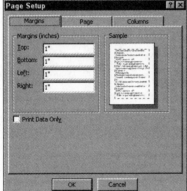

Figure 17-5:
Set the margins of your report on the, uh, Margins tab.

1. **Double-click in the appropriate box and type a new setting.**

   Access automatically uses whatever Windows thinks is your local unit of measurement (inches, centimeters, or whatever else you measure with). On the right side of the dialog box, Access displays a sample image, which shows you how your current margin settings work on a page.

2. **Make all the changes you want to your report's layout and then click OK.**

3. **Look at your report in Print Preview to check your adjustments.**

   If you need to tweak it, simply go back to Page Setup and play with the options until everything looks just right.

The last item on the Margins tab is the Print Data Only check box. I guess the programmers can't think of anywhere else to put this box, because it has *nothing* to do with margin settings. If you select this option by checking its box, Access 2002 prints only the data in your records; field headings won't appear on the printed document. Use Print Data Only if you plan to use preprinted forms. Otherwise, leave it alone, because your report looks pretty odd without any field labels.

The Page tab

The Page tab tells Access 2002 about the sheet of paper you actually print your report on, including its size, layout, and what printer you keep the paper in. You make some of the most fundamental decisions about how your report looks from the Page tab of the Page Setup dialog box (see Figure 17-6).

Figure 17-6:
The Page tab enables you to choose a printer, page size, and more.

The Orientation box sets the direction that your report prints on paper:

- ✔ Portrait (the way that this book and most magazines appear) is the default choice.

- ✔ Landscape pages lie on their side, giving you more horizontal room, but less vertical space.

Deciding whether to go Portrait or Landscape is more important than you may think. For Tabular reports, Landscape orientation displays more information for each field, thanks to the wider columns. Unfortunately, the columns get shorter in the process. (After all, that piece of paper is only so big.) Columnar reports don't do very well in Landscape, because they usually need more vertical space than horizontal space.

Your other choices for the Page tab are determined by your printing capabilities. The Size drop-down list in the Paper section of the tab enables you to pick the size of the paper you want to use (refer to Figure 17-6). The source drop-down list gives you the option to use your regular paper feed (the AutoSelect Tray choice), another automatic source, or to manually feed your paper into the printer.

The last part of the Page tab lets you choose a specific printer for this report. You can use either the default printer (Access uses whatever printer Windows says to use) or the Use Specific Printer option (where you pick the printer yourself). Most of the time, you can leave this setting alone; it's only useful if you want to force this report to always come from one specific printer at your location. If you click the Use Specific Printer radio button, the Printer button comes to life. Click this button to choose from among your available printers.

The Columns tab

You get to make more decisions about your report's size and layout on the Columns tab (as shown in Figure 17-7).

Figure 17-7:
The Column
Layout box
on the
Columns tab
enables you
to format a
report with
snaking
columns,
like a
telephone
directory.

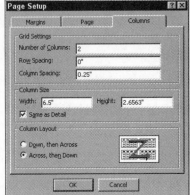

The Columns tab of the Page Setup dialog box is divided into three sections:

- ✔ **Grid Settings:** Controls how many columns your report uses and how far apart the different elements are from each other

- ✔ **Column Size:** Adjusts the height and width of your columns

- ✔ **Column Layout:** Defines the way that Access 2002 places your data in columns (and uses a very easy-to-understand graphic to show you as well)

The default number of columns is one column to a page, but you can easily change the setting to suit your particular report. Just keep in mind that with more columns, your reports may show less information for each record. If you use so many columns that some of the information won't fit, Access 2002 conveniently displays a warning.

If the number of columns you select fit (or if you're willing to lose your view of the information in some of your fields), click OK to see a view of how your document looks with multiple columns.

The Grid Settings section of the Columns tab also adjusts row and column spacing:

- ✔ **Row Spacing:** To adjust the space (measured in your local unit of distance) between the horizontal rows, simply click the Row Spacing box and enter the amount of space that you want to appear between each row. Again, this setting is a matter of personal preference.

- ✔ **Column Spacing:** Adjust the width of your columns. If you narrow this width, you make more room, but your entries are more difficult to read.

The bottom section of the Columns tab, called Column Layout, lets you control how your columns are organized on the page. You have two options here:

- ✔ **Down, then Across:** Access 2002 starts a new record in the same column (if the preceding record has not filled up the page).

    For example, Record 13 starts below Record 12 on the page (provided there's enough room), and then Records 14 and 15 appear in the second column.

- ✔ **Across, then Down:** Access starts Record 13 across from Record 12, and then puts Record 14 below Record 12, and Record 15 below Record 13, and so on.

Chapter 18

Wizardly Help with Labels, Charts, and Multilevel Reports

* *

In This Chapter

▶ Printing labels with Label Wizard

▶ Adding charts with the Chart Wizard

▶ Organizing your report

▶ Using the Report Wizard

▶ Creating grouping levels

▶ Adding summaries

* *

AutoReports (I cover those in Chapter 17) are just the tip of the Access report iceberg. If you're so inclined, you can use Access 2002 to generate much more complex reports. You can even create useful printouts that you probably never thought of as reports — mailing labels and charts. Don't be daunted — Access provides kind, gentle wizards to help you along your report-creating journey.

Creating Labels

When the bulk-mailing urge strikes, there's nothing like a good stack of mailing labels to really make your day. At moments like this, Access 2002 rides to the rescue with the Label Wizard, one of the many report wizards in Access.

The Label Wizard formats your data for use with any size or type of label on the planet. Mailing labels, file labels, shipping labels, name tags — the list goes on forever. Best of all, the Label Wizard does all the hard stuff with the wave of a wand.

In the past, one of the hardest aspects of making labels was explaining the label layout to the software. At some point, Microsoft engineers obviously endured this hardship themselves because they built the specifications for hundreds of labels from popular manufacturers right into the Label Wizard. If you happen to use labels from Avery, Herma, Zweckform, or any other maker listed in the wizard's manufacturer list, just tell the wizard the manufacturer's product number. The wizard sets up the report dimensions for you according to the maker's specifications. Life just doesn't get much easier than that.

Before firing up the Label Wizard, figure out what information you want on the labels. Unless you want a label for everything in the table, you need to create a query that picks out the right pieces from your table, sorts them into order, and generally gets them ready for their trip to the sticky-backed paper. Refer to Part III to review the procedures for creating queries.

With your table or query in hand, you can make the labels. Follow these steps to create your Label report:

1. **Click the Reports button under the Objects bar on the database window.**

   Access lists the reports in your database.

2. **Click New to create a new report.**

   The New Report dialog box appears, showing you all the available report types, including the all-important Label Wizard.

3. **Click Label Wizard.**

   The little picture to the left of the list changes into a page of labels to confirm that Access 2002 heard you correctly (see Figure 18-1).

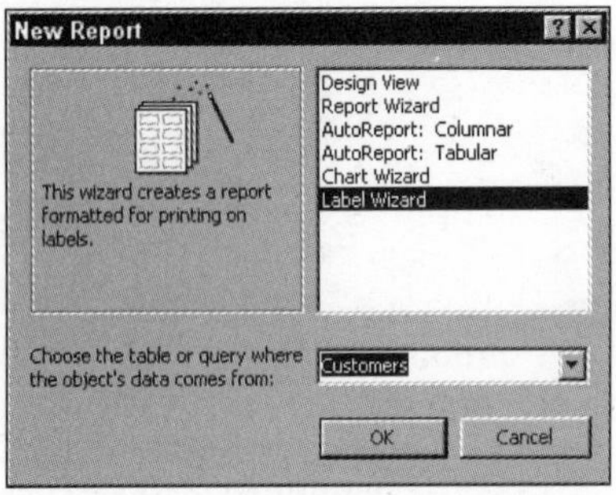

Figure 18-1:
Access 2002 prepares to prepare your labels.

New Report

This wizard creates a report formatted for printing on labels.

Design View
Report Wizard
AutoReport: Columnar
AutoReport: Tabular
Chart Wizard
Label Wizard

Choose the table or query where the object's data comes from: Customers

OK   Cancel

4. **Click the down arrow near the bottom of the dialog box.**

   A drop-down list appears, asking you to choose the table or query that you want the object's data to come from.

5. **Click the query or table that you want to use with the labels.**

   The wizard is ready, and the data awaits!

6. Click OK to start the Label Wizard.

In a flurry of disk activity, the Label Wizard dialog box appears, as shown in Figure 18-2.

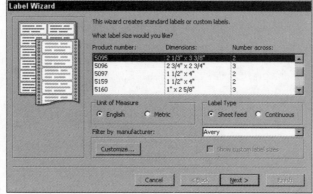

Figure 18-2:
The Label
Wizard
knows
almost
every label
type ever
made.

7. Click the down arrow next to the Filter by Manufacturer box and select your label's manufacturer from the drop-down list that appears.

Access 2002 makes creating labels as painless as possible — provided that you use labels from a company that the Microsoft developers know about.

- If your label manufacturer is on the Label Wizard's list, click the company name. In the top of the Label Wizard window, Access displays all of that company's labels by product number. Scroll through the list until you find the number that matches the one on your label box. When you find it, skip merrily along to Step 9 (Lucky you!). If the number isn't on the list, proceed to the next step.

- If your label manufacturer isn't on the Label Wizard's list, take another look at your box of labels. Because Avery controls so much of the label market, other manufacturers often put the equivalent Avery code number onto their product, usually with the notation like Avery xxxx labels, with the xxxx part replaced by an Avery code number. If you see that on your label box, select Avery as the label maker, then look for the right label number in the list. If you find it, skip ahead to Step 9. If you still don't find the number, go to Step 8.

- If all else fails and you simply cannot find in the list a label like yours, you can easily define one. Simply click the Customize button and follow the prompts. The biggest trick is telling Access the size of your labels (use a ruler for that) and how many labels across there are on a sheet (use your fingers to count those).

8. **If the Label Wizard doesn't know the details of your labels, click Customize to add them to the Wizard's repertoire.**

   Building a customized label entry isn't hard, but it *does* take a few steps.

9. **Click Next.**

   A dialog box appears, offering you a slew of font choices (see Figure 18-3).

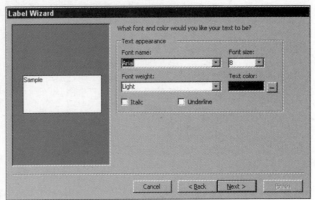

Figure 18-3:
Choose your
font wisely;
the entire
label will
use it.

10. **Pick the font, size, weight, and color for the text on your label and then click Next.**

    You can choose any font available in Windows: change the text size, change how bold it looks (what the technogeeks call *font weight*), or even add italics, underline, and a new text color (you need a color printer for that). As you make changes, the sample text screen on the left side of the window shows your current settings.

    Keep in mind that the formatting you choose applies to *all* the text on *every* label. If you add italics, then the *whole label* — every label — comes out that way. Add special formatting sparingly because a little goes a long way.

11. **Select the data you want to appear on the label and type any other text that you want to print.**

12. **Select the fields from the Available fields list and click the > button to transfer the field to the Prototype label box, as shown in Figure 18-4.**

    If you want fields on separate rows, press Enter or use an arrow key to move to the next row. When you double-click a field (or click the > button), that field always transfers to the highlighted line in the Prototype label box. Access 2002 figures out how many lines can print on your label, based upon the label's size and the font size you're using.

If you want to print a particular character, word, or other text message on every label, just click wherever you want it to appear and then type your text. For example, to insert a comma between the city, state, or province on your mailing labels, select the City field, type in a comma, press the spacebar, and then select the State/Province field. When Access prints each label, it puts the city name, adds a comma, and then fills in the rest of the information.

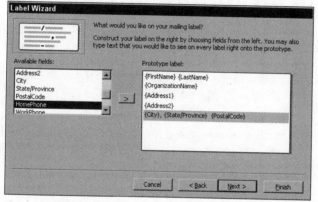

Figure 18-4: Pick the fields that you want Access to print on your labels.

13. **Click Next when the fields look simply marvelous (or at least passably cute).**

14. **Choose the field for Access to sort your labels (see Figure 18-5) and click Next.**

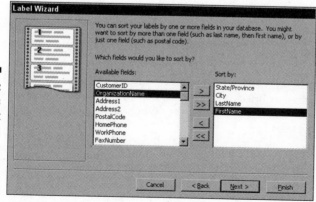

Figure 18-5: Tell Access in what order you want the labels to print.

15. **Type a name for the label report and then click Finish to see your creation in action.**

    If the labels are *almost* right but still need a few tweaks, click the Design view button on the toolbar (the one that looks like a triangle and pencil) and modify the design as needed.

Using the Chart Wizard in Your Report

Generally, reports are just a collection of words and numbers, organized to allow you to make sense of the information. But sometimes, words and numbers don't paint enough of the story. At times like these, a graph makes the perfect antidote, filling in the heads, tails, and other sundry parts of your report's informational picture. As the saying goes, a picture is worth a thousand words (so add a few graphs and save a bunch of trees).

Access 2002 includes an artsy wizard for just such occasions. Say hello to the Chart Wizard, creator of preeminent pies, beautiful bars, and luscious lines — and all at the wave of a wand (plus a few mouse clicks for good measure).

To build a chart (or graph, because Access 2002 uses the terms interchangeably), you need *at least* two fields (but no more than six). One field contains the numbers making up the bars, lines, pie slices, or other graphical representations in your graph. The other field should hold labels identifying the various numbers (otherwise, your graph looks swell but says nothing). All the fields must come from a single table or query.

Because the wizard is fluent in several types of charts, finding a layout that works perfectly for your data is easy. The Wizard offers five major types of charts:

- **Area charts:** A cross between a line chart and pie chart, these graphs show how the total of a *group* of figures changed over time. Perfect for showing how costs and profits add up to total revenue over several quarters.

- **Bar, Cone, and Column charts:** Variations of the line chart, these charts use vertical or horizontal bars to display your data. Good for comparing groups of data against each other (such as sales by quarter over a period of years).

- **Line charts:** The classic chart from geometry class is reborn into the digital world and great for showing trends over time.

- **Pie and Donut charts:** These charts take a series of numbers and display them as percentages of a total. Perfect for showing how much each division contributed to total corporate profit, how many people from various countries buy a product, and anything else that requires a *slice of the pie* approach. (Of course, they also add a nice touch to breakfast meetings, particularly when accompanied by a steaming cappuccino or nice cup of hot chocolate.)

✔ **XY and Bubble charts:** These charts are the odd uncles and peculiar third cousins of the Access chart family. Technically speaking, they chart two data points as they relate to a third data point (such as the number of women who visited the club each month, displayed by income group). In the vernacular, that translates to *unless you have a darn good reason, don't even bother with these charts.* These charts are wonderful for engineers, economists, scientists, statisticians, and anyone else who probably needs more to do with their free time.

Building the chart-of-your-heart only takes a few minutes, thanks to the wizard's helpful and competent assistance. Follow these steps to build a chart:

1. **Click the Reports button on the database window and then click <u>N</u>ew.**

   The New Report dialog box appears, proudly displaying your report options.

2. **Select Chart Wizard.**

3. **Click the down arrow next to the Choose the Table or Query text box and select a table or query for your chart.**

4. **Click OK.**

   Access opens the table or query you selected, takes a look inside, and then displays the fields available for the chart.

5. **Select the numeric and text fields for your chart and then click Next.**

6. **Use the > and < buttons to add or remove fields in the list.**

   The >> and << buttons move *all* the available fields.

7. **Click <u>N</u>ext.**

   Access displays samples of every graph it knows how to make.

8. **Click the picture of your chart type and then click <u>N</u>ext.**

   As you click a chart (see Figure 18-6), the wizard briefly describes the chart and offers a few technical thoughts on how it works. The wizard explains how to display the data in your chart, but ultimately lets you make whatever changes you want.

9. **Click <u>N</u>ext when the chart meets your expectations (or when you simply tire of messing with the whole affair).**

10. **Drag and drop fields from the column on the left of the window into the various positions in the graph. Double-click the graph items to change their summary options, and make whatever changes you want.**

11. **Click the Preview Chart button (as shown in Figure 18-7) to see how the chart looks as you make changes.**

12. **Click Next when you're satisfied with your chart.**

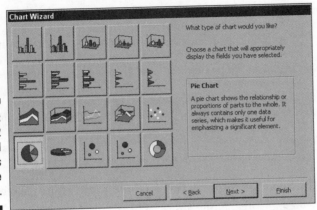

Figure 18-6:
Access 2002
displays and
describes
its available
graphs.

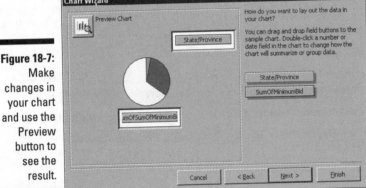

Figure 18-7:
Make
changes in
your chart
and use the
Preview
button to
see the
result.

13. **Type a name for your new chart in the window that appears.**

14. **Click Finish to see the product of your labor.**

Creating More Advanced Reports

The AutoReport Wizard (refer to Chapter 17 for details) quickly creates simple reports from a single query or table. When you (or, more likely, your boss) need something *right now*, the AutoReport Wizard is a great tool.

Sometimes, your reporting needs call for more detail, more organization, or simply more data. For these more complex reports, seek help from the Report Wizard. This master of informational presentation lets you add fields from as many tables as you want, and organize those fields into as many levels as you choose. Each new level gets its own personalized section of the report, complete with a custom header and footer. After a spin with the Report Wizard, your data won't want to go anywhere else.

Creating complex reports involves more steps than the simple ones, but the results are *definitely* worth the extra effort. Because complex reports include a lot more options, the steps to build the report are split into several sections according to topic. Each section includes some explanations of what the settings do and how to use them.

Starting the wizard and picking some fields

In the end, a multilevel report looks a lot different than a basic report, but they both start out the same way. Begin your report creation safari by following these steps:

1. **Click the Reports button under the Objects bar on the database window.**

   As usual, Access displays the reports currently in your database.

2. **Click New to create a new report.**

   The New Report dialog box appears, showing you all the report types you can choose from. (Bored? Don't worry — the cool stuff comes soon!)

3. **Click Report Wizard and then click OK.**

   The dialog box shown in Figure 18-8 appears.

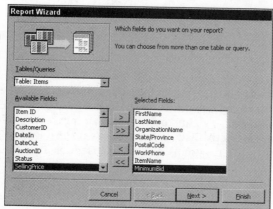

Figure 18-8: The Report Wizard enables you to add fields from one or more tables or queries in your database.

4. **Click the down arrow in the Tables/Queries box and, from the drop-down list that appears, select the first table or query that contains the fields you need for the report.**

   The Available Fields list updates to show everything that the selected item contains.

5. **Select the fields that you want in the report by either double-clicking the field names or clicking the greater than (>, >>) or less than (<, <<) buttons.**

   The greater than buttons move fields *into* the Selected Fields list, whereas the less than buttons move fields *out of* the list.

   Although clicking the buttons is fun, the easiest way to move a field from one side to another is by double-clicking it. No matter which side the field starts on, double-clicking moves the field to the opposite list.

6. **Repeat Step 4 for each table or query you need that contains fields for the report. Click Next after all the fields are listed in the Selected Fields side of the dialog box.**

   The dialog box shown in Figure 18-9 appears.

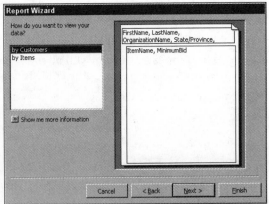

Figure 18-9:
Report Wizard lets you choose how you want your information grouped.

Report Wizard lets you pick the field to use when organizing your report. You also see a sample page based on the Report Wizard's extensive analysis of your data (yes, that means the wizard *guessed*). Access 2002 may or may not correctly discern how you want the data to appear (remember, it's only a program), so take a close look at each of the report-organization choices and decide which one displays the information in the most effective way. To see a different organization, click one of the *by* choices on the left side of the dialog box.

If you don't see the dialog box shown in Figure 18-9, that's okay. It simply means that you're using only one table or query in your report.

If you don't want the records sorted into groups, click the very last entry in the *by* list (in this case, the *by Customers* entry). For reasons beyond my comprehension (but that probably make sense to a demented programmer somewhere), this action makes Access 2002 lump together all the records, displaying them without sorting them into groups.

Creating new groupings

Access 2002 takes organization a step further by adding more grouping options — groups based on different fields than just the one you specified in the previous section. The dialog box shown in Figure 18-10 lists the available fields on the left side of the window. Pick as many or as few as you want. To add a new group, based on a particular field, click the field name and then click the greater than (>) button. The wizard adjusts the sample page to show what your report looks like with the additional group, as shown in Figure 18-11.

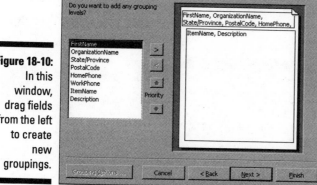

Figure 18-10: In this window, drag fields from the left to create new groupings.

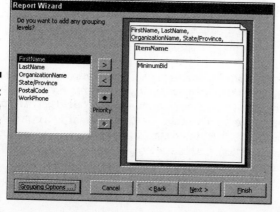

Figure 18-11: Narrow the reports organization by adding more groups.

You can rearrange the grouping if you want. For example, you can click ItemName and then click the up arrow between the two windowpanes (refer to Figure 18-11). The wizard groups the report first by ItemName and then by the customer information.

Each of the fields you select to organize your report creates a new section. Each of these sections has its own header and footer area that can hold information from your database or information that you add directly to the report through Design View after the wizard finishes its work.

Sorting out the details

Access 2002 calls the fields that aren't grouped as headers *detail records*. Report Wizard lets you sort those records by the remaining fields, which you can organize in either ascending or descending order, as shown in Figure 18-12. To sort records by any given field, click the down arrow and select the field from the drop-down list. Then click the button at the right to change the sorting order from ascending (with the letters going from A at the top to Z at the bottom) to descending (with the letters going from Z at the top to A at the bottom). See Chapter 10 for more details about sorting on more than one field.

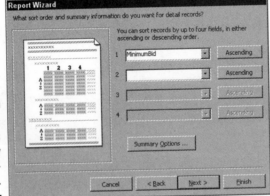

Figure 18-12:
Sort this
report by
Minimum-
Bid.

Click the Summary Options button to reveal the Summary Options dialog box, as shown in Figure 18-13. (If you don't see a Summary Options button, it's because your report doesn't include any number fields.) The Summary Options dialog box lets you tell Access 2002 to summarize your data with a number of statistical tools, including totals (Sum), averages (Avg), minimums (Min), and maximums (Max). Check the boxes next to the operations that you want performed on the fields in your report.

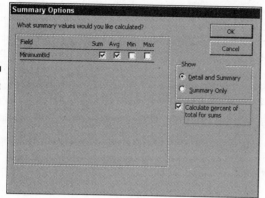

Figure 18-13:
I can
summarize
my data
nine ways to
Sunday . . .
too much!

For example, the auction company wants Access 2002 to add up all the minimum bids for each group (that's what the *Sum* checkmark does) and display the average minimum bid for each group (refer to Figure 18-13).

If you want to see both the data *and* the summary, click the Detail and Summary radio button in the Show section of the dialog box. If you need to see only the summarized information, click the Summary Only radio button. If you click the Calculate Percent of Total for Sums check box, Access 2002 calculates the total amount of the field and tells you the percentage of each record's contribution to that total.

Picking a layout style

The Report Wizard offers a series of ready-to-use layouts to make your report look great and read easily (see Figure 18-14):

1. **Click a radio button in the Layout section to choose a style.**

   Access shows you a sample of the layout on the left side of the window. Your choices here vary depending on the data in your report.

2. **Click a radio button in the Orientation section to choose how you want to lay out your report.**

   Generally, if you have a lot of small fields or several large fields, Landscape orientation works better. For fewer fields of any shape or size, try Portrait.

3. **Check or clear the Adjust the Field Width So All Fields Fit on a Page check box.**

   If this box is checked (the default), Access 2002 force-fits all of your fields onto one page, even if it has to squish some of them to do it. During the highly-scientific squishing process, the field may end up being too small to display the data it contains. For example, a field holding the name *Harriet Isa Finkelmeier* may only display *Harriet Isa Fink* after it's squished. The rest of the name isn't lost — it just doesn't appear on the report. If you *don't* check the box, Access 2002 packs as many fields onto the page as it can *without* changing any of the field widths. Fields that don't fit are left off the page, but the fields that *do* print appear in their normal, glorious size.

4. **Click Next when you're satisfied with the layout of your report.**

   A dialog box appears, enabling you to choose from six predetermined styles for your report. The window at the left gives you a basic idea of what the style looks like. Again, this is a matter of taste, not what is "correct." Pick the one you like the most.

5. **Click Next and give your report a name.**

   Your report is saved with a title. You also have the choice of previewing your report in Print Preview, modifying your report, or simply screaming for help.

6. **Click Print Preview to preview your report.**

7. **Click the Modify report's design button if you want to make changes to your report's design. Otherwise, click Finish.**

   Access 2002 opens the Design view of your report, and you can tinker with the report to your heart's content.

Chapter 19 explains how to modify and format your reports to create your own unique look.

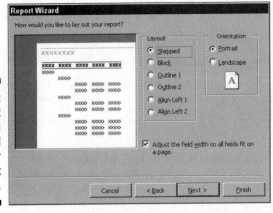

Figure 18-14:
Access 2002
gives you
several
options for
report
layout.

Chapter 19

It's Amazing What a Little Formatting Can Do

In This Chapter

▶ Getting into Design view

▶ Working with report sections

▶ Marking text boxes and labels

▶ Previewing your stuff

▶ Putting AutoFormat to work for you

▶ Drawing lines and boxes

▶ Adding graphics to your reports

▶ Exporting reports to Microsoft Word and Excel

*T*he Access 2002 Report Wizard is a pretty swell fellow. After a brief round of 20 compu-questions, it sets up an informative, good-looking report for you automatically. Well, at least the report's *informative* — just between you and me, I think that the Report Wizard can use a little design training.

Although the Access 2002 Report Wizard does the best job it can, the results aren't always exactly what you need. Those clever engineers at Microsoft foresaw this problem and left a back door open for you. That door is called *Design view*. In Design view, you can change anything — and I mean *anything* — about your report's design. Reorganize the text boxes, add some text, emphasize certain text boxes with boxes and lines, or do whatever else your heart desires.

This chapter guides you through some popular Design view tweaking and tuning techniques. With this information in hand, your reports are sure to be the envy of the office in no time. (And there's nothing like a well-envied report to start your day off just right.)

Taking Your Report to the Design View Tune-Up Shop

The first stop in your quest for a better-looking report is Design view itself. After all, you can't change *anything* in the report until the report is up on the jacks in the Design view. Thankfully, Access offers several easy ways to tow in your report for that much-needed tune-up. Precisely how you do it depends on where you are right now in Access 2002:

- ✔ After creating a report with the Report Wizard, the wizard asks if you want to preview your creation or modify its design (even the wizard knows that its design skills are lacking!). Click the Modify the Report's Design radio button to send the wizard's creation straight into Design view.

- ✔ If the report is on-screen in a preview, hop into Design view by clicking the Design View button on the toolbar.

- ✔ To get into Design view from the database window, click the Reports button below the Objects bar and then click the name of the report you want to work on. Click the Design button (just above the report list in the Database window) to open the report in Design view.

No matter which method you use, Access 2002 sends you (and your report) to a Design view screen that looks a lot like Figure 19-1. Now you're ready to overhaul that report!

Striking Up the Bands (And the Markers, Too)

When you look at a report in Design view, Access 2002 displays a slew of *markers* that are grouped into several bands (or *sections,* as they're called in Access 2002). The markers show where Access 2002 plans to put the text boxes and text on your final report. They also give you an idea of how the program plans to format everything.

Access 2002 uses two kinds of markers, depending on what information the report includes:

- ✔ **Text boxes:** Boxes that display a particular field's data in the report. Every field you want to include in the final report has a text box in the Design view. If the report doesn't include a text box for one of the fields in your table, the data for that field won't end up in the report.

✔ **Labels:** Plain, simple text markers that display a text message on the report. Sometimes, labels stand alone (such as "The information in this report is confidential. So there."); often, they accompany a text box to show people who read the report what data they're looking at ("Customer ID," or "Right Shoe Size," for example).

Markers are organized into sections that represent the different parts of your report. The sections govern where and how often a particular field or text message is repeated in your report. The report design in Figure 19-1 displays the three most common sections:

✔ Report Header

✔ Page Header

✔ Detail

Arrows to the left of the section names show you which markers each section contains.

The sections work in teams that straddle the Detail area. The teams are pretty easy to figure out (Report Header works with Report Footer, and Page Header works with Page Footer, for example). Figure 19-2 shows the mates to the sections shown in Figure 19-1.

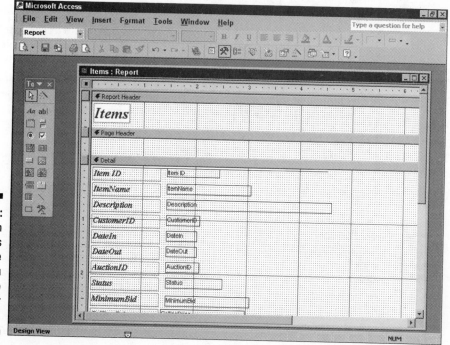

Figure 19-1: The Design view gives you all the tools you need to modify your reports.

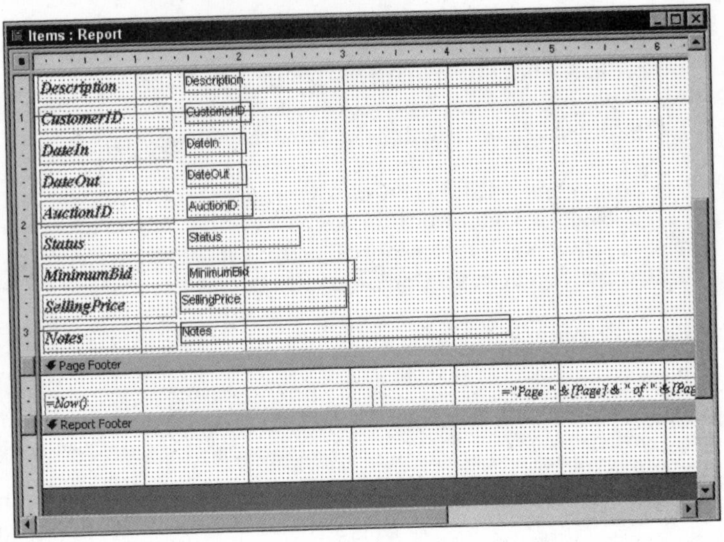

Figure 19-2:
The Page
Footer and
Report
Footer
mirror their
headers.

Here's how the most common sections work (including such important details as where and how often the sections appear in your printed report):

- ✔ **Report Header:** Anything that appears in the Report Header prints at the very start of the report. The information prints only once and appears at the top of the first page.

- ✔ **Page Header:** Information in the Page Header prints at the top of every page. The only exception is the report's first page, where Access 2002 prints the Report Header and *then* the Page Header.

- ✔ **Detail:** The meat of the report, the stuff in the Detail section fills the majority of each report page. The Detail section is repeated for every record included in the report.

- ✔ **Page Footer:** When each page is nearly full, Access finishes it off by printing the Page Footer at the bottom.

- ✔ **Report Footer:** At the bottom of the last page, immediately following the Page Footer, the Report Footer wraps up the display.

Being familiar with Glenn Miller, Claude Bolling, or John Philip Sousa won't help you when it comes to report bands in Access 2002. (Sorry, but I just can't let the term *band* go by without making a musical note.) Because the how-to of bands (or, if you prefer, *sections*) is so important to your reports, Chapter 20 explores the topic in exhausting detail. Chapter 20 includes information on inserting and adjusting sections, and convincing them to perform all kinds of automated calculations.

Formatting This, That, These, and Those

You can artfully amend almost anything in a report's design with the help of the Formatting toolbar in Figure 19-3. Whether you want to change text color, font size, or the visual effect surrounding a text box, this toolbar has the goodies you need.

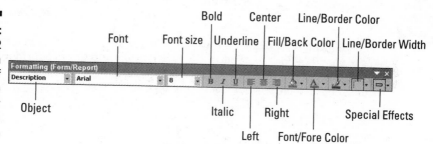

Figure 19-3: Access 2002 provides a suite of tools to help format your report.

To adjust items in your report with the tools in the Formatting toolbar, follow these steps:

1. Click the item you want to format.

Any text box, label, line, or box is okay — Access 2002 is an equal opportunity formatter. When you click something, a bunch of little black boxes appear around it, much like Figure 19-4. (The little black boxes are a good sign.)

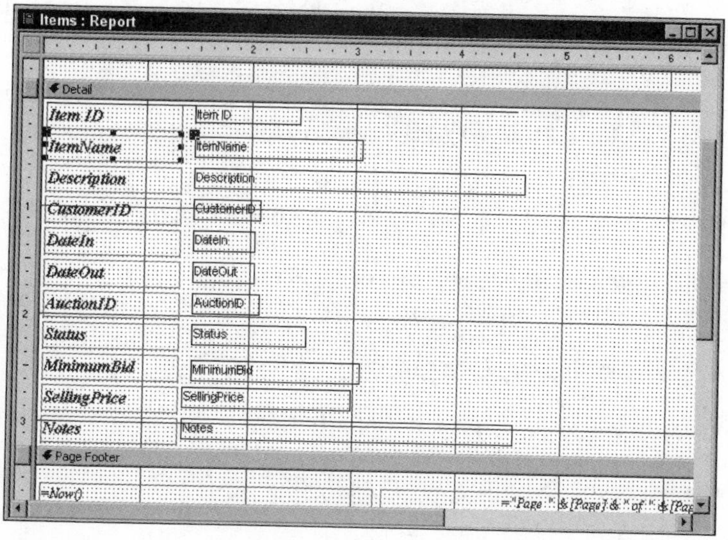

Figure 19-4: The ItemName field is selected.

2. Click the toolbar button for the formatting effect you want.

With most formatting tools, the new format immediately takes effect. Some tools (color, border, and 3-D effect) also offer a pull-down list of choices.

I cover these options in more detail later in the chapter.

3. Repeat Steps 1 and 2 for all of the text boxes you want to modify.

If you make a mistake while formatting, just choose Edit➪Undo Property Setting. Poof! Access removes the last formatting you applied.

The following sections step through some of the most common formatting tasks ahead of you. Just follow the instructions and your report looks like a cross between the Mona Lisa and a state tax form. (That's a compliment, I think, but I'll have to get back to you on that.)

Colorizing your report

Nothing brightens up a drab report like a spot of color. Access 2002 makes adding color easy with the Font/Fore Color and the Fill/Back Color buttons. These buttons are located on your friendly Formatting toolbar (no surprises there).

Both buttons change the color of text markers in your report, but they differ a little in precisely how they do it:

✔ The Font/Fore Color button changes the color of text in a text box or label marker.

✔ The Fill/Back Color button alters the marker's background color but leaves the text color alone.

To select a color to use, click the arrow at the right of the Font/Fore Color or Fill/Back Color button. When the menu of colors appears, click the color you want to use.

Your color choice also appears along the bottom of the toolbar button.

To change the color of a text box or label on your report, click the marker that you want to work with. To change the font color, click the Font/Fore Color button; to change the background, click Fill/Back Color, instead. The new color settings appear right away on-screen.

You can also use the Font/Fore Color button to change the color of the text in a text box or any label. You can easily create special effects by choosing contrasting colors for the foreground and background, just like the white text floating on a black background in Figure 19-5.

Taking control of your report

In addition to the normal goodies found on an everyday Access report (like labels and text boxes), you can also include all kinds of fascinating items called *controls*. You add controls to the report by using the Design view Toolbox (the floating island of buttons sitting somewhere around your screen).

Some controls work with specific types of fields. For example, a check box can graphically display the value of a Yes/No field. (Plus, controls look cool on the page.)

Anything this neat simply *must* be a little complicated, and the controls certainly live up to these expectations. Access 2002 includes several control wizards to take the pain out of the process. These wizards, like their brethren elsewhere in the program, walk you through the steps for building your controls in a patient, step-by-step manner. The control wizards *usually* come to life automatically after you place a control in the report.

If you create a new control but the control wizard doesn't show up to help, make sure that the Wizard button at the top of the Toolbox (the button emblazoned with a magic wand) is turned on. If it's on, the button looks as though it's pushed down a bit. If you aren't sure, click it a couple of times so you can see the difference.

Some of the controls (specifically the Line, Rectangle, Page Break, and image controls) are covered later in this chapter. Chapter 20 includes tips about using controls to create summaries in your report.

Figure 19-5:
Set the foreground and background colors.

Be careful when choosing your colors — if you make the text and background colors the same, the text seems to disappear! If this happens, just choose Edit⇨Undo Property Setting to bring back the original color setting.

Moving elements around

Feel like reorganizing a little bit? You can easily move just about any element (text box, label, line, and such) in a report. In fact, moving elements is *so* easy that you need to go slow and take extra care not to move elements you shouldn't.

To move a line, box, label, or text box, follow these steps:

1. **Click the item you want to move.**

   A bunch of black squares surround the item, letting you know that it's selected.

   If you have trouble selecting a line, try clicking near its ends. For some reason, Access 2002 has a tough time recognizing when you want to grab a line. Clicking right at the line's end seems to help the program figure out what you want to do.

2. **Move the mouse pointer to any edge of the selected item.**

   When you do this step, the mouse pointer turns into a little hand. Too cute, isn't it?

3. **Press and hold the left mouse button and then drag your item to a new position.**

   As you move the mouse, the little hand drags an outline of whatever object you selected. (Depending on your computer's video card, you *may* see the whole object move instead of just watching the outline box wander around the screen.)

4. **Release the mouse button when the item is hovering over its new home.**

   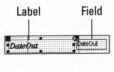

   If something goes wrong, and you want to undo the movement, choose Edit⇨Undo Property Setting or just press Ctrl+Z (the universal Undo key).

In some Access 2002 reports (specifically the ones created by the Columnar Report Wizard), the text box and label for each field in the report are attached to each other. If you move one, the other automatically follows. In this case, you have to adjust the procedure a bit if you want to move one *without* moving the other. Follow the preceding steps, but instead of moving the cursor to the edge of the marker, move it to one of the big square handles, as shown in Figure 19-6. Here's a summary of what the handles do:

Figure 19-6:
Use the big handles to move the label or text box separately.

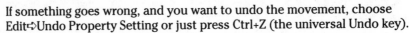

Label   Field

✔ The handle on the far left moves the label.

✔ The handle in the middle of the two markers moves the text box.

As the mouse pointer enters the handle, the cursor changes to a pointing finger. That's your sign that you can proceed with Step 3 — press and hold the mouse button and then start moving. Release the mouse button when you have the text box positioned where you want it. If the mouse pointer changes to a double-ended arrow instead of a pointing hand, try moving your mouse pointer onto the big handle again. That double-ended arrow tells Access to *resize* the item, not move it.

Other types of reports, such as Tabular Reports or Labels, don't combine the label and the text box together the way Columnar reports do. In such reports, either no label appears, or the label appears only once in the Page Header section. When labels aren't linked to their respective text boxes, they each appear separately — without the special large handles shown in Figure 19-6.

Use the smaller handles around the edge of a text box to resize the text box. For example, if you discover that the information in one of your text boxes is getting cut off, you can click the text box and use the small handles to make that text box longer. Or if a text box contains a lot of information, you can make the text box taller. Access wraps the information to the next line.

The amount of space between the markers controls the space between items when you print the report. Increasing that spacing gives your report a less crowded look; decreasing the space enables you to fit more information on the page.

Bordering on beautiful

Organizationally speaking, lines and marker borders are wonderful accents for your report. They draw your reader's eye to parts of the page, highlight sections of the report, and generally spruce up an otherwise drab page. The toolbar contains three buttons to put lines and borders through their paces:

- Line/Border Color
- Line/Border Width
- Special Effects

Coloring your lines and borders

The Line/Border Color button changes the color of lines that mark a text box's border and lines you draw on your report using the Line tool. This button works just like the Back Color and the Font/Fore Color buttons did for text, so you probably know a lot about using it already. (Comforting feeling, isn't it?)

To change the color of a line or a marker's border, follow these steps:

1. **Click the marker or line to select it.**

   Remember to click near the end of a line to select it; otherwise, you may end up clicking all around the line, but never highlighting it.

2. **Click the arrow next to the Line/Border Color button.**

   A drop-down display of color choices appears on-screen (see Figure 19-7).

3. **Click your choice from the rainbow of options.**

Figure 19-7:
Choose
from an
entire
palette of
colors.

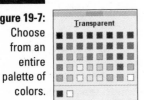

Widening your lines and borders

In addition to colorizing lines and borders, you can also control their width:

1. **Click the line or text marker you want to work with.**

2. **Click the arrow next to the Line/Border Width button to display line and border width options.**

   Your choices for line and border width are represented in terms of *points* (a geeky publishing word that means $\frac{1}{72}$ inch). The menu offers options for a hairline (half-point) line, 1 point, 2 points, 3 points, 4 points, 5 points, and finally the 6-point Monster Line that Devoured Toronto. (A 6-point line is $\frac{1}{12}$ inch thick, but actually appears quite heavy on a report.)

3. **Click the line width option you want.**

   That's all there is to it! As with everything else, choosing Edit⇨Undo Property Setting repairs any accidental damage, so feel free to experiment with the options.

Adding special effects to your lines and borders

You can change the style of a marker's border by using the Special Effects button. Six choices are available under this button, as shown in Figure 19-8. Here's a rundown of what these options do:

✔ The Sunken and Raised options actually change the colors on two sides of the text box, but the effect makes the text box look three-dimensional.

Selecting a sunken border makes the label or text box appear as though it is pushed into your text; a raised border makes it seem as though your text box is rising from your text.

✔ The Chiseled option gives a text box the appearance of having the bottom portion of its border raised upward, and the Etched option gives the effect of the border being etched into the background around the text box.

✔ The Shadow option places a shadow around the lower right of the text box.

✔ The Flat option simply puts a standard, single-line border around the entire text box.

Figure 19-8:
The six
Special
Effects
border
options.

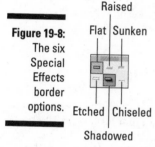

Raised

Flat | Sunken

Etched | Chiseled

Shadowed

To add special effects to a markers border, follow the same basic steps as you do for changing a border's color or width:

1. **Click the marker whose border you want to change.**

2. **Click the arrow next to the Special Effects button to display the six options.**

3. **Click the special effect you want to add.**

Tweaking your text

To change the font or the font size, simply click the arrow to the right of the Font or Font Size list box and select from the drop-down list that appears. To turn on or off the bold, italic, or underline characteristics, select a block of text and click the appropriate button. If the feature is off, clicking on the button turns it on. If the feature is on, clicking on the button turns it off. When one of these formatting features is turned on, the button appears to be pressed into the surface of the toolbar.

You can also control the alignment of the text within labels and text boxes. To change the alignment of the text for a label or text box, simply select the marker and then click one of the three alignment buttons on the toolbar.

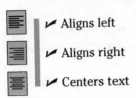

- ✔ Aligns left

- ✔ Aligns right

- ✔ Centers text

To make the best-looking report possible, pay attention to the little details such as label and data alignment. Numeric data should be right-aligned so that the numbers line up. Most other types of data should be left-aligned. Headings generally should be centered. Your effort may mean the difference between a hard-to-read report and an object of informational beauty.

Taking a Peek at Your Report

After fiddling around long enough in Design view, you inevitably reach a point where you want to view the *actual* report, rather than just looking at the technical magic being used to create it. No matter how good your imagination is, it's difficult to visualize how everything will look when it all comes together in the printed report. Access 2002 provides two distinct tools for previewing your report.

- ✔ **Layout Preview:** When you choose the Layout Preview, Access 2002 takes a portion of your data and arranges it to give you an idea of how your data will appear in the finished report.

  The preview shows only a sampling of your data (without performing any final calculations that you included). The idea is to see what the report *looks like,* not to review your calculations. To view Layout Preview, click the down-arrow next to the Report View button and then select Layout Preview from the drop-down list, as shown in Figure 19-9.

- ✔ **Print Preview:** If you want to see a full preview of your report, complete with the calculations and all the data, select Print Preview by clicking on the Print Preview button. Or you can go the long way around and click the down arrow next to the Report View button and then select Print Preview from the drop-down list (see Figure 19-9).

Regardless of which approach you use, you see a Print Preview screen similar to the one shown in Figure 19-10. The various items of your report appear as they will when you print the report. You can then use the controls at the top of the Print Preview window to change the appearance of the screen.

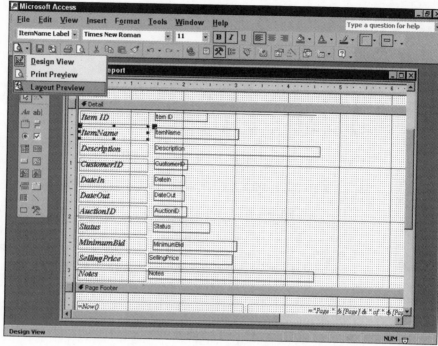

Figure 19-9:
Choose
Layout
Preview to
get a taste
for how the
report will
look; choose
Print
Preview to
see the
report in full.

See Chapter 17 for more information about using Print Preview.

Figure 19-10:
Print
Preview
shows you
exactly how
the report
will look.

AutoFormatting Your Way to a Beautiful Report

When you want to change the look of the whole report in one (or two) easy clicks, check out the AutoFormat button. When you click this button, Access 2002 offers several different format packages that reset everything from the headline font to the color of lines that split up items in the report.

To use AutoFormat, follow these steps:

1. **Click in the empty gray area below the Report Footer band.**

   This may sound like a strange first step, but there's reason behind my peculiarity (or at least there is *this* time). Clicking in this area is the easiest way to tell Access 2002 that you don't want *any* report sections selected. If any one section is selected when you do the AutoFormat command, then AutoFormat *only* changes the contents of that one section. Although that precision may be nice sometimes, most of the time you want AutoFormat to redo your whole report.

2. **Click the AutoFormat toolbar button.**

   A dialog box appears, listing your various package-deal formatting choices.

3. **Click the name of the format you want and then click OK (as shown in Figure 19-11).**

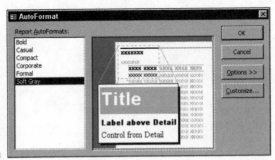

Figure 19-11: Pick the look that you like and apply it to the whole report.

Access 2002 updates everything in your report with the newly selected look.

If just a few text boxes in one section change, but the majority of the report stays the same, go back to Step 1 and try that *click in the gray area* step again. The odds are good that you had one section selected when you clicked AutoFormat.

The Customize button allows you create your own AutoFormats.

Lining Up Everything

When you start moving various items around on your report, you can easily wind up with a report that's out of alignment. For example, you may have put the column headings in the Page Header and the actual information farther down the page in a Detail line. Of course, you want the text boxes to line up with the headers, but simply moving the items around the page by hand and eyeballing the results may not do the trick.

The grid in the background of the screen can help you position screen elements by aligning them with the vertical lines or with the various dots on the Design screen. When you move an object on the report, you can choose Format➪Snap to Grid to control whether the object stays lined up with these dots that are "snapped to the grid," or whether you can move the object freely between the dots.

When you move an object with Snap to Grid turned on, the object's upper-left corner always aligns with one of the dots on the grid. Choose this command when you resize an object, and the side of the object that you move stays aligned with the dots on the grid.

Other commands on the Format menu that you may find useful for arranging objects on your reports include:

- ✔ **Align:** You can choose two or more objects and align them to each other or to the grid.

  Selecting Left, Right, Top, or Bottom causes the left, right, top, or bottom sides of the selected items to line up. For example, if you select three objects and then choose Format➪Align➪Left, the three objects move so that their left edges line up. By default, Access 2002 moves objects to line up with the object that is the farthest to the left.

- ✔ **Size:** You can change the size of a group of objects by selecting the objects and then selecting an option from the Size submenu.

  For example, you can

  - Choose Size➪to Fit, which adjusts the size of the controls so that each one is just large enough to hold the information it contains. Choose Size➪to Grid to adjust the controls so that all control corners are positioned on grid points.

- Adjust the controls relative to each other. If you choose <u>S</u>ize⇨to <u>T</u>allest, <u>S</u>ize⇨to <u>S</u>hortest, <u>S</u>ize⇨to <u>W</u>idest, or <u>S</u>ize⇨to <u>N</u>arrowest, each box in the selected group changes to that characteristic. If you select a group of controls and then choose <u>S</u>ize⇨to <u>T</u>allest, each of the selected controls is resized to the same height as the tallest control in the selected group.

- ✔ **Horizontal Spacing, Vertical Spacing:** These commands space a selected group of objects equally. This feature can be very useful if you're trying to spread out the title items for a report. Select the items in your group and then choose F<u>o</u>rmat⇨<u>V</u>ertical Spacing⇨Make <u>E</u>qual to have Access 2002 space the items equally.

Drawing Your Own Lines

An easy way to make your report a bit easier to read is to add lines that divide the various sections. To add lines to your report, follow these steps:

1. **Open the Toolbox by clicking on the Toolbox toolbar button.**

2. **Click the Line tool from the Toolbox.**

   Your cursor changes to a cross-hair with a line trailing off to the right.

3. **Click where you want to start the line, drag to the location where you want to end the line, and release the mouse button.**

You can use the various toolbar buttons (discussed earlier in this chapter) to dress up your lines. For example, to change the line's color, thickness, and appearance, use the Line/Border Color, Line/Border Width, and Special Effects buttons.

The Box tool draws boxes around separate items on your report. Click the point that you want to be the upper-left corner of your box, and drag the box shape down to the lower-right corner. When you release the mouse button, presto, you have a box.

Inserting Page Breaks

Most of the time, page breaks aren't high on the list of report priorities. Instead, you worry about challenges like making the summaries work, lining the data up into neat columns and rows, and selecting the proper shade of magenta (or was that more of a pinky russet?) for the lines and label borders.

Occasionally, you get the urge to tell Access 2002 precisely where a report page should end. Maybe you want to end each page with a special calculation, or just keep some information grouped on the same page. Regardless of the reason, inserting a page break into your report is as quick as a click.

To insert a page break into your Access 2002 report, follow these steps:

1. **Click the Page Break button in the Toolbox.**

   The mouse pointer changes into a crosshair with a page next to it.

2. **Position the crosshair wherever you want the page break and then click the left mouse button.**

   A couple of small black marks appear on the left side of the report. This is the page break marker. From now on, a new page always begins here.

If you want to remove a page break that you so carefully added, click the page break marker and then press Delete. That page break's outta there.

Sprucing Up the Place with a Few Pictures

When you click either the Image or the Unbounded Object Frame tool, you get a plus-sign pointer, with the button's image at the lower right. You can use this tool to draw a box on your screen.

- ✔ **If you're using the Image tool:** Access opens the Insert Picture dialog box, which you can use to locate the image you want to insert.

- ✔ **If you're using the Unbound Object Frame tool:** Access opens the Insert Object dialog box so you can choose the type of object to insert.

Images are great, but I strongly encourage you to add images only to the Report Header or Page Header. An image in the Detail section repeats many times.

If you don't have an image that you're ready to use, but rather have an image in progress, you may choose to use the Unbound Object Frame to add an OLE object. *OLE* (which stands for *object linking and embedding*) enables you to put an object onto your page, while maintaining the object's link to its original file. Any changes to that original file are reflected in the object you place into the report. You can link to an image or to *any* type of file that supports OLE.

Passing Your Reports around the (Microsoft) Office

You can do an awful lot with Access 2002, but sometimes a different program can get the job done better and make your life a little easier. The key to this trick is to choose Tools⇨Office Links on the main menu. This menu includes three options: two for sending your report to Microsoft Word and one for shipping it off to Excel.

Chapter 20

Headers and Footers for Groups, Pages, and Even (Egad) Whole Reports

. . . .

In This Chapter

▶ Getting into sections

▶ Grouping and sorting your records

▶ Adjusting the size of sections

▶ Fine-tuning the layout of your report

▶ Controlling your headers and footers

▶ Putting expressions into your footers

▶ Adding page numbers and dates

. . . .

*W*izards are great for creating reports, but they can only do so much for you. Even when you're working with a wizard, you still need to know a little something about how to group the fields of your report to get the optimum results. And someday after you've created your report, you may need to alter its organization or fine-tune its components to meet your changing needs. To tweak an existing report, you need to go into Design view and manually make the changes you want.

Don't despair! This chapter is designed to help you through these thorny issues. In this chapter, I explain the logic behind grouping your fields in a report, and I show you several options for your groups. I also walk you through the Design view thicket — a thorny place if ever there was one.

Everything in Its Place

The secret to successful report organization lies in the way you position the markers (known to programmers as *controls*) for the labels and fields within the report design. Each portion of the report design is separated into *sections* (called *bands* in other database programs) that identify different portions of the report. Which parts of the report land in which section depends on the report's layout:

- ✔ **Columnar:** In a standard columnar report (see Figure 20-1), field descriptions print with every record's data. The layout behaves this way because both the field descriptions and data area are in the report's Detail section. Because the report title is in the Report Header section, it prints only once, at the very beginning of the report.

- ✔ **Tabular:** The setup is quite different in a standard tabular report, as shown in Figure 20-2. The title prints at the top of the report, just as in the columnar report, but the similarity ends there. Instead of hanging out with the data, the field descriptions move to the Page Header section. Here, they print once per page instead of once per record. The data areas are by themselves in the Detail section.

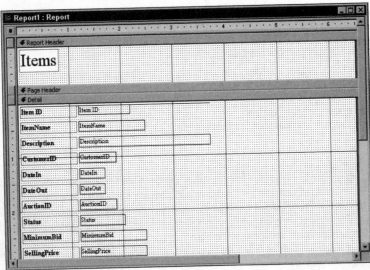

Figure 20-1: In a columnar report, labels are to the left of the fields and repeat for each record.

Understanding the whole section concept is a prerequisite for performing any serious surgery on your report or for running off to build a report from scratch. Otherwise, your report groupings don't work right, fields are out of place, and life with Access 2002 is less fulfilling than it can be.

The most important point to understand about sections is that the contents of each section are printed *only* when certain events occur. For example, the information in the Page Header is repeated at the top of *each* page, but the Report Header only prints on the *first* page.

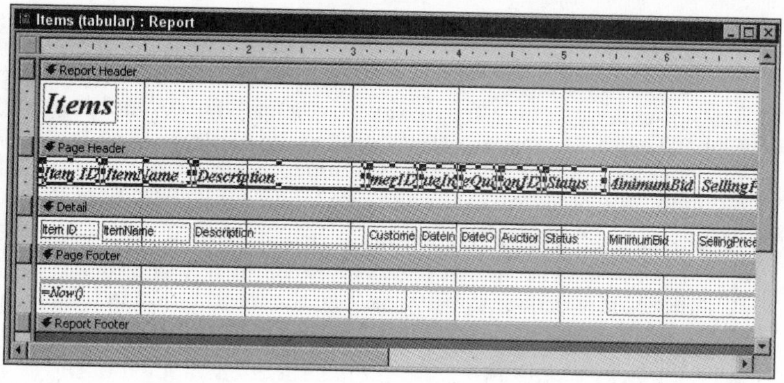

Figure 20-2:
In a tabular report, the labels become column headings.

Getting a grip on sections is easy when you look at the innermost section of your report and work your way outward, like so:

- ✔ **Detail:** Access prints items in this section each time it moves on to a new record. Your report includes a copy of the Detail section for each record in the table.

- ✔ **Group headers and footers:** You may have markers for one or more *group sections.* In Figure 20-3, information in the report is grouped by AuctionID, and then by LastName (you can tell by the section bars labeled AuctionID Header and LastName Header — the section bars identify which field is used for grouping).

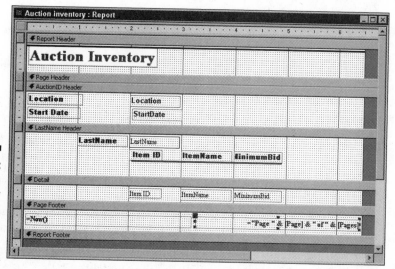

Figure 20-3:
Grouping records by AuctionID and then by LastName.

Group sections always come in pairs: the *group header* and the *group footer*. The header section is above the Detail section in the report design; the footer is always beneath Detail. Information in these sections repeats for every unique value in the group's field. For example, the report shown in Figure 20-3 reprints everything in the AuctionID Header for each unique auction number. Within the section for each auction, Access repeats the information in the LastName Header for each customer.

✔ **Page Header and Page Footer:** These sections appear at the top and bottom of every page. They're among the few sections not controlled by the contents of your records. Use the information in the Page Header and Footer sections to mark the pages of your report.

✔ **Report Header and Footer:** These sections appear at the start and end of your report. They make only one appearance in your report — unlike the other sections, which pop up many times.

So when Access produces a report, what does it do with all these sections? The process goes this way:

1. Access begins by printing the Report Header at the top of the first page.

2. Next, it prints the Page Header, if you choose to have the Page Header appear on the first page. (Otherwise, Access reprints this header at the top of every page except the first one.)

3. If your report has some groups, the Group Headers for the first set of records appear next.

4. When the headers are in place, Access finally prints the Detail lines for each record in the first group.

5. After it's done with all the Detail lines for the first group, Access prints that group's footer.

6. If you have more than one group, Access starts the process over again by printing the next group header, and then that group's Detail lines, and then that group's footer.

7. At the end of each page, Access prints the Page Footer.

8. When it finishes with the last group, Access prints the Report Footer — which, like the Report Header, only appears once in a given report.

Here's what you can do with headers and footers:

✔ The Report Header provides general information about the report. This is a good place to add the report title, printing date, and version information.

✔ The Page Header contains any information you want to appear at the top of each page (such as the date or your company logo).

✔ The headers for each group usually identify the contents of that group and the field names.

✔ The footers for each group generally contain summary information, such as counts and calculations. The footer section of the AuctionID group, in this example, may hold a calculation that totals up the Minimum Bids.

✔ The Page Footer, which appears at the bottom of every page, traditionally holds the page number and report date fields.

If keeping the information in your report private is critical, consider typing something like **Company Confidential** in the footer (won't your corporate lawyers be proud!).

✔ By the time the Report Footer prints, about the only information left is a master summary of what happened during the report. You may also include contact information (whom to call with questions about the report) if you plan to distribute the report widely throughout the company.

Grouping your records

If you're designing a report from scratch, you can use the Sorting and Grouping dialog box to create your groups and control how they behave. Perhaps more importantly, if you use a wizard to create a report for you, you can still use this dialog box to control how that report behaves and where information appears.

When the Report Wizard creates a report for you, it automatically includes a header and footer section for each group you want. If you tell the Report Wizard to group by the field AuctionID, it automatically creates both the AuctionID Header and the AuctionID Footer sections. You aren't limited to what the wizard does, though; if you're a little adventuresome, you can augment the wizard's work with your own grouping sections.

The key to creating your own grouping sections is the Sorting and Grouping dialog box, as shown in Figure 20-4. This dialog box controls how Access organizes the records in your report. Each grouping section in your report is included in the sorting and grouping list automatically (regardless of whether you created the section or the wizard did). You can also have additional entries that sort the records, although these entries don't generate their own section headers.

To build your own groupings, follow these steps:

1. **Choose View⇨Sorting and Grouping.**

   The Sorting and Grouping dialog box appears.

2. **Click a blank field under Field/Expression.**

   The blinking toothpick cursor appears, along with a down arrow.

3. **Click the down arrow.**

   A list of fields that you can use for the group appears.

4. **Select a field.**

Access 2002 adds a new line for that field to the Sorting and Grouping list. By default, Access plans to do an ascending sort (smallest to largest) with the data in that field.

5. **Click in the Group Header area at the bottom of the dialog box.**

You're telling Access 2002 that you want the entry to be a full-fledged group.

6. **Click the down arrow that appears in the box and select Yes from the drop-down menu that appears.**

Behind the scenes, Access 2002 adds a new group section to your report design. To include a footer for your new group as well, repeat this step in the Group Footer entry of the dialog box.

7. **Close the dialog box after you finish.**

That's it — your new group is in place.

Figure 20-4:
The Sorting and Grouping dialog box enables you to adjust the organization of your report.

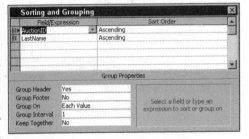

 To remove a group, click the gray button next to the group's Field/Expression line and then press Delete. Access asks whether you really want to delete the group. Click Yes.

 If you want to change the order of the various groups, just dash back to the Sorting and Grouping dialog box (choose View⇨Sorting and Grouping). Click the gray button next to the group you want to move; then click and drag the group to its new location. Access automatically adjusts your report design accordingly.

 Be careful when changing the grouping order! It's easy to make an innocent-looking change and then discover that nothing in your report is organized correctly anymore. Before making any big adjustments to the report, take a minute to save the report (choose File⇨Save). That way, if something goes wrong and the report becomes horribly disfigured, just close it (File⇨Close) without saving your changes. Ahhh. Your original report is safe and sound.

Group on, dude!

Groups are one of the too-cool-for-words features that make Access 2002 reports so flexible. But wait — groups have still *more* untapped power, thanks to the Group On setting in the Sorting and Grouping dialog box. This setting tells Access when to begin a new group of records on a report. The dialog box contains two settings for your grouping pleasure: *Each Value* and *Interval*.

✔ Each Value tells Access to group identical entries together. If any difference exists between values in the grouping field, Access puts them into different groups. Each Value is a great setting if you're grouping by customer numbers, vendor numbers, or government identification numbers. It's not such a great choice if you're working with names, because every little variation (Kaufield instead of Kaufeld, for example) ends up in its own group.

✔ Interval tells Access that you're interested in organizing by a range of entries. Exactly how Access interprets the Interval setting depends on whether you're grouping with a number or text field.

If you're grouping a number field with the Interval setting, Access counts by the Interval setting when making the groups. For example, if your Interval is 10, then Access groups records that have values from 0 to 9, 10 to 19, 20 to 29, and so on.

With text fields, Access works a little differently. Suppose, for example, you specify an Interval of 1 — Access will then group records by the first character of the text field. In other words, all the A's will form one group followed by all the B's and so on. If you set an Interval of 2, Access will group the records by the first two characters in the text field so Maine and Massachusetts would group together (both begin with Ma) but Maine and Mississippi would be in separate groups.

The properties for the currently selected group appear at the bottom of the Sorting and Grouping dialog box.

✔ **Group Header and Group Footer:** Specify whether you want this group to include a section for a Group Header, a section for a Group Footer, or both in your report.

✔ **Group On:** Determines how Access 2002 creates the groups for that value — check out the sidebar, "Group on, dude!"

✔ **Keep Together:** Controls whether all the information within a group must be printed on the same page; whether the first Detail line and the headings for that group must be printed on the same page; and whether Access can split the information any way it wants as long as it all gets printed on one page or another.

You have three choices under the Keep Together property:

- **No:** Tells Access to do whatever it pleases.

- **Whole group:** Tells Access to print the entire group, from Header to Footer, on the same page.

- **With first detail:** Tells Access to print all the information from the Header for the group through the Detail section for the first entry of the group in that group on the same page. Choose this option to ensure that each of your pages starts with a set of headings.

Changing a section's size

One problem you may have with designing your own report is controlling how much space appears in a section. When you print a section — be it a Page Header, a Section Header, or a Detail line — it normally takes up the same amount of space as shown on the Design screen. You generally want to tighten the space within the group so that little space is wasted on your page, but your section needs to be large enough to contain all the markers and such that go into it. (To find out how to create sections that change size based on the information in them, flip ahead to the next section, "Fine-Tuning the Layout.")

Changing the size of a section is easy — put your cursor on the edge of the bar immediately below a section, and then drag up or down to decrease or increase the size.

Fine-Tuning the Layout

Most of the control you have over your report comes from setting the report's properties. Although *setting properties* is a formatting topic, it becomes useful only after you start dividing your report into sections.

Dressing up your report as a whole

To adjust the formatting of an entire report, double-click the small box in the upper-left corner of the report window in Design view. Up pops the Report dialog box shown in Figure 20-5.

Playing with page headings

Of particular interest in the Report properties dialog box are controls on the Format tab that affect when the Page Header and Page Footer print:

✔ The default setting for the Page Header and Page Footer is All Pages, meaning that Access prints a header and footer on every page in the report.

✔ Choose Not with Rpt Hdr (or Not with Rprt Ftr for the footer) to tell Access to skip the first and last pages (where the Report Header and Report Footer are printed), but print the Page Header on all the others.

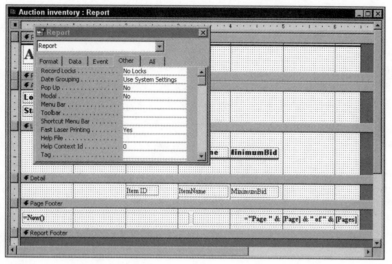

Figure 20-5: Double-click the little box in the upper-left corner to open the Report dialog box for the report.

The Page Header itself comes with a bunch of options, too. Double-click the Page Header to bring up the PageHeaderSection properties dialog box, which probably looks quite similar to the one shown in Figure 20-6. Here are your options:

✔ **Visible:** You can use this dialog box to control whether the Page Header appears at all.

✔ **Height:** Access automatically sets this property as you click and drag the section header up and down on the screen.

To specify an exact size (for example, if you want the header area to be *precisely* four centimeters tall), type the size in this section. (Access automatically uses the units of measurement you chose for Windows itself.)

✔ **Back Color:** If you want to adjust the section's color, click in this box and then click the small gray button that appears to the right of the entry. This button brings up a color palette. Click your choice and then let Access worry about the obnoxious color number that goes into the Back Color box.

Although you can control the color of your Page Header's background from the Report properties dialog box, an easier method is to click the section in Design view and use the drop-down lists on the Formatting toolbar.

✔ **Special Effect:** This property adjusts the visual effect for the section heading, much as the Special Effect button does for the markers in the report itself. Your choices are somewhat limited here, though. Click in the Special Effect box and then click the down arrow to list what's available. Choose Flat (the default setting), Raised, or Sunken.

Figure 20-6:
You can control how the page header looks with the PageHeader Section properties dialog box.

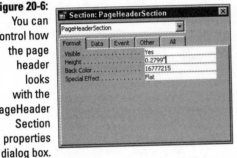

Keeping the right stuff together

The Keep Together option on the Format tab of the Report properties dialog box affects the Keep Together entry, which you set in the Sorting and Grouping dialog box (see "Grouping your records," earlier in this chapter).

Choose Per Page to apply the Keep Together criteria to pages. Or, in a report with multiple columns, choose Per Column to apply the Keep Together criteria to columns.

Formatting individual sections of your report

What if you don't want to change the format of the whole report, but just of one section of it — for example, the header for one group? Simple. In Design view, double-click the GroupHeader to call upon the dialog box shown in Figure 20-7.

With the Force New Page option, you can control whether the change for that group automatically forces the information to start on a new page. When you set this option, you can determine whether this page break occurs only before the header, only after the footer, or in both places. Similarly, you can control the way in which section starts and endings are handled for multiple column reports (such as having the group always start in a separate column). As with the preceding dialog boxes, you can control whether the group is kept together and whether the section is visible.

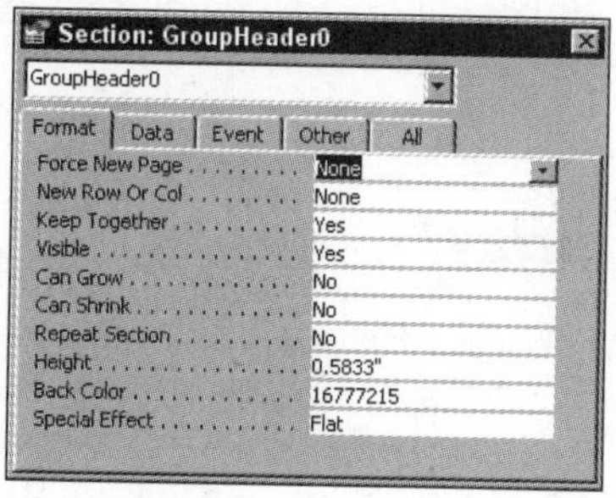

Figure 20-7: The Group-Header dialog box allows you to specify how groupings are handled.

Take particular note of Can Grow, Can Shrink, and Repeat Section. Here's what happens when you enable these settings:

- **Can Grow:** The section expands as necessary, based upon the data within it.

  Can Grow is particularly useful when you're printing a report that contains a Memo field. You set the width of the field so that it's as wide as you want. Then you can use the Can Grow property to enable Access 2002 to adjust the height available for the information.

- **Can Shrink:** The section can become smaller if, for example, some of the fields are empty. To use the Can Grow and Can Shrink properties, you need to set them for both the section and the items within the section that are able to grow or shrink.

- **Repeat Section:** Controls whether Access 2002 repeats the heading on the new page (or pages, if the section is so big that it covers more than two pages when a group is split across pages or columns).

Taking it one item at a time

Double-clicking doesn't just work for sections. When you want to adjust the formatting of any item of your report — a field, a label, or something you've drawn on your report — just double-click that item in Design view. Access 2002 leads you to a marvelous dialog box from which you can perform all manner of technical nitpicking.

Filling in Those Sections

Although Access includes several default settings for headers and footers, those settings aren't very personalized or imaginative. You can do much more with headers and footers than simply display labels for your data. You can build expressions in these sections or insert text that introduces or summarizes your data. Now that's the kind of header and footer that impresses your friends, influences your coworkers, and wins over your boss.

At the head of the class

How you place the labels within the report's Header sections controls how the final report both looks and works, so you really oughta put some thought into those Headers. You want to make sure that all your headings are easy to understand and that they actually add some useful information to the report.

When you're setting up a report, feel free to play around with the header layouts. Experiment with your options and see what you can come up with — the way that information repeats through the report may surprise you.

For example, when you use a wizard to create a grouped report in Access, Access puts labels for your records into the page header by default. Figure 20-8 shows such a report in action. Notice that the column headings are printed above the site name. The descriptions for the column headings appear at the top of each and every page because they're in the Page Header section. This example is certainly not a bad layout, but you can accomplish the same goal in other ways.

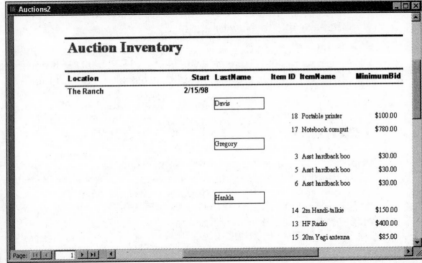

Figure 20-8: The Auction Inventory Report with the labels in the page header.

Figure 20-9 shows an alternate arrangement. In this case, the DateIn, Minimum Bid, and Item Name headings repeat every time the last name is printed because they have been dragged into the LastName Header section of the report. This arrangement is a little easier to read than the version shown in Figure 20-8 because the column descriptions are right above their matching columns.

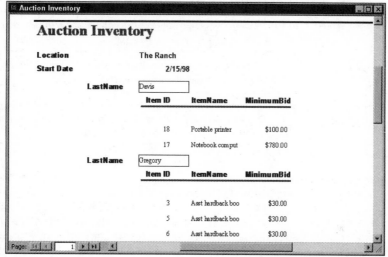

Figures 20-9: The Auction Inventory Report where you drag the labels from the page header to the LastName header.

Figures 20-8 and 20-9 show some of the labels (such as LastName) moved from where the Wizard placed them and various sections resized to make the reports more aesthetically pleasing. In addition, the pair of lines used to mark the top and bottom of the Page Header was removed to close that space.

Expressing yourself in footers

Typically, the markers in the footer simply print the page number or some other text. That doesn't mean that you *can't* put something more complex in there, however. These fields can involve complex-looking formulas that mix some text with the current value of a field in the report to produce an informative note for the report.

These feet were made for summing

Access 2002 contains many functions, but the ones listed in Table 20-1 win the award for Most Likely to Be Used in a Normal Human's Report. These functions create different summaries of the fields in your report.

Table 20-1	Summary Functions	
Function	*Description*	*Example*
Sum	Adds up all of the values in the field	Sum([MinimumBid])
Maximum	Finds the largest value in the values listed in this section for this field	Max([MinimumBid])
Minimum	Finds the smallest value in the values listed in this section for this field	Min([MinimumBid])
Average	Finds the average value of all of the values listed within this section for this field	Avg([MinimumBid])
Count	Counts how many values are listed in this section for this field	Count([MinimumBid])

Double-click a calculated field in a report to open the Properties dialog box. You can use the first line of the Format tab to select a format for displaying the information in the field. This control is most useful for setting the look of your report. You also have options for whether duplicates within the field are shown or whether the fields after the first instance of the same entry are left blank. For the most part, you'll use these options in the Detail section, where you may want to show only the first record of several records with the same entry in a field.

You can control how calculations are performed and displayed by following these steps:

1. **Double-click the field.**

   The field's Properties dialog box appears.

2. **Click the Data tab to view data-oriented properties.**

3. **Modify the summary formula in the Control Source box.**

   Click in the field and then click the ellipsis that pops up to the right of the field to open the Expression Builder to create your calculations (Chapter 15 covers this).

   The Input Mask field allows you to specify an input mask. I show you how to work with input masks in Chapter 7.

   At the bottom of the Data tab is an option for whether or not the entry is a Running Sum. This tells Access whether to reset the total at zero when the corresponding Header appears, or if it should keep on summing and build a massive total.

Running Sum can be a little difficult to understand. Here are the possible settings:

- **Over All:** The value from preceding groups is carried forward — you get a running total, such as a grand total or a grand average.

- **Over Group:** The calculation is continued across all the groups contained within that section (any sections that fall between the header for the group and the footer for the group).

- **No:** The value is reset to zero each time a new record is encountered. If the field is in a grouping, the value is set to zero when a new grouping starts.

Page numbers and dates

Access can insert certain types of information for you in either the headers or the footers. Most notably, Access can insert page numbers or dates, using the Page Number command and the Date and Time command under the Insert menu.

Hey, what page is this?

Choosing Insert⇨Page Numbers displays the dialog box. From this dialog box, you have several options for your page-numbering pleasure:

- **Format:** Choose Page N to print the word "Page" followed by the appropriate page number. Or choose Page N of M to count the total number of pages in the report and print that number in addition to the current page (as in "Page 2 of 15").

- **Position:** Tell Access whether to print the page number in the Page Header or the Page Footer.

- **Alignment:** Set the position of the page number on the page. Click the arrow at the right edge of the list box to scroll through your options.

- **Show Number on First Page:** Select this check box to include a page number on the first page of your report. Deselect it to keep your first page unnumbered.

To change the way that the page numbers work on your report, first manually delete the existing page number field by clicking it and pressing the Delete key. After the number is gone, choose Insert⇨Page Numbers to build the new page numbers.

When did you print this report, anyway?

Choose Insert⇨Date and Time to display the dialog box. The most important options are Include Date and Include Time. You select the formats from a set of choices.

Part V
Wizards, Forms, and Other Mystical Stuff

The 5th Wave   By Rich Tennant

"You ever get the feeling this project could just up and die at any moment?"

In this part . . .

Part V defies rational explanation. (How's *that* for a compelling tag line?) It introduces a wide range of stuff that's all individually useful, but collectively unrelated. When you get down to it, the only thing tying these topics together is the fact that they're not related to anything else.

Chapter 21 (appropriately enough) takes you and your databases into the 21st century with Internet integration — one of the much-heralded features of Access 2002.

Also, be sure to check out Chapter 22 to find out all about forms in Access 2002. (Uh-oh — my *inner nerd* is starting to get excited. . . .) Forms are really powerful and flexible . . . and they're fun to make — that's right, I said *fun*.

Chapter 23 delves into the wonderful world of importing and exporting data. Chapter 24 shows you how to analyze the heck out of your tables. (Perhaps you should just go ahead and read the part while I try to get the nerd back under control.)

In Chapter 25, I describe how you can tell Access what to do without touching your keyboard.

Chapter 21

Spinning Your Data into (And onto) the Web

· ·

In This Chapter

▶ What Access 2002 knows about the Internet

▶ Entering and using hyperlinks

▶ Publishing stuff on the Web

▶ Advanced topics to challenge your hair retention

· ·

Access 2002 is a powerhouse of Internet and intranet information. If you're itching to join the online revolution, or if you yearn for fun and profit on the electronic superhighway, Access 2002 (and the rest of the Office 2002 suite, for that matter) is ready to get you started.

This chapter takes a quick look at the online capabilities of Access 2002 and discusses some of the details of hyperlinks and online database publishing. The chapter closes with some advanced topics for your further research pleasure. (These topics are just too high on the old technonerd scale for this book.)

Access 2002 and the Internet: A Match Made in Redmond

These days, it seems that all software makers are touting their products' cozy linkage with the Internet. Whether it's a natural fit or the marketing equivalent of a shotgun wedding, everyone's joining the rush to cyberspace.

Thankfully, Internet integration with Access 2002 is on the *natural fit* end of the scale. Databases are a perfect complement to the Net's popular World Wide Web information system. The Web always offers lots of interactivity and a flexible presentation medium. But until now, publishing a database on the Web was a complex process requiring time, effort, and a willingness to cheerfully rip your hair out by the roots.

To make the data-publishing process much easier and less hair-intensive, Microsoft came up with a way to bring the Net right into Access 2002. The key to the behind-the-scenes magic is Microsoft's ActiveX technology.

You sometimes hear terms like OLE (Object Linking and Embedding), COM (Component Object Model), and even DNA (Distributed interNet Architecture). Believe it or not, these terms are all essentially synonymous with ActiveX. (Microsoft has an unfortunate habit of periodically giving its technology a new name for somewhat dubious marketing purposes.) Basically, ActiveX (or OLE or COM or whatever) is the technology that allows different programs to share information. Don't stress out about the technology — you don't need to know *anything* technical about ActiveX to make Access 2002 sing duets with either the Internet or your company's intranet.

The Internet power of Access 2002 comes directly from the Microsoft Web browser, Internet Explorer, through a cool ActiveX pipeline. When you work with hyperlinks, browse the Net from a form, or search your company's intranet, Internet Explorer does all of the work behind the scenes. Even when it looks as though Access 2002 is in charge, the Internet information is coming directly from Internet Explorer. The ActiveX technology makes everything appear seamless.

To make Access 2002 do its Internet tricks, you must be running Internet Explorer 5.0 or above. In addition, you need a connection to the Internet (or to your company's intranet).

Can't Hyperlinks Take Something to Calm Down?

Sitting right in the center of the whole Internet discussion is the term *hyperlink*. Although "hyperlink" sounds vaguely like a frenzied game show host, hyperlinks are actually the special storage compartments for whatever you want to link with. Hyperlinks can connect to a variety of Internet or intranet locations, as Table 21-1 shows.

Table 21-1	Hyperlinks in Access 2002
Link	*Description*
file://	Opens a local or network-based file
ftp://	File Transfer Protocol; links to an FTP server
gopher://	Links to a Gopher server on the network or Internet

Link	Description
http://	Hypertext Transfer Protocol; links to a World Wide Web page
mailto:	Sends e-mail to a network or Internet address
news://	Opens an Internet newsgroup

Table 21-1 contains the most popular and commonly used tags. For a complete list of the hyperlink tags that Access 2002 understands, press F1 to open the Access 2002 Help system and then search for the term *hyperlink*.

If you surf the World Wide Web regularly, many of these tags should look familiar. Although most of them are geared toward Internet/intranet applications, Access 2002 can also use hyperlinks to identify locally stored Microsoft Office documents. This technology is so flexible, the sky's the limit.

Adding a hyperlink field to your table

You can't let hyperlinks just stand around without a permanent home, so Access 2002 sports a field type specifically for this special data. As you probably guessed, this type is called the hyperlink field. Figure 21-1 shows a table design containing a hyperlink field.

Adding a hyperlink field to a table doesn't require any special steps. Just use the same steps for adding *any* field to a table. The hyperlink field is no different from the other mundane fields surrounding it.

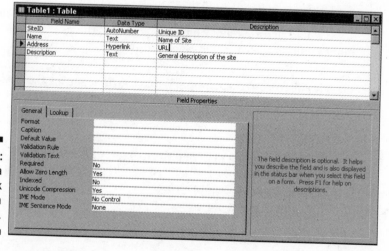

Figure 21-1:
Adding a
Hyperlink
field to a
table.

Typing and using hyperlinks

Hyperlinks can have up to four parts, all separated by pound signs. Table 21-2 lists these four parts.

Table 21-2	Formatting Hyperlinks in Access 2002
Hyperlink Part	**Description**
Display Text	The text that is displayed. If omitted, the URL is displayed.
Address	The URL (Uniform Resource Locator) such as a Web page; this is mandatory.
Sub Address	A link on the same page or document.
Screen Tip	Text that pops up if the user pauses his or her mouse cursor over the address.

Here are some examples of formatted hyperlinks:

- `www.microsoft.com` displays the URL `http://www.microsoft.com` only.

- `Microsoft Corporation# http://www.microsoft.com#` displays Microsoft Corporation.

- `Microsoft Corporation# http://www.microsoft.com# Information#` displays Microsoft Corporation and links to a topic called "Information" on that page.

- `Microsoft Corporation# http://www.microsoft.com# Information#Redmond#` displays Microsoft Corporation and links to a topic called "Information" on that page. When the user pauses the mouse pointer over the link, the word "Redmond" pops up.

- `Microsoft Corporation# http://www.microsoft.com##Redmond#` displays Microsoft Corporation. When the user pauses the mouse pointer over the link, the word "Redmond" pops up. Because the subaddress wasn't included, I had to use two pound signs after the URL and before "Redmond."

Your best bet in formatting hyperlinks is to experiment to achieve an attractive result. Figure 21-2 shows a formatted hyperlink as entered into a table and how it displays on an Access form.

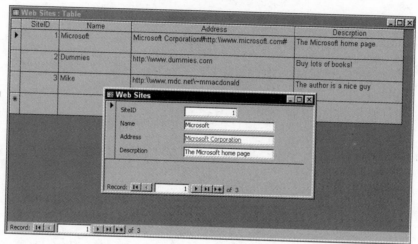

SiteID	Name	Address	Descrption
1	Microsoft	Microsoft Corporation#http:\\www.microsoft.com#	The Microsoft home page
2	Dummies	http:\\www.dummies.com	Buy lots of books!
3	Mike	http:\\www.mdc.net\~mmacdonald	The author is a nice guy

Web Sites

SiteID	1
Name	Microsoft
Address	Microsoft Corporation
Descrption	The Microsoft home page

Record: |◄| ◄| 1 |►| ►| ►*| of 3

Figure 21-2:
The
hyperlink
field
automati-
cally
formats
itself.

Record: |◄| ◄| 1 |►| ►| ►*| of 3

Although most hyperlinks store World Wide Web or other Internet addresses, they can point to just about anything in the known world. Thanks to their flexible tags, hyperlinks understand Web pages, intranet servers, database objects (reports, forms, and such), and even plain Microsoft Office documents on your computer or another networked PC.

Using the hyperlink is easy, too. Follow these steps:

1. **Either log onto your network or start your Internet connection.**

   Internet Explorer needs to see that everything is up and running before it consents to making an appearance.

2. **Open the Access 2002 database you want to use and then open the table containing those wonderful hyperlinks.**

   The fun is about to begin!

3. **Click the hyperlink of your choice.**

   If the hyperlink was to a Web page, Internet Explorer leaps on-screen, displaying the Web site from the link. If the link leads to something other than a Web site, Windows automatically fires up the right program to handle whatever the link has to offer.

A few words about the World Wide Web (and why you care)

Although hyperlinks may seem like just so much technohype, they really *are* important. Nearly all businesses have a Web presence and many (if not most) are moving information to the World Wide Web. Companies are also creating in-house *intranets* (custom Web servers offering information to networked employees).

The abilities of Access 2002 put it in the middle of the Web and intranet excitement — and that presents a cool opportunity for you.

The Web and intranet technology is not new but it continues to rapidly evolve. Duties that used to belong exclusively to *those computer people*

are landing in graphic arts, marketing, and almost everywhere else. New jobs are born overnight as companies wrestle with the Web's powerful communication features. It may sound a little chaotic, and that's okay — it is.

If you're looking for a new career path in your corporate life, knowledge of the Web may just be the ticket. Whether you move into Web site development, information management, or even your own Web-oriented consulting business, this is an exciting time full of new possibilities. Dive in and discover what's waiting for you!

Pushing Your Data onto the Web

Now that Access 2002 contains all of your coolest information, why not share your stuff with others in your company — or even publish it for the world? Whether you're building a commercial site geared toward fame and online fortune, or a cross-department intranet to supercharge your company, Access 2002 contains all the tools you need to whip your data into Web-ready shape in no time at all.

Although you don't need to know anything about HTML to build Web pages with Access 2002, you probably need to know some HTML before your project is done. For a painless introduction to HTML, check out *HTML 4 For Dummies,* by Ed Tittel and Steve James.

Access 2002 helps you publish data in two ways: static and dynamic. The method for your project depends on the equipment, goals, and expertise available in your immediate surroundings. Here's a quick comparison of the options:

> ✔ **Static:** This option is a straight conversion from Access 2002 into HTML. Its name reflects the fact that the stuff you convert doesn't change over time — it's a lot like taking a picture of your data. If you add more records to your table and want to include them in your Web-based stuff, you need to re-create the Web pages.

Static conversion is a great option for address lists and catalogs that don't change very often. It's also a good place to start when you're exploring the possibilities of the Web. You can convert almost any Access 2002 object — including tables, queries, forms, and reports — into a static Web page with the File⇨Export option. (I show you how to do just that in the next section.)

✔ **Dynamic:** Instead of creating a simple HTML page that contains all of your data, the Dynamic option builds a special goodie that Access 2002 calls a *data access page.* This is an HTML page that gives people *access* to your data, so they can see (and even change) your information through the corporate network or the Web. Data access pages work only with Access tables and queries.

Thanks to the Data Access Page Wizard, building a data access page isn't tough. But because all this technical magic requires some serious cooperation among the Web server, Access 2002, and your database, *implementing* the finished data access page isn't necessarily a task for beginners. If your page is to be viewed by more than a few people outside your company, you probably need to enlist the aid of a Web pro.

Although the details of making a data access page work may require some help from a trained computer professional, literally anyone can create a data access page by using the wizard. The process works a lot like the Form or Report Wizard. Here are the step-by-step details:

1. **Open the database containing data destined for your intranet or the Web.**

   The database window hops to the screen.

2. **Click the Pages Objects bar button on the left side of the window.**

   The database window changes, displaying three options dealing with data access pages.

3. **Double-click the Create Data Access Page by Using the Wizard option.**

   After a gratuitous amount of hard drive activity, the Data Access Page Wizard ambles forth (as shown in Figure 21-3).

4. **Click the down arrow in the Tables/Queries box.**

   A list of tables and queries in the current database appears.

5. **Click the one you want on the data access page.**

   The Available Fields window lists all of the fields in the selected table or query.

6. **For each field you want in the data access page, click the field name and then click the > button (greater than symbol).**

   The highlighted field hops into the Selected Fields list.

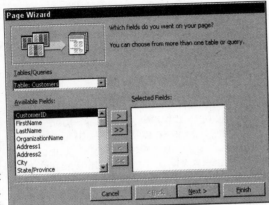

Figure 21-3:
The Data
Access
Page
Wizard
looks a lot
like the
Report
Wizard.

To copy all of the possible fields into the Selected Fields list, click the >> button (double greater than symbol). To remove a field, click its entry in the Selected Fields list, then click the < button (less than symbol). To clear the whole list out and start over, click the << button (double less than symbol).

7. **Repeat Steps 4 and 5 for each table or query you want to include. After all the fields are ready, click Next.**

    Data access pages understand how related tables work together so that you can include fields from several tables in one data access page. (Chapter 5 covers everything you ever wanted to know about relationships. For tips about other relationships, consult a good counselor.)

8. **To show your data in groups on your new data access page, click the fields you want to subtotal your records with and click the > button (greater than symbol) to add the new groups. After you finish, click Next.**

    With grouping complete, Access moves along to sorting and summary information.

    Groups in a data access page work just like groups in a report.

9. **To sort the detail records even further, select a field on the Sort order and summary information page. Click Next after you're finished.**

    Most of the time, you won't need yet *another* layer of organization for your data. By this time, the data is sliced and diced a couple of times, thanks to the grouping options. However, if you *do* need more layers, feel free to add up to four more levels of sorting and summarizing.

10. **Type the page title you want and then click Finish.**

    The Wizard clunks, shimmies, and generally ambles around for a bit. After making you wait just long enough to prove that the whole process is woefully complex, the Wizard delivers your finished data access page, as shown in Figure 21-4.

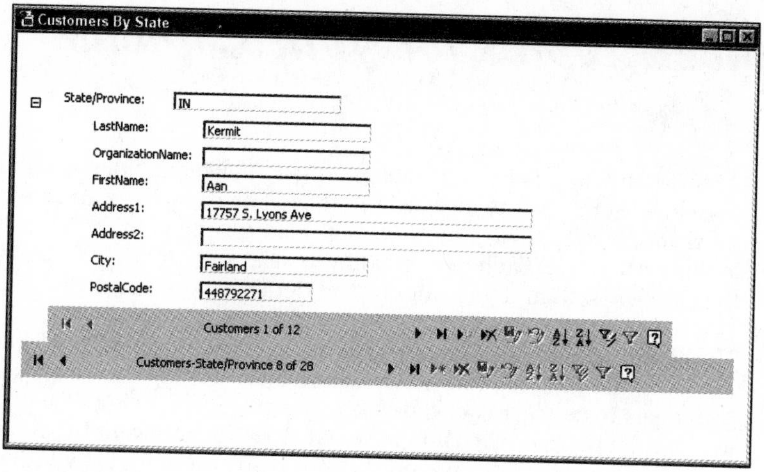

Figure 21-4:
The finished
data access
page —
looking
good!

11. **Test your new page by running your Web browser and loading the page for a quick look (as shown in Figure 21-5).**

You may not be able to deploy your data access page on a big commercial Web site. Just as ActiveX technology makes it easy to create the page, it also restricts where it can be displayed. As of this writing, only Internet Explorer (versions 5.0 and above) can display data access pages.

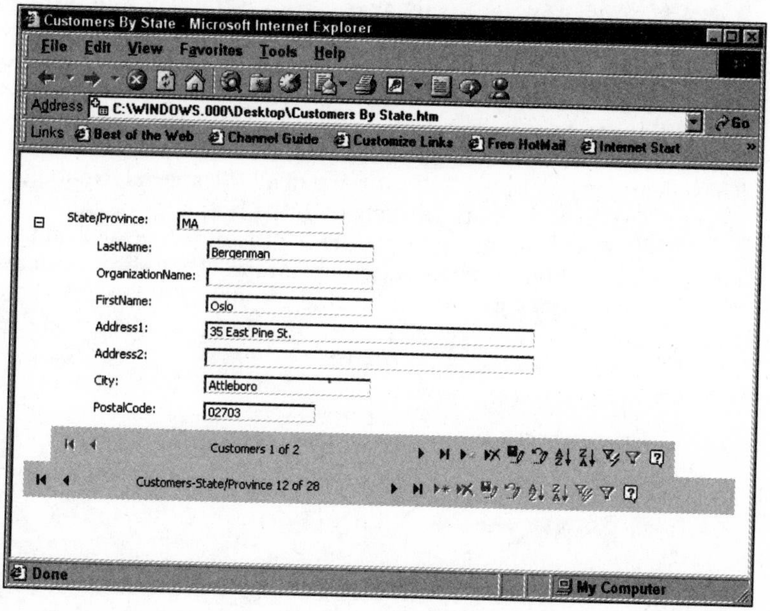

Figure 21-5:
The data
access
page
displayed
within
Internet
Explorer.

Advanced Topics for Your Copious Nerd Time

If all the stuff in this chapter doesn't quell your technological impulses, don't worry — there's plenty more where this came from. Here are a few ideas to keep your mind active, your Web pages sharp, and your Access 2002 forms looking truly cool. Each item includes a brief summary plus a term to give to the Office Assistant if you want all the details.

- ✔ Export datasheets, reports, and forms directly as static HTML pages with the File⇨Export menu selection. One or two quick clicks is all it takes to convert your data into a simple, unchanging Web page. This option is great when you're fluent in HTML and want to quickly generate a few pages of information that are ready for manual tweaking. Search for: **export to HTML**.

- ✔ Put hyperlinks right into your reports and forms. Access 2002 lets you attach hyperlinks directly to command buttons, labels, or images. Search for: **add hyperlink to form**.

- ✔ Build HTML template files to make your exported tables look, act, and dress the same. If you're building the mother of all database Web sites, template files are a big time-saver. Plus, they give your site a consistent, professional feel. Search for: **HTML template files**.

- ✔ Add a Web browser to any Access 2002 form. Navigate through Web documents directly from a form — no need to switch between Access 2002 and your Web browser! This feature has incredible possibilities for corporate intranets, plus a lot of promise on the Internet, too. Search for: **Web page on a form**.

These features just scratch the surface of all the special capabilities of Access 2002. In addition to working with the Net, Access 2002 also works closely with the other members of the Microsoft Office 2002 suite. There's so much to know about how the programs interact that Microsoft created a huge informational file on the subject. Amazingly, the file is available for free through the Internet. To get all the details, view the Office 2002 Resource Kit by visiting www.microsoft.com/office/ork.

In life, there are three certainties: death, taxes, and broken hyperlinks. If the above address doesn't work for you, follow these steps:

1. **Type** www.microsoft.com.

   A Support option appears at the top of the window.

2. **Click Support and choose Knowledge Base from the drop-down menu that appears.**

3. **Type the search term** Office Resource Kit **in the Knowledge Base window.**

   The search engine should return a link to the correct location.

Chapter 22

Making Forms That Look Cool and Work Great

In This Chapter

▶ Taking a look at forms in Access 2002

▶ Building a form with the Form Wizard

▶ Making simple forms with the AutoForm Wizard

▶ Improving on the Form Wizard's creation

Paper forms are the lifeblood of almost every enterprise. If they weren't, life would probably be simpler and we'd have more trees, but that's beside the point. Because real life is the mirror that software engineers peer into (and frequently faint while looking at) when they design programs, Access 2002 includes the ever-cherished capability of viewing and working with forms.

Fear not! Electronic forms are infinitely friendlier than their old-fashioned counterparts, the dreaded PBFs *(paper-based forms)*. In fact, you may even discover that you *like* messing around with forms in Access 2002. (If that happens to you, don't tell anyone.) This chapter looks at what forms can do for you, explores a couple different ways to make forms, and tosses out some tips for customizing forms so that they're exactly what you need.

Tax Forms and Data Forms Are Very Different Animals

All forms are *not* created equal. Paper forms make cool airplanes, take up physical space, are hard to update, and (depending on the number of forms involved) may constitute a safety hazard when stacked. Access 2002 forms, on the other hand, are simple to update, easy to store, and are rarely a safety risk (although designing a form *can* be hazardous to your productivity, because it's kinda fun).

Forms in Access 2002 are something like digital versions of their paper cousins, but the similarity ends with the name. Access 2002 forms have all kinds of advantages over old-fashioned paper forms — and they'll spoil you if you're used to wandering through your data in Datasheet view. Here's a sampling of how forms in Access 2002 make viewing your data easier. You can:

- **Escape the clutches of Datasheet view:** Instead of scrolling back and forth through a datasheet, you focus on one record at a time, with all the data pleasantly laid out on a single screen.

- **Modify at will:** When your needs change, update the form in Design view. And, unlike with its paper cousins, you don't have to worry about recycling 10,000 leftover copies of the old form.

- **See your data any way you want:** Access 2002 lets you take one set of data and present it in as many different forms as you want — all without re-entering a bit of data for the new form. Create a special form for the data-entry folks, another for your analysts, and a third for yourself. Well-designed forms give the right information to the right people *without* revealing data they don't need to reveal.

- **View the entries in a table or the results of a query:** Forms pull information from tables or queries with equal ease. Forms based on queries are especially flexible because they always display the latest information.

- **Combine data from linked tables:** One form can display data from several related tables. Forms automatically use the relationships built into your database.

Like reports and queries, forms are stored in the database file under their own button, as shown in Figure 22-1. Forms are full-fledged Access 2002 objects, so you can do all kinds of cool tricks with them.

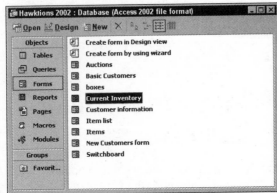

Figure 22-1:
Click Forms
to see all
your Access
forms.

Depending on your needs, you can make forms in three ways:

- ✔ The Form Wizard walks you through a series of questions and proudly produces a rather bland-looking form.

- ✔ The three AutoForm tools make the same forms as the Form Wizard but don't ask any questions.

- ✔ Access 2002 sets up a blank form, drops off a toolbox full of form-related goodies, shakes your hand, and then wanders off to do something fun while you make a form from scratch.

I believe in keeping systems as simple as possible, so this chapter explains how to enlist the Form Wizard and the AutoForm tools to build basic forms *for* you. The chapter closes with tips and tricks for manually tweaking these Masterpieces of Vanilla into Truly Cool Forms.

Creating a Form at the Wave of a Wand

The easiest way to create the best in computer-designed forms (not stunning forms or incredibly useful forms) is by using the Form Wizard. As with all the other Access 2002 wizards, the Form Wizard steps you through the creation process.

To get the Form Wizard up and running, follow these steps:

1. **Open your database file and click the Forms button on the Objects bar on the left side of the window.**

   Access 2002 displays a list of the forms currently in your database. Don't fret if the list is currently empty — you're about to change that.

2. **Click New.**

   The New Form dialog box appears.

   The next time you want to create a form, you also can double-click the Create Form by Using the Wizard option instead of using New. Think of this option as a shortcut to the wizard's lair.

3. **Double-click Form Wizard in the dialog box (as shown in Figure 22-2).**

   At this point, the computer's hard disk usually sounds like it's having a massive fight with itself. When the noise dies down, the Form Wizard poofs into action.

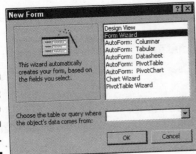

Figure 22-2:
Invoking the
Form
Wizard.

4. **Click the down arrow in the Tables/Queries box to list the tables and queries in your database and then select the one that contains the fields you want to view with this form.**

   The Form Wizard lists the available fields.

5. **Double-click a field name in the Available Fields list to include the field in your form.**

   If you want to see *all* the fields, click the >> button in the middle of the screen. To remove a field that you accidentally picked, double-click its name in the Selected Fields list. The field jumps back to the Available Fields side of the dialog box.

6. **Repeat Step 5 for each field destined for the form (see Figure 22-3). After you're done with all the fields, click Next.**

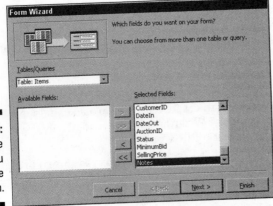

Figure 22-3:
Select the
fields you
want to see
on the form.

If you select fields from more than one table, the Form Wizard takes a moment to ask how you want to organize the data in your form.

7. Click your choice in the By (field name) list on the left side of the dialog box and then click Next.

The Form Wizard asks how you want to display data on the form.

8. Leave the option set to Columnar (or Datasheet, if that's the default option on your screen) and then click Next.

If you want to use an option other than the default, check out the section, "Giving the Form Just the Right Look," later in this chapter.

9. Choose color and background styles to display your data and then click Next.

I chose Standard, as shown in Figure 22-4. Most of the color and background combinations really slow down the performance of your forms. If you absolutely must have some color in your forms, try the Colorful or Stone settings. They provide some lively highlights without affecting your form's performance.

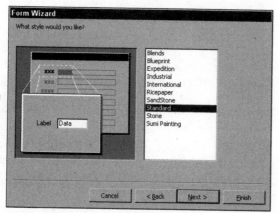

Figure 22-4: It's tempting to be fancy, but for now keep it simple.

10. Type a descriptive title for your form in the "What title do you want for your form?" box at the top of the Form Wizard screen.

By default, the Form Wizard offers you the name of the table that you used to feed the form, but *please* use something more descriptive than that.

11. Click Finish.

Your new form appears on-screen, ready for action (see Figure 22-5).

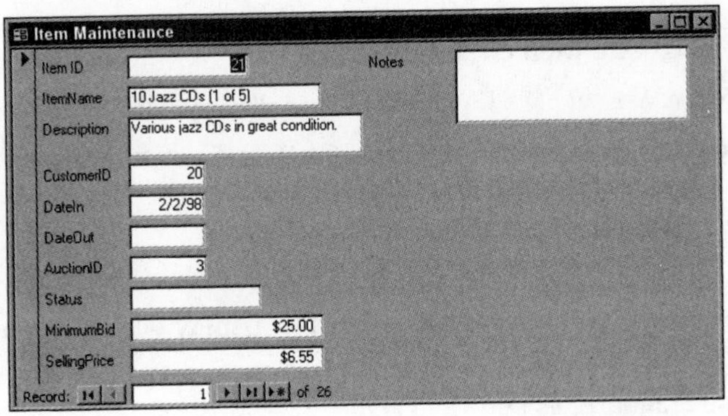

Item Maintenance

Item ID	21
ItemName	10 Jazz CDs (1 of 5)
Description	Various jazz CDs in great condition.
CustomerID	20
DateIn	2/2/98
DateOut	
AuctionID	3
Status	
MinimumBid	$25.00
SellingPrice	$6.55

Notes

Record: 1 of 26

Figure 22-5:
The new form's not pretty, but it's a place to start.

The Form Wizard automatically saves the form as part of the creation process, so you don't need to manually save and name it.

Giving the Form Just the Right Look

Depending on the data you select for your form (for example, whether you use more than one table), you have different options for displaying your data:

- ✔ **Columnar:** A classic, one-record-per-page form. Most data entry forms use Columnar.

- ✔ **Tabular:** A multiple-records-per-page form (see Figure 22-6). Be ready for some cosmetic surgery (rearranging and resizing to make the form more attractive) to grind away the rough edges and make the form truly useful. This type of layout is good for reports.

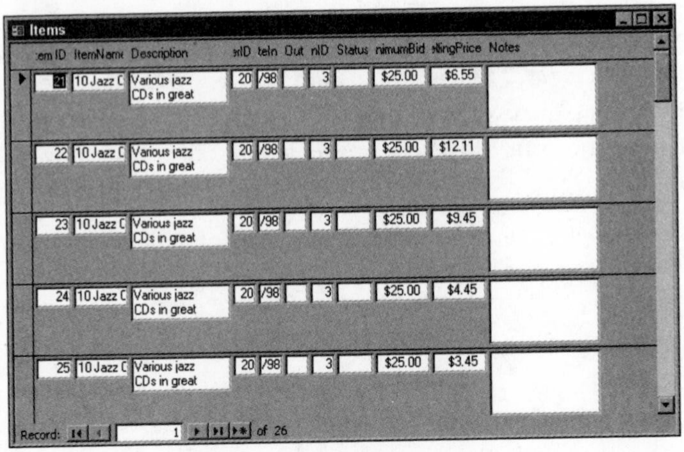

Items

emID	ItemName	Description	rnID	teIn	Out	nID	Status	nimumBid	ellingPrice	Notes
21	10 Jazz C	Various jazz CDs in great	20	/98		3		$25.00	$6.55	
22	10 Jazz C	Various jazz CDs in great	20	/98		3		$25.00	$12.11	
23	10 Jazz C	Various jazz CDs in great	20	/98		3		$25.00	$9.45	
24	10 Jazz C	Various jazz CDs in great	20	/98		3		$25.00	$4.45	
25	10 Jazz C	Various jazz CDs in great	20	/98		3		$25.00	$3.45	

Record: 1 of 26

Figure 22-6:
This Tabular form is functional but needs a little work to make it prettier.

✔ **Datasheet:** A spreadsheet-like grid. Essentially, this is an Access Datasheet View embedded in a form and is appropriate where an Excel style presentation suits your needs.

✔ **Justified:** The data is laid out across the whole form over multiple rows (see Figure 22-7). This is an interesting layout and may be especially useful where you have memo fields.

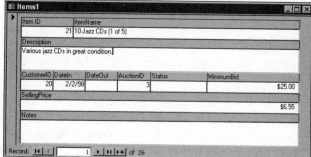

Figure 22-7: The Justified form layout.

✔ **Pivot Table:** New to Access 2002. Summarizes data and allows for its analysis by dragging data items and showing or hiding detail.

✔ **Pivot Chart:** New to Access 2002. A Graphical analysis of data (see Figure 22-8) which lets you drag items you want to analyze.

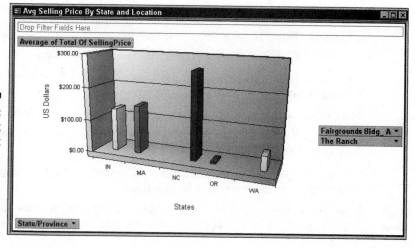

Figure 22-8: The Pivot Chart layout allows the viewer to pick and choose data to analyze.

Mass Production at Its Best: Forms from the Auto Factory

When I was a kid, I became fascinated with business and how it worked. The move from hand-built products to Henry Ford's automated assembly line particularly amazed me. (Yes, I *was* a little different. Why do you ask?) The assembly line had its good and bad points, but the quote that always defined the Ford assembly line for me was, "You can have any color you want, as long as it's black."

With that thought in mind, let me welcome you to the AutoForm Factory. Our motto: "You can have any form you want, as long as it's one of the three we make." Ah, the joys of flexible production management. . . .

Access 2002 claims that the AutoForms are wizards, but because they're so limited — er, I mean *focused* — I don't think of them as full-fledged purveyors of the magical arts. Semantics aside, you can use AutoForms to build any of the form types that I list in the previous section.

Using the AutoForms is a quick process. Despite their alleged *wizard* status, AutoForms are more like office temps: Just point them at data, stand back, and before you know it, the form is done. Follow these steps to use AutoForms:

1. **With your database open, click the Form button on the Objects bar on the left side of the database window and then click <u>N</u>ew.**

   The New Form dialog box hops onto the screen, ready to help.

2. **Click the layout that you're looking for.**

   Access 2002 highlights the appropriate mini-wizard name.

3. **Click the down arrow next to the Choose the Table text box below the Wizard list.**

   A drop-down list of tables and queries in the current database appears.

4. **Click the table or query that you want to provide information for this form and then click OK.**

   The appropriate mini-wizard begins its focused little job, and your new form appears on-screen in a few moments.

5. **Save your form by choosing <u>F</u>ile➪<u>S</u>ave and typing a name for the form in the dialog box that appears. You can also click the Save button on the toolbar.**

6. **Click OK.**

   Unlike the Form Wizard, AutoForms *don't* automatically save the form they create, so you have to save the form manually. The form is added to your database on the Forms button.

Ultimate Beauty through Cosmetic Surgery

Tell me the brutal truth, okay? I want your honest opinion on this. Ready? Would you rather slavishly toil away in the data-entry sweatshop of Figure 22-5 or casually pop a few records into Figure 22-9 between tennis sets? Take your time to answer.

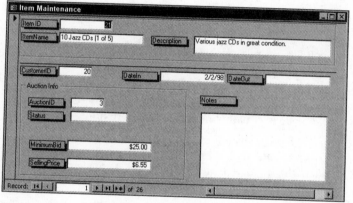

Figure 22-9: This is the same form as Figure 22-5 (honest!) after five or six minutes of surgery.

Believe it or not, those images are the *same kind of form.* Yup, it's true. The *Before* image in Figure 22-5 is a standard columnar form straight from the AutoForm Factory of the preceding section. The *After* image is also a standard columnar form, but I transformed it by moving some fields around, adding some graphics to segment the form, and changing the tab order to make data entry more intuitive.

In the next section, I show how you too can make your forms more, well, more sexy. (And if you find these forms sexy, you are probably breaking some law.) Access gives you the basic tool kit used by top form surgeons around the country. In no time at all, your frumpy forms are sleek data-entry machines, both functionally useful and visually appealing.

Taking a form into Design view

Before you can make *any* of these changes, the form has to be in Design view. Access provides two easy ways to get there:

- **From the database window:** Click the Forms button on the Objects bar to list the available forms. Click the form you want to change and then click Design.

✔ **From a form window:** Click the Design button on the toolbar or choose View➪Form Design from the menu.

Don't let Design view stress you out. It *looks* more complicated than normal life, but that's okay. If something goes wrong and you accidentally mess up your form, just choose File➪Close from the menu. When Access 2002 asks about saving your changes, politely click No. This step throws out all the horrible changes you just made to the form. Take a few deep breaths to calm your nerves and then start the design process over again.

Moving fields

To move a field around in Design view, follow these steps:

1. **Put the mouse pointer anywhere on the field that you want to move.**

   You can point to the field name or the box where the field value goes. Either place is equally fine for what you're doing.

   If the field is already selected (the name has a box around it that's decorated with small, filled-in squares), click any blank spot of your form to deselect the field; then start with Step 1. Otherwise, Access gets confused and thinks you want to do something *other* than just move the field.

2. **Press and hold down the left mouse button.**

   The mouse pointer turns into a hand, which is how Access 2002 tells you that it's ready to move something. Strange response, isn't it?

3. **Drag the field to its new location.**

   As you move the field, a pair of white boxes moves along with the cursor to show you precisely where the field goes.

4. **When the field is in position, release the mouse button.**

   The field drops smoothly into place.

   If you don't like where the field landed, either move it again or press Ctrl+Z to undo the move and start over from scratch.

Adding lines and boxes

Two buttons near the bottom of Design view enable you to create the following on your form:

 ✔ Lines

 ✔ Boxes (or borders)

Here's how to use these tools:

1. **Click the tool of your choice.**

   The tool appears pushed in, just like a toggle button.

2. **Put the mouse pointer where you want to start the line or place the corner of a box; then press and hold down the left mouse button.**

   Aim is important, but you can always undo or move the graphic if the project doesn't work out quite right.

3. **Move the cursor to the spot where the line ends or to the opposite corner of your box and then release the mouse button.**

   The line or box appears on-screen.

You can apply special effects to your line or box graphics:

- ✔ Lines can be *flat* or *raised*. Even though the other options seem to be available, they don't look any different from *raised* when you're working with a line.

- ✔ Boxes have six different special effects: Flat, Etched, Raised, Shadowed, Sunken, and Chiseled.

To use these special effects, draw a line or box and then right-click it (if it's a line, right-click one end). Choose Special Effects from the pop-up menu and then click the particular effect you like best.

If you want to further customize your line or box, give the following Border settings a try. Open the Special Effects dialog box and then click the Format button.

- ✔ **Border Style:** Adjusts how the line looks, with options ranging from solid to dotted.

- ✔ **Border Color:** Changes the line's color.

- ✔ **Border Width:** Makes the line anything from a wispy hairline to a bold 6-point behemoth.

Experiment with the settings to come up with the best combination for you. As with the special effects settings, click the X button at the top-right corner to close the Properties box after you're done.

Changing the field tab order

When you have a window open inside of any program and press the Tab key, the cursor moves from control to control in a pre-defined order. Access allows you to create a tab order so that the cursor moves through your forms in a rational manner (such as going to Last Name from First Name). You accomplish this by changing the Tab Index property of each control as follows:

1. **With the form open in Design view, choose View⇨Tab Order.**

   The Tab Order dialog box opens, listing the fields in their current tab order.

2. **Click the small square to the left of the field you want to work with (as shown in Figure 22-10).**

   The field appears highlighted.

Figure 22-10: In the Tab Order dialog box, you can rearrange the order that the cursor moves through your fields.

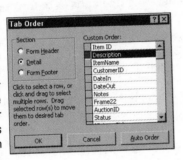

To have Access 2002 automatically set the tab order for all the fields in the form, click the Auto Order button at the bottom of the Tab Order dialog box. Access 2002 sets the order according to where the field is in the form. It starts from the upper-left side of the form and goes across, and then moves down one line and repeats the process. Fields end up in order horizontally (fields on line one, fields on line two, and so on).

3. **Click and drag the field to its new position in the tab order.**

   As you drag the field, a dark gray bar moves with it, showing where the field goes into the tab order. When the bar is in the right place, release the button. Access moves the field into its new position in the tab order.

4. **Repeat Steps 2 and 3 for any other fields you want to change.**

   Access doesn't care how much you work with the tab order, so play to your heart's content.

5. **Click OK after you're done adjusting the tab order.**

   The Tab Order dialog box runs off to wherever dialog boxes hang out when they're not on-screen.

6. **Click the Form View button on the toolbar and test your work.**

   If any fields are still out of order, note which ones they are and then work back through these steps to fix the order.

Chapter 23

If Love Is Universal, Why Can't I Export to It?

In This Chapter

▶ Pulling data into Access 2002

▶ Deciding when to import and when to link data

▶ Speaking in foreign data tongues

▶ Pushing your comfortable data into the cold, cruel outside world

To achieve true success these days, speaking only the tongue of the country that bore you isn't enough. You need to be comfortable with several languages before the pinnacle of achievement is within your grasp. I, for example, am fluent in American English, a language that the British view as a poor substitute for grunting and knocking rocks together. For work, I also studied several variants of the vernacular Nerd, including Windows, DOS, the pictorial troubleshooting tongue $%@&#!, and the esoteric dialect Macintosh (which is particularly challenging because all the words in it look and act alike).

Access 2002 is multilingual as well, because its electronic world is filled with more disagreeing tongues than the United Nations in general session. To simplify your life, Access 2002 understands a couple of spreadsheets, several competing databases, and even plain old text files. Because of this capability, you can exchange data with almost any source out there. Access 2002 is one of the most flexible programs I've ever seen (and I've seen a *bunch* of programs).

This chapter looks at the import and export capabilities of Access 2002, how they work, and what you can do with them. If you work with Access 2002 and almost *any* other program, you need this chapter, because sometime soon, some data will be in the wrong place — and guess whose job it is to move it....

Importing Only the Best Information for Your Databases

Access 2002 includes two ways of sucking data into its greedy clutches. *Importing* involves translating the data from a foreign format into the Access 2002 database file format (which, according to Microsoft, all the world's data should be stored in). The other method is *linking,* where you build a temporary bridge between the external data and Access 2002.

If you worked with older versions of Access, linking used to be called *attaching.* The concept is the same; only the name has been changed to confuse the innocent.

Translating file formats

Regardless of whether you import or link the data, Access 2002 understands only certain data formats. Table 23-1 lists the most common file types that Access interacts with. Believe it or not, the entries in this table cover the majority of data stored on PCs around the world.

Table 23-1		Access 2002 Language Fluencies	
Program	**File Extension**	**Versions**	**Comments**
Access	.MDB	2.0, 7.0/95, 8.0/97, 9.0/2000, 10.0/2002	Although they share the same name, these versions use slightly different file formats than Access 2002.
ODBC	N/A	N/A	Use Open Database Connectivity to connect to other databases such as Oracle.
dBASE	.DBF	III, IV, 5	One of the most popular formats out there; many programs use the dBASE format.
FoxPro	.DBF	2.x, 3.0, 5.0, 6.x	The other desktop database program of Microsoft; not directly compatible with dBASE in some cases.
Paradox	.DB	3.x, 4.x, 5.0	A competing database from Borland.

Program	File Extension	Versions	Comments
Excel	.XLS	3.0, 4.0, 5.0, 7.0/95, 8.0/97, 9.0/2000, 10.0/2002	Although it's a spreadsheet, many people use Excel as a simple flat-file database manager.
Lotus 1-2-3	.WKS, .WK1, .WK31, .WK4	All	At one time, the most popular spreadsheet.
Text	.TXT	N/A	The "if all else fails" format; Access 2002 understands both delimited and fixed-width text files.
XML	.XML	All	XML, eXtensible Markup Language, stores and describes your data.
HTML	.HTM, .HTML	1.0 (lists), 2.0 (tables), 3.x (tables)	The Web page codes that make a Web page a Web page.

Although Access 2002 is pretty intelligent about the translation process, you need to watch out for some quirks. Here are some specific tips to keep in mind as you play The Great Data Liberator and set imperiled information free to enjoy a new life in Access 2002:

✔ When working with dBASE and FoxPro files, keep careful track of the index files that go along with the database files. Access 2002 needs the index to work with the table. If Access can't find the index or if it's corrupt, try canceling the prompt that requests the index file and see if the import worked.

✔ Access 2002 has problems linking to Paradox tables that don't have a primary key. Specifically, Access 2002 can't write changes to the unkeyed Paradox table. To fix the problem, use Paradox to create a primary key in the table and *then* link the table to Access 2002.

✔ Remember that data in Paradox tables *isn't* stored in a single file. Having a .PX (the primary index) and a .MB (memo data — I don't know what the *B* is supposed to stand for) file lurking around the .DB file is common. If you copy a Paradox table from one computer to another, take care to copy *all* of the associated files!

✔ Double-check information coming from any spreadsheet program to be sure that it's *consistent* and *complete*. Above all, make sure that all of the entries in each column (field) are the same type (all numbers, text, or whatever). Otherwise, the import won't work right (and you know how forgiving software is of such "little" problems).

✔ If you have difficulty importing a given format, you can try using the old database product to open the respective file, and exporting the database tables as text files (the data techies use its formal name, *ASCII*). Text may be cumbersome to manage, but it's the most widely recognized form of data known to man (or computer).

Always back up your data before importing, exporting, or even leaving the office for a short vacation. The computer person's advice always begins "Well, nothing should go wrong," but wise folks prepare for the worst. Make copies of your databases *before* trying the techniques in this chapter.

Importing or linking your files

The precise details of importing and linking depend greatly on the type of file you're importing, but here are the general steps to get you started in the right direction. Although the instructions are written mainly for importing, they include supporting notes about linking as well.

Ready to take a spin at the *Data Import Polka?* Here goes:

1. **Open the Access 2002 database that you're pulling data into.**

   If you're not familiar with this step, *stop* — don't go any further. Flip to Chapter 1 and spend some time getting comfy with Access 2002 before attempting an import.

2. **Choose File⇨Get External Data⇨Import.**

   The dialog box shown in Figure 23-1 appears.

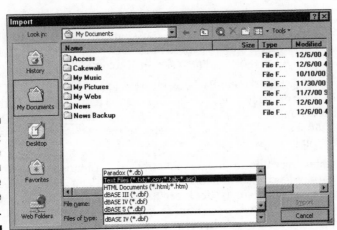

Figure 23-1: Make sure that you pick the correct file type.

3. **Click the down arrow in the Files of Type box (at the bottom of the window) and click the kind of data you're importing. (If necessary, use the Look In list box to navigate your way to the files.)**

The dialog box displays the matching files for your selection pleasure. Make sure that you choose the correct file type. Otherwise, Access doesn't list the file you're looking for in the dialog box!

If your database file has a strange, nonstandard extension on the end of the filename (like .FOO, .DTA, or .XXX), Access 2002 may not be able to make heads or tails of the file. In that case, seek help from your technical support people or local computer jockey.

4. **Double-click the file that you want to import.**

Here's where the process takes off in wildly different directions depending on the file format you're importing and whether you're linking or importing. The only sage advice I can give is to cross your fingers, follow the on-screen instructions carefully, refer to the preceding tips, hope for the best, and take comfort in the knowledge that you made backup copies of your databases before starting this sordid process. (You *did* make those backups, right?)

If you're importing and the process is taking *forever,* Access is probably struggling with errors in the inbound data. Press Ctrl+Break to stop the import process and check the data that's being imported for obvious errors (bad or corrupt data, badly organized spreadsheet data, invalid index, and so on).

Sending Your Data on a Long, One-Way Trip

In the interest of keeping you awake, I'll keep this explanation short: Exporting is just like importing, except where it's different.

Hmm . . . perhaps that explanation was a little *too* short.

Exporting a table involves reorganizing the data it contains into a different format. Like importing, Access 2002 can translate the data into a variety of "languages," depending on your needs. The master list of export formats is the same one governing imports, described earlier in the chapter.

The main problem to keep an eye out for when exporting is *data loss*. Not all storage formats are created equal (after all, Microsoft didn't come up with them *all,* which is arguably a good situation). Just because the data looked glorious in your Access 2002 table doesn't mean a suitable home is waiting when you ship the information off to, say, Paradox or FoxPro. Special Access 2002 data types such as *AutoNumber, Yes/No, Memo,* and *OLE* are almost sure to cause problems. Be ready for some creative problem solving to make the data work just the way you want it to work.

Likewise, field names can be trouble. Access 2002 is very generous about what you can put into a field name. dBASE, on the other hand, is downright totalitarian about field names. This attitude can lead to multiple fields with the same name — a frustrating (if slightly humorous) problem. If you export an Access 2002 table with fields called Projected2000Sales, Projected2000Net, and Projected2000Overhead, ending up with three fields named *Projected1* is distinctly possible — *not* a pleasant thought. Be ready to spend some time tuning the export so that it works just the way you want it.

The steps to exporting a table are much simpler than they are for importing. Here goes:

1. **With the database open, click the table that you want to export.**

   As you may expect, the table name is highlighted for the world to see.

2. **Choose File⇨Export from the main menu.**

   The Export Table dialog box bounds merrily onto the screen.

3. **Click the down arrow in the Save As Type box to list the available exporting formats; then select the one you want (as shown in Figure 23-2).**

Figure 23-2:
I choose to export a table as HTML.

If the format you're looking for is in Table 23-1 but is not in your list on-screen, run the Access 2002 setup program again (oh joy, oh rapture!) and install that format on your system.

4. Brace yourself and click Export.

Depending on the file type you export to, you may get absolutely no feedback that the export was successful other than lack of an error message. You *should* be able to go to the other program and see your table there.

If you export to HTML or to XML, you can check Autostart (refer to Figure 23-2). Internet Explorer opens, displaying your data, as shown in Figure 23-3.

When exporting to HML or XML, experienced developers will next edit the file that Access created. While the Web page that was created in Figure 23-3 was easy, it's not real attractive. You can edit the file and add appropriate formatting, colors, and so on.

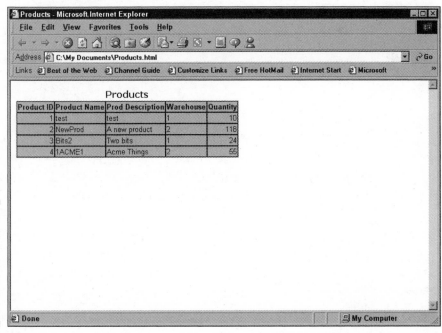

Figure 23-3:
Internet Explorer proudly displays my Products table.

To import or to link — the answer is, it depends

Because Access 2002 offers two different ways to get data in, a logical question comes up: Which method should I use? Because this question involves a computer, the simple answer is that it depends.

The answer mainly depends on the other program and its fate within your organization. Are you still using the other program to update the data? Do other people use the program to access the data? If so, use a link with Access 2002. This option lets you play with the data while keeping it in the original format so that everyone else can use it as well.

On the other hand, if the other application was mothballed and you're rescuing data, import the data permanently and give it a comfortable new home. Preserving a data format that nobody cares about anymore makes no sense.

Chapter 24

The Analyzer: Your Data's Dr. Freud, Dr. Watson, and Dr. Jekyll

In This Chapter

▶ Becoming relational with the Table Analyzer

▶ Making the database document

▶ Steering clear of the Performance Analyzer

*I*f I didn't know better, I'd file this chapter under the heading *Oh Sure, That's What It Does* (said with heavy sarcasm). After all, the Analyzer promises to do the three tasks nearest to a database person's heart:

✔ Convert flat files into relational databases automatically

✔ Document the database and all its sundry parts (including tables, queries, forms, reports, and more)

✔ Analyze the structure of your tables to make sure that everything is set up in the best possible way

Although technology has come a *long* way in recent years, it's not as advanced as you may expect. That caveat is true of the Analyzer, too — it promises more than it delivers. On the bright side, it delivers a great deal, so the Analyzer gets a chapter of its own, a place to extol its two virtues and reveal its shortcoming. (I guess one out of three isn't bad.)

It Slices, It Dices, It Builds Relational Databases!

Arguably, the Analyzer's biggest promise is hiding under Tools➪Analyze➪Table. This piece of software claims it can turn a flat file table into a relational database with minimal human intervention *and* check for spelling errors in the data at the same time.

Truth be told, the Analyzer *tries* awfully hard to convert the flat file into a relational database. But, like most software, sometimes it gets confused and vaults off in the wrong direction. I still recommend giving the Analyzer a try, simply because it *may* work on your table, and if it does, you just saved a ton of time and effort.

The Analyzer works best with a flat file table that contains plenty of duplicate information. For example, I created a table with records containing customer information, order information, and room for up to four items to be purchased on that order. Because orders are on the customer record, every time a customer places an order, the customer information has to be entered all over again. Likewise, because item descriptions are stored in the same table, every time a customer orders an item, item information has to be entered over and over again. I've created a relational nightmare!

With that thought in mind, here's how to invoke the Table Analyzer Wizard:

1. **Open your database and choose <u>T</u>ools⇨<u>A</u>nalyze⇨<u>T</u>able.**

   After a period of thought punctuated by hard disk activity, the Table Analyzer Wizard dialog box appears on-screen (as shown in Figure 24-1).

Figure 24-1:
Introducing
the Table
Analyzer.

Table Analyzer Wizard

The Table Analyzer: Looking At the Problem

Your table or spreadsheet may store the same information many times. Duplicating information can cause problems.

First, duplicating information wastes space.

Show me an example.

Second, duplicating information can lead to mistakes.

Show me an example.

Products and Suppliers

Product	Supplier ID	Supplier	Address
Ravioli Angelo	PAST	Pasta Buttini s.	Via dei Gelsomir
Gnocchi di nonr	PAST	Pasta Buttini s.	Via dei Gelsomir
Carnarvon Tige	PAVL	Pavlova, Ltd.	74 Rose St.
Outback Lager	PAVL	Pavlova, Ltd.	74 Rose St.
Pavlova	PAVL	Pavlova, Ltd.	74 Rose St.
Vegie-spread	PAVL	Pav, Ltd.	74 Rose St.

Supplier name is misspelled.

Supplier information is repeated.

Cancel   < Back   Next >   Finish

2. **Read the first two screens if you want (they're strictly educational); click <u>N</u>ext after each one.**

   Another Table Analyzer Wizard screen appears (see Figure 24-2).

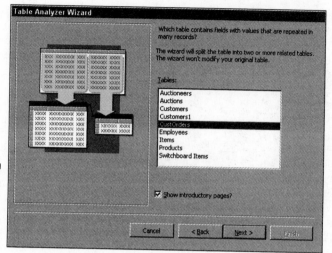

Figure 24-2:
Select a
table to
analyze.

3. **Click the name of the table on which you want to do relational magic and then click Next.**

   In the dialog box that appears, the wizard asks whether it can analyze the table and offer suggestions about how the table ought to work.

4. **Click the Yes radio button (if it's not already selected) and then click Next.**

   This step is the pivotal one in the whole process. The wizard leaps into the task, displaying a couple of horizontal bar charts to show how the project is progressing. When the Analysis Stages bar gets all the way to the end, the wizard is done. The results look like those shown in Figure 24-3.

5. **If you like what the wizard came up with, name the tables by clicking each table and then clicking the Name Table button (the one that looks like a pencil doodling on a table). Or, you can use your mouse to drag and drop fields from table to table and rename the tables. When you're done, click Next.**

   If the wizard recommends that you don't split your table, carefully click the Cancel button and pat yourself on the head for a job well done. That's the wizard's way of saying that it thinks your table is fine just as it is.

6. **Designate a key field by clicking a field in the table and then clicking the Key button.**

   This step lets you replace many of the Generated Unique ID entries that the wizard put in the tables. Make sure that each table has a key field before continuing!

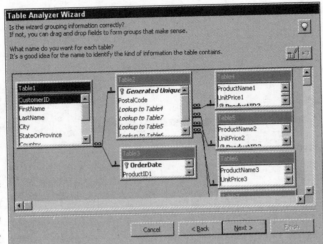

Figure 24-3:
Unfortu-
nately,
Access
didn't do a
good job of
analyzing
the
database.

Now that the structure is basically complete, the wizard turns its attention to typographical errors within the database. Essentially, the Wizard acts as a spell checker by searching for fields that *seem* to be the same except for minor differences.

You don't have to do anything to make the "typo-checker" kick in. Typo-checking happens automatically after Access analyzes the database structure. Depending on the condition of your data, you may have *many* records to correct. Be patient — the wizard really *is* helping!

After the wizard makes corrections, it offers to create a query that looks and acts like your original table. If you have reports and forms that work with the flat file, they'll work with the new table(s).

7. **Click the No radio button if you've changed your mind and want to forget the whole thing. Otherwise, click Finish to exit the wizard.**

Access now creates a query that runs against your original table. The query looks and acts like a "real" table. The original table is renamed and any reports and forms will now automatically use the query instead of the original table.

The Table Analyzer is highly unlikely to correctly split a flat file database into a properly designed relational database. You're *much* better off bringing the database to a qualified human and letting him or her properly redesign it.

Documentation: What to Give the Nerd in Your Life

Pardon me while I put on my technoweenie hat and taped-together glasses for a moment. The world needs more (can't ever have enough, in fact) *documentation*. If life were better documented, it would be easier.

In truth, documentation is probably the task furthest from your mind right now, but it's still important, especially if you're creating something for your business. I know that you barely have time to get the database running and tested, but you *absolutely* need to document what you're creating.

Like many problems, documenting your work is a tradeoff between a dire need and a lack of time. What's a person to do? Call the Documenter!

This second piece of the Analyzer puzzle browses through everything in your database (and I do mean *everything*) and documents the living daylights out of it all. This collects information so obscure that I'm not even sure the programmers know what some of it means.

The neat part of the Documenter is that it works *by itself*. Really. You start it, sic it on a database, and nip off for a spot of lunch. When you come back, the Documenter's report is done and waiting. {Poof!} Instant documentation.

Here's how to put the Documenter to work on your database:

1. **Open the database file and choose Tools⇨Analyze⇨Documenter.**

   The Database Documenter appears on-screen.

2. **In the Documenter dialog box, click the All Object Types tab and then click the Select All button to document your entire database (see Figure 24-4). When you're ready, click OK to start the process.**

Figure 24-4:
Click the
All Object
Types tab
and then
click
Select All.

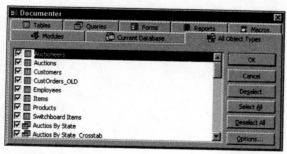

The Documenter begins by examining all the objects in your database, starting with the tables, and moving on to the queries, forms, reports, and so on. During the process, your forms appear on-screen for a moment — that's normal.

The process often takes a while, so this is a good time for lunch or a little coffee break.

When the Documenter finishes, it leaves a report packed with information about your database (as shown in Figure 24-5).

3. **Click the Print button on the toolbar or choose File⇨Print to get a paper copy.**

   If you want to store the report for posterity, choose File⇨Save As Table and then give the table a name.

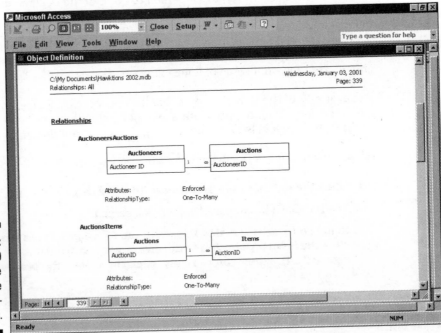

Figure 24-5: Page 339 shows some of the table relationships.

Performance: Toward a Better Database

WARNING!

Like the Design Analyzer, the Performance Analyzer is far from perfect. When you run it (and you should), take the suggestions with a grain of salt.

To use the Performance Analyzer, follow these steps:

1. **Open the database file and choose Tools⇨Analyze⇨Performance.**

   The Database Performance Analyzer appears on-screen.

2. **Choose the objects that you want to analyze and click Next.**

   I recommend clicking the All Object Types tab and clicking the Select All button the same way as you did for the Documentation tool. The screen is identical to that shown in Figure 24-4.

3. **Select each result (as shown in Figure 24-6) and review the comments.**

   If Access can make the changes for you, the Optimize button will be enabled. Otherwise, use a pencil and paper and jot down any good thoughts that Access may have had.

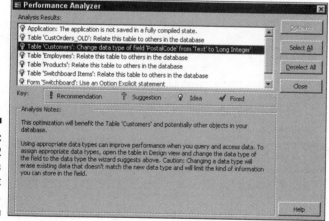

Figure 24-6:
Access 2002 tells you its innermost thoughts.

Chapter 25

Talking to Your Computer

- -

In This Chapter

▶ Understanding speech recognition

▶ Using speech recognition to dictate text

▶ Using speech recognition Command mode

- -

*I*t wasn't long ago that talking to your computer marked you as a disturbed person or a Trekkie. Perceptions have changed. All of the Office suite, including Access, has the Lernout & Hauspie (L & H) speech recognition engine built-in. That means that you can pretty much tell Access 2002 what to do and have a reasonable expectation that it won't talk back. (Did you ever wish your significant other would do the same?)

Most people find speech recognition in Access to be of limited usefulness unless their database contains a lot of lengthy text fields where dictation may come in handy. Yet, if you're are among the many thousands who have trouble using keyboards, voice recognition may well be a savior.

In this chapter, I provide you with an explanation of how speech recognition works in Access 2002 and how to use it.

What Is Speech Recognition (And What Can I Do with It)?

Speech recognition is an amazing technology. The computer "listens" to what you say by breaking electronic signals from a microphone into individual *tokens* and then combining those tokens into words based on a predefined vocabulary that the software understands. (So, if you said "gastroenterologist," the software would likely be confused unless you had previously bought and installed a medical vocabulary.) However, it gets even more complicated than that.

Consider the phrase "To be or not to be." For the computer to understand what you're saying, it has to discern among several possibilities for each word. For example, is the first word "to," "too," or "two?" They all sound alike. The second word might be "be" or "bee" and the third could be "or" or "ore." So, the computer has to apply some grammatical rules to discern among "to," "too," and "two."

Further complicating the process of speech recognition is the fact that we all talk differently and we may be in a noisy environment. Accurate speech recognition is nothing short of a miracle and yet is far from perfect. All that said, people with repetitive strain injuries or other handicaps may find speech recognition a boon.

You can use the speech recognition feature in two ways:

- **Dictation:** Place the cursor in the customer last name field, and say "Smith." Access 2002 responds by typing the word "Smith" for you. You can use dictation pretty much anywhere you can type text.

- **Command:** Dictate commands such as Print to print a document.

Installing Speech Recognition

Naturally, your PC has to be able to handle speech recognition. Microsoft recommends the following *minimum* configuration for your computer:

- A high-quality headset-based microphone with gain adjustment (built-in amplification). Microsoft recommends a USB microphone.

- A 400 MHz or faster CPU.

- 128MB memory.

- Windows 98 or later or Windows NT 4.0 or later.

- Microsoft Internet Explorer 5.0 or later.

As a practical matter, the key requirement in the above list is the memory — I tested speech recognition on a 350 MHz PC with 256MB of memory, and speech recognition worked well. On the other hand, I also tested on 400 MHz and 733 MHz PCs, both with 128MB of memory. The performance on the 733 MHz PC was not great; the performance on the 400 MHz PC was dismal.

Your results may not match my own. Certainly, running a lot of software simultaneously increases how powerful your computer needs to be.

As you may expect, before you can use speech recognition, you have to install it. You may have selected speech recognition as an option when you installed Access. If not, you can install speech recognition by choosing Tools⇨Speech.

All of the Office applications share the speech recognition feature. You need install it only once. If you prefer, you can install it from Word or Excel the same way.

Sending Access to Voice Training School

Before you can use speech recognition effectively, you need to train it to recognize your speech patterns. Bostonians, with their rapid speech and refusal to sound out the letter R, sound very different than do residents of Biloxi and New Orleans with their slow, Southern drawls. The training process helps the computer to understand how *you* say "hello" and "goodbye."

Access enters training mode automatically the first time you try to use speech recognition. If you find that the computer isn't doing a good job of understanding you, you can give it more training by selecting Training on the Speech toolbar (which opens any time you invoke speech recognition).

To train Access to recognize your speech patterns, follow these steps:

1. **Put on the headset and place the microphone about an inch from your mouth.**

   Avoid putting the microphone directly in front of your mouth, where it will detect breathing sounds. Try to position the microphone the same way every time you use the speech recognition feature.

2. **Choose Tools⇨Speech.**

   Access displays the Welcome box as shown in Figure 25-1.

Figure 25-1:
Welcome to
Office
Speech
Recognition.

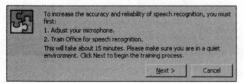

To increase the accuracy and reliability of speech recognition, you must first:
1. Adjust your microphone.
2. Train Office for speech recognition.
This will take about 15 minutes. Please make sure you are in a quiet environment. Click Next to begin the training process.

Next >   Cancel

3. **Follow the prompts on the next few screens to set up the optimal volume on your microphone.**

Office adjusts your volume settings behind the scenes as you read a few sentences. You're ready to train the computer to recognize your voice!

4. **Follow the prompts to read displayed text into the microphone (see Figure 25-2).**

Access keeps track of your progress and highlights words as it understands them. If it doesn't recognize a word, Access leaves that word unhighlighted. Simply repeat the word or phrase. You're finished!

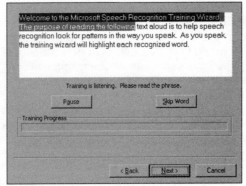

Figure 25-2:
Access highlights words as it understands them.

When you finish speech recognition training, you see the window shown in Figure 25-3. Note that Access promises only about 85 percent accuracy at first. The more you use speech recognition, the better it understands you.

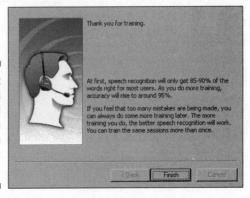

Figure 25-3:
Access has completed the training course on understanding *you*.

If recognition accuracy is too low, you can return to training mode for additional reading exercises. Retraining is a quick way to improve accuracy.

Speaking to Access

To turn on speech recognition, choose Tools⇨Speech. The Language toolbar appears, as shown in Figure 25-4. Turn the Microphone on or off by clicking the Microphone icon.

The first time you choose Speech, you launch into training mode automatically.

Figure 25-4:
The Language toolbar is your access to the world of speech recognition.

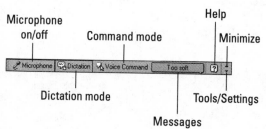

Microphone on/off

Command mode

Help

Minimize

Dictation mode

Messages

Tools/Settings

The Language toolbar gives you access to several alternative input methods besides speech recognition. For example, if you have a graphics tablet attached to your PC, you can write on the tablet with a stylus and use Office's handwriting feature to turn your writing into text.

You can use speech recognition in either dictation or command mode. Understanding the difference between the two modes is important. Suppose, for example, you say the word "open." How Access responds depends on whether it's in dictation or command mode. In dictation mode, Access types the word, whereas in command mode, it displays the File Open dialog box.

The next sections cover each mode in turn.

"Access, take a letter please"

Dictation mode works just like it sounds — you speak into the microphone and Access types what you say (or at least what it *thinks* you said). To go into dictation mode, follow these steps:

1. **If you're in Command mode, click the Dictation button on the Language toolbar or say "dictation."**

    The Speech bar always displays the current mode: Dictation or Command.

2. **Click in the box where you want to type and start speaking.**

    Speak in a normal voice, enunciating each word, but not pausing between words.

Watch the Language toolbar for any prompts. For example, in Figure 25-4, Access tells me that I'm speaking too softly. Figure 25-5 shows the result of my dictating to Access. In the first record, Access recognized what I said with no errors. In the second record, I said, "This is record number three. I have already deleted record number two." Figure 25-5 shows what Access *thought* I said. See the section "Correcting dictation errors" later in this chapter for details about smoothing out the misunderstandings.

To get out of Dictation mode, click Voice Command on the Language toolbar or say "voice command." Alternatively, you can turn off the microphone by clicking the Microphone button on the Language toolbar.

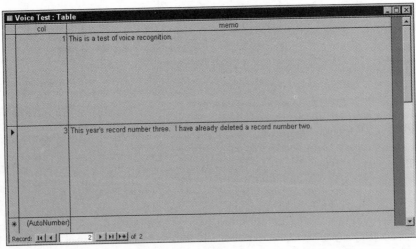

Figure 25-5:
The results of dictating three sentences — one is perfect, one is close, and one is pretty well mangled.

When dictating, you can spell out any word by saying "spelling mode," pausing a moment, and then saying the letters.

Built into dictation mode are a number of special things you can say. Table 25-1 lists some of the more common commands.

For a complete list of dictation mode commands, search the Help file for "Things you can do and say with speech recognition."

Table 25-1	Select Dictation Mode Commands Access 2002 Understands
What You Say	**What's Inserted**
Dot or period	.
At sign	@
Comma	,
Backslash	\
Slash	/
Equals	=
Plus or Plus sign	+
New line	Enter
New paragraph	Enter Enter
1	One (numbers less than 20 are spelled out)
21	21 (numbers 20 or greater are inserted as digits)

Correcting dictation errors

You can correct errors anytime during dictation. Microsoft recommends that you wait until you're done dictating so that you don't interrupt your train of thought. I tried dictating several pages of text and then went back to correct errors. I couldn't even recall what I was trying to say. It's up to you how and when you correct errors — experiment to see which method suits you.

You can correct errors in three ways:

- **Retype the errors.** Select the text in error and simply retype it. This method is often the easiest.

- **Dictate over the errors.** Highlight the incorrect text by using your mouse or keyboard and re-dictate.

If you decide to dictate over an error, you're best off highlighting a whole phrase. For example, in Figure 25-5 I said, "This is record number three" but the computer heard "This year's record number three." I could have highlighted the word "year's" and re-dictated "is." But speech recognition is more accurate with phrases. Selecting and re-dictating "This is record" or perhaps even the whole sentence serves you better.

✔ **Spell over the errors.** Select an error by using the mouse or keyboard, say "spelling mode," pause a moment, and then say each letter of the word, pausing between letters. Say "dictation mode" when you're done.

Using Command mode

Command mode lets you tell Access what to do. For example, if you open a datasheet and say "print," Access sends the datasheet to the printer immediately.

If you're in dictation mode, you can go into command mode by saying "voice command." (You can also click Voice Command on the language toolbar.) Here are some guidelines for using command mode:

✔ To select toolbar items, say the name of the toolbar button, such as Save or Spelling. If you don't know the name of a toolbar item, pause the mouse cursor over it to display a screen tip.

✔ To open a menu, say its name. For example, saying "file" prompts the File menu to drop down. If you then say "insert," the Insert menu drops down.

✔ To select a menu item, say its name while the menu is open. For example, to display the About box, say "help" to open the Help menu and then say "about Microsoft Access."

✔ To "click" a button, say its name. For example, saying "okay" activates the OK button.

✔ To work with windows and dialog boxes, say the caption of the control that you want to work with. For example, Figure 25-6 shows the Options dialog box in Access. To move to the Spelling tab, say its name. To check the top check box, say "suggest from main dictionary only." Saying "suggest from main dictionary only" a second time causes the box to be unchecked. To access the drop-down list of languages, say "dictionary language."

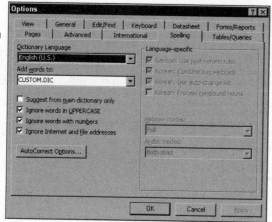

Figure 25-6:
While in
Command
mode, you
can work in
any window
or dialog
box without
touching the
mouse or
keyboard.

As with dictation mode, command mode recognizes some specific commands. Table 25-2 lists commands and their actions.

Table 25-2	Select Command Mode Commands Access 2002 Understands
What You Say	*What Happens*
Left or go left	Left Arrow
Right or go right	Right Arrow
Page down	Page Down
Page Up	Page Up
Tab	Tab
Delete	Delete
Right-click	Open context menu
Escape	Press ESC
Return or Enter	Press ENTER
Space	Press Spacebar

Improving Speech Recognition

The following are some tips on increasing speech recognition accuracy in Access 2002. For more tips, consult the Help file and also check out the Microsoft Office Web site by clicking Office on the Web on the Access Help menu.

- ✔ Work in a quiet environment. If you work in a noisy office, Access tries to detect what everyone else around you is saying.

- ✔ Use a high-quality microphone. Make sure it provides signal boost and that it's unidirectional ("listens" in only one direction).

- ✔ Wear the headset and microphone in the same position each time you dictate. Make sure the microphone is about an inch from your lips but not right in front of your lips (it's best if the microphone is just below or to the side of your mouth).

- ✔ Use a high quality sound card. If you detect hissing through your headset, so does Access. Try moving the sound card as far away from the power supply as possible.

- ✔ Speak in phrases rather than pausing between words. Enunciate clearly.

- ✔ Turn off the microphone when you're not dictating.

- ✔ Train your computer by reading prepared texts in the training wizard.

- ✔ Add new words to the dictionary by choosing Tools➪Add/Delete words. Type the new word and then pronounce it.

Part VI
The Part of Tens

The 5th Wave   By Rich Tennant

"This isn't a quantitative or a qualitative estimate of the job. This is a wish-upon-a-star estimate of the project."

In this part . . .

All hail the traditional Part of Tens, purveyor of numerically organized information, keeper of the sacred decimal count, and upholder of the proud *For Dummies* tradition.

Every *For Dummies* book closes with a Part of Tens. I guess it's the *For Dummies* version of denouement. Anyway, this book's final part includes stuff you can use today, stuff you may need tomorrow, and stuff for *way* on down the road. I tried to include a little something for everyone, so read every chapter *very* closely and see if you can find the stuff that I put in just for you.

By the way, no animals were harmed, exploited, or even consulted in the quest to bring you this information (although I did remember to feed my dog periodically throughout the project). One technoweenie was slightly miffed, but I'm sure he'll get over it.

Chapter 26

Ten Timesaving Keyboard Shortcuts

• •

*J*ust because Windows is supposed to be the ultimate graphical user environment doesn't mean that you won't need the keyboard anymore. In fact, Access 2002 has some cool shortcuts up its sleeve that are available only through this special, keyboard-based offer.

This chapter highlights ten cool shortcuts designed to make your life a little easier. Some keystroke combinations enter data automatically, some make editing quicker, and others are for fun.

Select an Entire Field — F2

This shortcut is particularly handy when you're replacing a lengthy address or description field. Instead of wrestling with the mouse to make sure that you have *everything* in the field highlighted, simply press F2 and you *know* that it's done. The keystroke works in both Datasheet view and Form view.

Insert the Current Date — Ctrl+; (Semicolon)

This keystroke combination and the following one not only save time, but also increase accuracy. Ever mistype a date because you were in a hurry (or because the keyboard can't spell)? Ctrl+; resolves the issue completely by working for you. To properly execute this command, press the Ctrl button first and while holding down the Ctrl button, press the semicolon button at the same time. The keystroke works in Datasheet view and Form view.

Insert the Current Time — Ctrl+: (Colon)

This shortcut is another nod to accuracy. To insert the current time, you press the Ctrl button and Shift button first, and while holding down the two buttons, press the semicolon button at the same time. Although Ctrl+: is the actual keystroke to get a colon, you have to do the Shift+; (semicolon) routine. The keystroke works in Datasheet view and Form view.

Insert the Same Field Value as the Last Record Ctrl+' (Apostrophe)

While entering data, you often come across a whole bunch of records containing similar information — for example, people from the same city and state. Instead of manually typing the duplicate information in every record, the Ctrl+' (apostrophe) keystroke quickly enters it for you in both the Datasheet view and Form view.

Ctrl+' (apostrophe) isn't psychic, though. Instead, it merely says, "Well, I see that you're in the City field. In the last record, the city was *Tucumcari,* so I bet that's what you want in this record, too." And then it promptly copies the value from the preceding record into the current one. (Of course, this works for any field, not just address information.)

Insert a Line Break — Ctrl+Enter

When a long entry in a memo or large text field feels like it's never going to quit, end the monotony with a line break. Well-placed line breaks make your data more legible, too. The keystroke is available in Datasheet view and Form view.

Add a New Record — Ctrl++ (Plus Sign)

Although Ctrl++ looks funny (just how *do* you write *plus* + without spelling it out?), this keyboard shortcut keeps you on the go when you're in a hot-and-heavy edit mode. Because you don't have to keep switching between the keyboard and the mouse to insert new records, your speed increases, as does your accuracy. This keystroke may seem strange but this one works with Ctrl+= (equal) also. I guess the Access gurus figured that because the + sign and = sign are on the same button on many keyboards, it's easier to remember that + means adding something such as a record, then the = sign. No doubt to your surprise, this shortcut works in Datasheet view and Form view.

Delete the Current Record — Ctrl+– (Minus Sign)

Do you suffer from pesky, unsightly, or unneeded records in your tables? Ctrl+– painlessly excises the records that you want to delete. And just like this shortcut's cousin, Ctrl++, this shortcut works in both Datasheet view and Form view.

Save the Record — Shift+Enter

After a long, hard edit, make sure that the record is saved with a quick Shift+Enter. That signals Access 2002 that you're truly done working on this one and are ready to store it for posterity. The software takes the cue and saves your changes immediately. Use this key combo in Datasheet view or Form view. It's a real time-saver!

Undo Your Last Changes — Ctrl+Z

Everyone should have this one memorized. The Undo keystroke is a golden oldie. With the propensity of Access 2002 to automatically save changes every time you turn around, it can really save your bacon. When something goes wrong, don't panic — try Ctrl+Z instead. This keystroke combination works almost everywhere in Access 2002 and even beyond in many Windows applications.

Open the Selected Object in Design View — Ctrl+Enter

Hey, what's this? Ctrl+Enter does *two* functions in Access 2002? You're right.

- ✔ When you're editing a table in *Datasheet* view or *Form* view, Ctrl+Enter inserts a line break.
- ✔ When you're in *Database* view, use Ctrl+Enter to whip open something in Design view.

Let the *ordinary folks* use the mouse — be different and do it from the keyboard!

Chapter 27

Ten Common Crises and How to Survive Them

In This Chapter

▶ Mysteriously changing numbers

▶ Misplacing tables

▶ Vanishing files and records

▶ Unasked questions

*W*here there are computers, so also is there software, because a computer is nothing without its software. Where there is software, so also are there problems, because software without problems is obviously outdated and in need of replacement.

Problems are a part of life. When the problems strike in or around your precious data, they seem all the more fearsome. This chapter touches on ten problems you may encounter while using Access 2002. If your problem is covered here, try the solution I outline. If your particular trouble isn't on the list, refer to Chapter 3 for some other spots to seek help.

And good luck. (I mean it!)

You Type 73.725, but It Changes to 74 by Itself

Automatic rounding can frustrate the living daylights out of you, but fixing it is easy. By default, Access 2002 sets all number fields to accept *long integers* — numbers without decimal places. You need to change the setting to *single*, which is short for *single precision number*, not *hey you swinging text field, let's go party with the forms*.

To fix the problem, open the table in Design view and then click the field that's giving you fits. On the General tab of the Properties area at the bottom of the screen, click in the Field Size box. Click the down arrow on the end of the box; then select Single from the drop-down menu that appears. Save the table and your automatic rounding problem is over.

You Run a Query but the Results Are Screwy!

Well, you could look under the bed but that probably won't help. And if you have a bed in your cubicle, *someone* is in trouble. Getting unexpected results from a query is common. The problem always stems from one of these three issues:

- ✔ **You got your selection criteria wrong.** For example, in Chapter 13, I talk about how to mix and match And and Or. Nevertheless, getting confused when using Ands and Ors in your queries is easy. So, if you get some peculiar results from a query, double-check your search criteria and refer to Chapter 11 for a review of the Query Designer.

- ✔ **You joined the tables incorrectly or not at all.** If your query results show *way* too many records coming back and the query uses two or more tables, improper joining is the likely cause. Flip back to Chapter 12 where I cover joining one table to another.

- ✔ **You joined the tables correctly, but Access 2002 isn't finding a legitimate match between the tables.** If your query involves two or more tables and you get fewer records than you expected, this is the likely cause. For example, if you have an order entry database and run a query listing all customers and their orders, by default you would see only those customers who have placed an order. To see all customers whether or not they have placed an order, do this:

  1. **In the Query Designer, right-click the join (the line connecting the two tables) and choose Join Properties.**

     If you need a refresher about joining tables in the Query Designer, check out Chapter 12.

  2. **Examine the types of joins offered and choose the one that says something like "Include ALL records from 'Customers' and only those records from 'Orders' where the joined fields are equal."**

     The actual text you see differs according to the names of your tables. In technical mumbo-jumbo, this is called an *outer join*. Very cool.

  3. **Click OK and run the query.**

You should now have all records from the Customers table whether or not there are corresponding records in the Orders table.

If your query is complex and involves calculated fields, trying to build the query all at once is a common mistake. Instead, break the query into small pieces and get each to work before moving on to the next one. (See Chapter 15 for more on that approach.)

Don't forget that you can always use the Expression Builder to help you put together particularly tricky questions.

This may be the best advice in this whole book: If your query is messed up no matter what you do, stand up, clear your throat, and at the top of your lungs, shout "Help!" (If that doesn't work, try calling over to your comrade-in-bondage in the next cubicle in a soft and civilized tone.) Odds are, if someone else looks at your query they'll take all of two seconds to look at it and then point to the problem. After 20 years in this field, I can tell you that when it comes to queries, we're the ones who can't see our own mistakes.

And When You Looked Again, the Record Was Gone

"The record was there — right there!" The key word in that sentence is the verb, because it indicates that the record *isn't* there now. Precisely *where* the record went is a moot point because only the computer knows, and machines have a code of silence about these details. (It's a subset of the rules that make all the copiers break at the same time.)

Don't panic. Panicky people make strange changes, and you need your wits about you for the next few minutes. You can panic later after the dust settles.

Before doing anything technical with Access 2002 (or hitting the computer with a baseball bat), press Ctrl+Z. That's the Undo command. If the record comes back, you're done. In that case, close the table and go have a panic attack in the break room.

If the Undo command didn't accomplish anything, you're in slightly more trouble. The next best solution is to copy the record from a backup of the database file. This solution works only if you backed up your database at some point. If you have a paper copy of the data, you can always manually re-enter it into the database. If that record was your only copy of the information, then raise your hand, look at the computer, and wave good-bye, because it's gone now (you have my deepest sympathy).

Please, oh *please,* keep current backups of your information. You never know when bad things will happen (insert eerie organ music here).

The Validation That Never Was

Validations are one of my favorite features of Access 2002. But like anything, validations can cause problems if they're not used properly.

The biggest concern is a validation rule that *can't* be valid. For example, suppose that someone (certainly not you or I, but *someone*) wants to limit a particular field so that it only accepts entries between 0 and 100. To accomplish that feat, the person creates a validation that says <0 And >100. Unfortunately, that rule won't work — ever! The person mixed up the symbols and created a rule that accepts only a number that's less than 0 *and* greater than 100. According to my college math professor, not too many numbers like that are running loose in the world.

Don't let this problem happen to your validations. To avoid such crises, write your rule on paper and then test it with some sample data. Be sure to include examples of both good and bad entries to make sure that the rule works just like it's supposed to.

The Sometimes-There, Sometimes-Gone Menus

Thanks to someone in the *Conceptually Cool, But Functionally Frustrating New Feature Division* of Microsoft, the menus in Access 2002 (and all of its brethren in Office XP) don't automatically show all of the possible menu items available. Instead, they show only the most commonly used menu items, plus a little down-pointing chevron at the bottom of the menu. (Yes, this is *supposed* to make your life easier. Isn't that nice to know?)

That little chevron is your key to the full menu. When you click the chevron, the menu magically expands to its full size, proudly displaying all of the options available on it. At this point, click whichever menu item you want.

After you click the chevron and select an item from the full menu, Access 2002 automatically adds that item to the *short* version of the menu.

You Can't Link to a dBASE Table

This is probably nothing more than your using the wrong dBase version. If you chose dBase 5 and it didn't work, try dBase IV or dBase III.

You Can't Update A Linked dBASE or Paradox Table

If you can't update a dBase or Paradox table to which you have linked, you probably need to get the techies involved. The default drivers delivered with Access 2002 allow read-only access to dBase and Paradox tables; you need to have the "Borland Database Engine" (BDE) installed on your computer. As of this writing, your only option was to contact a third party vendor for an appropriate driver. Vendors include Merant (www.merant.com and choose the DataDirect line of products), or Inprise (www.inprise.com and choose Downloads and then BDE). If you need more information, go to the Microsoft Knowledge Base (http://search.support.microsoft.com) and enter a search for "Borland Database Engine."

You Get a Key Violation While Importing a Table

When you get a key violation while importing a table, Access 2002 is trying as hard as it can, but the data you're importing contains a duplicate key value. Because Access 2002 can't arbitrarily change the data in question, you need to do the repair. Go back to the master program, find the offending record, and build a good key to replace the duplicated one. After you're sure that the key values are all unique, then try, try again.

Try as You May, the Program Won't Start

After picking Access 2002 from the Start menu, the oh-so-cool Access 2002 splash screen (the pretty picture that keeps you entertained while the program takes too long to load) flows smoothly onto the screen. Suddenly, the serene moment shatters as a small warning box bursts in, shouting that Windows can't find ODD_ESOTERIC_FILE.MDB. The Access 2002 splash screen fades and you're left facing the Windows desktop.

This sequence really does happen from time to time. Honestly, such events are just part of life with computers. I teach my troubleshooting classes a simple mantra to cover precisely this problem: *It's a file. Files go bad.*

Because the error message was kind enough to give you a filename (not all errors are so generous), use the Explorer to look for the file. If it's there, odds are that the file is corrupt. If the file isn't there, well, at least you know why Access 2002 didn't find it.

Either way, you need to replace the file with a healthy version from your original Access 2002 program disks. If you have a CD-ROM copy of Access 2002, this process is easy. Just point the Explorer at the installation CD-ROM, find the file, and copy it to the Access 2002 subdirectory.

If Access 2002 lives on your company's network, contact your friendly Information Systems support folks for guidance. In that case, the problem is very likely out of your hands. Wish the computer gurus luck, and then take a coffee break while they work on the problem.

The Wizard Won't Come Out of His Castle

This one is a more focused version of the preceding problem where Access 2002 won't start. Now the problem is localized to a particular wizard. The solution is the same: Look for the missing file, replace it from the master disks, and then see whether that solves the problem.

If all else fails (which may happen), pick up a bag of nacho chips and call in your favorite nerd for some assistance.

By default, the Access 2002 menus and other dialog boxes show *all* of the *possible* options — not just the options currently installed on your computer. This means that as you use Access 2002, it may periodically say that a menu option you select doesn't exist on your computer. In that case, whip out the Access 2002 CD-ROM and install it. If your computer is part of a network in a business, contact your computer support folks, because they probably need (or want) to handle the installation themselves.

Chapter 28

Ten Tips from the Database Nerds

*L*ike 'em or loathe 'em, the technical experts are always with you. In their more lucid moments, the technical experts possess incredible nuggets of wisdom. This chapter is a distillation of good advice that I picked up over the years. Some of it is very focused, while other parts are downright philosophical. Such is life with the technical experts (but you knew that already).

Document As if Your Life Depends on It

Yes, it's a pain. Yes, it's a bother. Yes, *I* do it myself (kinda scary when a guy actually listens to his own advice). If you build a database, make sure that you document every little detail about it. Here's a list of items to start with:

- ✔ **General information about the database:** Include file locations, an explanation of what the database does, and information on how it works.

- ✔ **Table layouts, including field names, sizes, contents, and sample contents:** If some of the data comes from esoteric or temporary sources (like the shipping report that you shred right after data entry), note that fact in the documentation so that people know.

- ✔ **Report names, an explanation of the information on the report, and lists of who gets a copy of the report when it's printed:** If you need to run some queries before creating a report, document the process. (Better, get a nerd to help you automate the work.) Documenting who receives the report is *particularly* important. Jot down the job title in the documentation as well as the current person in the position.

- ✔ **Queries and logic:** For every query, provide a detailed explanation of how the query works, especially if it involves multiple tables or data sources outside of Access (like SQL tables or other big-time information storage areas).

- ✔ **Answer the question "Why?":** As you document your database, focus on *why* your design works the way that it works. Why do the queries use those particular tables? Why do the reports go to those people? Granted, if you work in a corporate environment, you may not *know* why the system works the way it does, but it never hurts to inquire.

✔ **Miscellaneous details:** Provide information such as the backup process and schedule, where backup tapes are located (you *are* making backups, right?), and what to do if the computer isn't working. If your database runs a particularly important business function, such as accounting, inventory, point-of-sale, or order entry, make sure that a manual process is in place to keep the business going if the computer breaks down — and remember to document the process!

Every 6 to 12 months, review your documentation to see whether some updates are needed. Documentation is only useful if it's up-to-date and if someone other than yourself can understand it. Likewise, make sure you (or your counterparts in the department) know where the documentation is located. If you have an electronic version, keep it backed up and have a print-out handy.

Don't Make Your Fields Way Too Big

When you're building a table, take a moment to make your text fields the appropriate size for the data you're keeping in those fields. By default, Access 2002 sets up text fields to hold 50 characters — a pretty generous setting, particularly if the field holds two-letter state abbreviations. Granted, 48 characters of space aren't anything to write home about, but multiply that space across a table with 100,000 customer addresses in it and you get 4.8MB of storage space that's very busy holding absolutely *nothing*.

Adjust the field size with the Field Size setting on the General tab in Design view.

Real Numbers Use Number Fields

Use number fields for *numbers*, not for text *pretending* to be a number. Computers perceive a difference between UPC (universal product code) 47999 and the number *47,999*. The UPC is stored as a series of characters that all happen to be digits, but the number is stored as an actual number that you can use for math and all kinds of other fun numeric stuff.

When choosing the type for a new field with numbers in it, ask yourself a simple question: Are you *ever* going to make a calculation or do anything math-related with the field? If so, use a number type. If not, store the field as text and go on with your life.

Better Validations Make Better Data

Validations work hand in hand with masks to prevent bad data from getting close to your tables. Validations are easy to make, quick to set up, and ever vigilant (even when you're so tired you can't see straight). If you aren't using validations to protect the integrity of your database, you really should start. Flip to Chapter 7 and have a look at the topic.

Use Understandable Names

When building a table or creating a database, think about the names you use. Will you remember what they mean three months from now? Six months from now? Are they intuitive enough for someone else to look at the table and figure out what it does, long after your knowledge of Access 2002 puts your career on the fast track?

Windows allows long filenames; please use them. You don't need to get carried away, but now you have no excuse for files called *99Q1bdg5*. Using *Q1 1999 Budget Rev 5* makes *much* more sense to everyone involved.

Take Great Care When Deleting

Whenever you're deleting field values from a table, make sure that you're killing the values in the *right* record, check again, and — only when you're sure — delete the original. Even then, you can still do a quick Ctrl+Z and recover the little bugger.

Why all the checking and double-checking? Because after you delete a field value *and do anything else in the table,* Access 2002 completely forgets about your old value. It's gone, just as if it never existed. If you delete a record from a table, then the record is really gone because there is no Undo available for an entire record. If that record happened to be important and you don't have a current backup file, you're out of luck. Sorry!

Keep Backups

There's no substitute for a current backup of your data, particularly if the data is vital to your company. Effective strategies often include maintaining back up copies at another location just in case a disaster destroys your work facility. Don't believe me? Let the phrase *no receivables* float through your mind for a while. How do you feel about backups now? I thought you'd see it my way.

Think First and Then Think Again

Apply this rule to any Access 2002 step that contains the word *delete* or *redesign.* Think about what you're doing. Then think again. Software makes handling large amounts of data easier than ever before, but it also offers the tools to screw up your data on a scale not seen since the time of P.T. Barnum.

Get Organized and Keep It Simple

Although they may seem different at first blush, these two tips work together to promote classic nerd values like *a place for every gadget* and *my query ran faster than yours, so there.* By keeping your computer orderly and organizing your entire workspace, you have everything you need at hand. Get yourself a recliner and a remote control, and you never need to leave the office again.

Yes, you can get *too* organized. In fact, overorganizing is altogether too easy. Temper your desire to organize with a passion for working with as few steps as possible. On your computer, limit the number of folders and subfolders you use — a maximum of five levels of folders is *more* than enough for just about anybody. If you go much beyond five levels, your organization starts bumping into your productivity (and nobody likes a productivity loss, least of all the people who come up with those silly little slogans for the corporate feel-good posters).

Know When to Ask for Help

If you're having trouble with something, swallow your ego and ask for help. Saying *I don't know* and then trying to find out holds no shame. This rule is *especially* important when you're riding herd on thousands of records in a database. Small missteps quickly magnify and multiply a small problem into a huge crisis. Ask for help *before* the situation becomes dire.

Index

• Numbers and Symbols •

& (ampersand)
  combining text fields with, 187–188
  in input masks, 92, 100
* (asterisk button), datasheet window, 27
@ (at sign), 92
\ (backslash), 99, 190
^ (caret), 190
: (colon), 100
! (exclamation point), 101, 189
> (greater than symbol)
  Advanced Filter/Sort criteria, 144
  formatting text, 92
  input masks, 99
  validation rules, 102
< (less than symbol)
  Advanced Filter/Sort criteria, 144
  formatting text, 92
  input masks, 99
  validation rules, 102
( ) (parentheses), 99
(pound sign), 164–165
? (question mark)
  input mask code, 100
  What's This? help, 39
" " (quotation mark), 99
; (semicolon), 100
[ ] (square brackets), 180–181
_ (underscore), 100
3-D effects
  form borders, 287
  Page Header, 256
  report borders, 238–239
  table cells, 114–115

• A •

ACCESS-L, 40
Across, then Down, 213
ActiveX, 266
adding
  Count function, 173–175
  Expression Builder, 188
  Running Sum, 260–261
  Summary Options, reports, 226–227
  Totals row, 171–173
addresses
  fields for, 50–51
  mailing labels, creating, 186–187, 215–220
Advanced Filter/Sort, 140–145
alignment, 240, 243
alphabetical sorting
  fields, 131–132
  filter results, 143–144
  query results, 147, 149, 160
Alt key, keyboard shortcuts, 4
America Online, support sites, 40
America Online For Dummies, 40
ampersand (&)
  combining text fields with, 187–188
  in input masks, 92, 100
Analyzer
  Documenter, 301–302
  Performance, 302–303
  Table, 297–300
AND
  combining with OR, 168–169
  versus OR, 163–164
  using, 164–166
  validation rules, using in, 102
Answer Wizard, 37
Any Part of Field, Match, 130

AOL (American Online), 40
Append query, 194
area charts, 220–222
area codes, 99, 101
arithmetic operators, 190
arrow buttons, datasheet window, 27
arrow keys, moving cursor with, 104–105
Ascending, Sort
  fields, 131–132
  filter results, 143–144
  query results, 147, 149, 160
ASCII text files, importing, 292–293
Ask A Question, 34
asterisk button, datasheet window, 27
at sign (@), 92
attaching files. *See* linking files
AutoFormat, reports, 242–243
automated editing queries, 192–193
automatic rounding, 93–94, 321–322
automatic saving, 17–18, 83
AutoNumber fields
  about, 49
  as primary key, 70, 72
  typing in, 83–84
AutoReport, 204–206
Avery labels, 217
Avg (average), 177, 226–227

• B •

background color
  forms, 281
  Page Header, 255–256
  reports, 234–235
  tables, 115
backing up
  databases, 20, 329
  documenting processes for, 328
  tables, 192
backslash (\), 99, 190

bands, report
  grouping, 251–254
  markers, 230–231
  resizing, 254, 257
  types of, 231–232, 247–251
bar charts, 220–222
Baroudi, Carol, 40
BDE (Borland Database Engine), 325
BETWEEN operator, 165
bold fonts, 114, 239
Boolean operators
  AND, 163–166, 168–169
  OR, 163–164, 167–169
borders, adding to
  forms, 286–287
  reports, 237–239
Borland Database Engine (BDE), 325
boxes
  forms, adding to, 286–287
  moving, 235–237
  reports, adding to, 244
brackets, square ([ ]), 180–181
breaks, page
  adding, 244–245
  Force New Page option, 256–257
  Keep Together option, 253–254
browser requirements, 266
bubble charts, 221–222

• C •

calculated fields
  creating, 180–183, 185–186
  defined, 179
  Expression Builder, 188–190
  footers, adding to, 260–261
  text, 186–187
  Update query, 199–200
  using in multiple calculations, 184–185
calculations
  functions, 176–177
  reports, 226–227

Running Sum, 260–261
totals, 171–173
Update query, 199–200
Can Grow, 257
Can Shrink, 257
canceling printing, 18
caret (^), 190
case
formatting text, 92
searching for, 130
Cell Effects, 114–115
centering text, 240
cents
Currency field, 49
decimal places, 93–94, 321–322
changing records, 17, 85, 192–193
character limits
field names, 52
field types, 49
formatting, text, 92
input masks, 96, 99, 100
chart layout, 283
Chart Wizard, 220–222
check boxes, 96, 235
checking spelling, 300
child records, 86
child tables, 75–76. *See also* relational
databases
Chiseled effect
forms, 287
report borders, 239
Clear Grid button, 137
clicking
with mouse, 3–4
using speech recognition, 312
closing
Access, 21
databases, 14
codes
Advanced Filter/Sort criteria, 144
ampersand (&), 187–188
exclamation point (!), 189

formatting text, 92
input mask, 99–101
pound sign (#), 164, 165
square brackets ([ ]), 180–181
text formatting, 92
validation rules, 102
colons in input masks, 100
color
font, 114
forms, 281
Page Header, 255–256
reports, 234–235, 237–238
tables, 115
Column spacing, reports, 213
Columnar forms, 282
Columnar reports
creating, 204–206
moving elements on, 236–237
orientation, 211
sections, 248
columns (fields)
adding in Design view, 118–120
adding with Database Wizard, 59
adding with Table Wizard, 62
calculated. *See* calculated fields
check boxes in, 96
counting, 173–175
Crosstab queries, 175–176
data entry wizard, 50
data validation, 101–102
defined, 47, 119
deleting, 121–122, 329
descriptions, adding, 67
designing, 55–56
editing, 17, 85
Expression Builder, 189
filtering, 143
formats, 91–96
freezing, 112–113
headings, reports, 210
hiding, 110–112

columns (fields) *(continued)*
  indexing, 77–78
  input masks, 96–101
  linking, 72
  moving, 109–110
  moving between, 104–105
  naming, 52
  placeholders, creating, 93
  primary key, 70–72
  properties, 90–91
  renaming, 122–124
  searching, 128–131
  Select queries, 146–147
  selecting (F2), 317
  Simple Query wizard, selecting in, 150
  size, 49, 67, 94, 328
  sorting, 131–132
  types of, 48–51, 65, 66
  typing in, 83
  width, changing, 106–108
Columns tab, Page Setup, 212–213
comma, thousands separator, 93
command mode, speech recognition, 312–313
compound key, 70
CompuServe, support sites, 40
CompuServe 2000 For Dummies, 40
cone charts, 220–222
constants, 180, 189
context-sensitive
  help, 39
  menus, 31, 324
Control Menu, 24–25
controls
  alignment, 240, 243
  borders, 237–239
  color, changing, 234–235
  defined, 230–231
  font settings, 239
  moving, 235–237
  spacing, 237
converting databases, 297–300

copying tables, 192
Count queries, 173–175, 177
Crawford, Sharon, 58
criteria
  AND, 163–166, 168–169
  Advanced Filter/Sort, 144–145
  Crosstab queries, 175–176
  functions, 176–177
  OR, 163–164, 167–169
  Select queries, 148
Crosstab queries, 175–176
Currency fields
  about, 49
  data validation, 101–102
  decimal places, 93–94, 321–322
  formats, 92–94
current date or time, inserting in
  Date/Time fields (Ctrl+;), 85, 317
  reports, 261
customer support, 39–41
customized field formats, 96

data
  access page, creating, 271–273
  defined, 47
  entry, 50, 318
  input masks, 96–101
  validation, 101–102
Data Types, 48–51, 65, 66
Database Wizard, 56–60
databases
  backing up, 20, 329
  closing, 14
  converting flat file to relational, 297–300
  creating, 56–60
  defined, 48
  designing, 55–56
  display options, 59
  documenting, 301–302, 327–328
  flat versus relational, 52–54

online publishing, 265–266, 270–273
opening, 11–13, 79–82
Performance Analyzer, 302–303
relational. *See* relational databases
searching for, 84
templates, 57
window, 13–14, 26
Datasheet forms, 283
Datasheet view
  cautions for making changes in, 112, 118
  renaming fields, 123–124
  tables, creating in, 65
  tables, displaying in, 103–105
  window, options available in, 27–28
date, inserting in
  Date/Time fields (Ctrl+;), 85, 317
  reports, 261
Date/Time fields
  about, 49
  data validation, 101–102
  formats, 94–95
  input masks, 96–101
  inserting current date or time, 85, 317
dates, in queries, 164–165
day format, 94
dBASE
  exporting to, 294
  files, importing, 290–293
  troubleshooting, 325
decimal places, 93–94, 321–322
decimals, converting percentages to, 18
definitions, 46–48, 119
Delete query, 194–196
Delete Record, 86, 329
Delete Rows, 121
deleting fields, 121–122, 329
Descending, Sort
  fields, 131–132
  filter results, 143–144
  query results, 147, 149, 160

Description, field, 67
Design button, Object bar, 26
Design view
  fields, adding in, 118–120
  forms, viewing in, 285–286
  keyboard shortcuts for, 320
  renaming fields, 122–123
  reports, opening in, 230
  tables, displaying in, 89–90
Detail query, 157
detail records, 226
Detail sections, reports, 248–249
dictation mode, speech recognition, 309–312
division, 188, 190
documentation, creating
  tips for, 327–328
  using Database Documenter, 301–302
dollars
  Currency field, 49
  decimal places, 93–94, 321–322
donut charts, 220–222
double-clicking, 3
Down, then Across, 213
dragging, 4
drivers, downloading, 325
duplicate data
  Find Duplicates Query Wizard, 158
  flat file versus relational databases, 52–53
  indexes, 78
  preventing, 77–78
  primary keys, 72
  Table Analyzer, 298
dynamic HTML conversion, 271–273

• E •

e-mail discussion lists, 40
e-mailing reports, 209
Each Value, grouping on, 253

Edit
  Delete Record, 83
  Delete Rows, 121
  Delete Tab, 137
  Find (Ctrl+F), 128–131
  Replace, 192–193
  Saved Record, 17
  Undo Delete, 121–122
  Undo Property Setting, 234
  Undo Saved Record, 83
editing queries, automated, 192–193
editing records, 17, 85
Enforce Referential Integrity, 76
entering data, 50, 318
equal spacing, 244
Equals criteria, 144
Etched effect
  forms, 287
  report borders, 239
Euro format, 93
Excel
  exporting to, 245
  files, importing, 291–293
exclamation point (!), 101, 189
Excluding Selection, Filter, 137–138
exiting Access, 21
Explorer, Internet, 266
exponents, 190
exporting
  to HTML, 270–274
  reports, 245
  tables, 293–295
Expression Builder, 188–190
Expression function, 177
expressions, 181–182
extensions, file formats, 290–291, 293

• *F* •

F1 (help key), 33
Favorites list, 81
fields
  adding in Design view, 118–120
  adding with Database Wizard, 59
  adding with Table Wizard, 62
  calculated. *See* calculated fields
  check boxes in, 96
  counting, 173–175
  Crosstab queries, 175–176
  data entry wizard, 50
  data validation, 101–102
  defined, 47, 119
  deleting, 121–122, 329
  descriptions, adding, 67
  designing, 55–56
  documenting, 327–328
  editing, 17, 85
  Expression Builder, 189
  filtering, 143
  formats, 91–96
  freezing, 112–113
  headings, reports, 210
  hiding, 110–112
  indexing, 77–78
  input masks, 96–101
  linking, 72
  moving, 109–110
  moving between, 104–105
  naming, 52
  placeholders, creating, 93
  primary key, 70–72
  properties, 90–91
  renaming, 122–124
  searching, 128–131
  Select queries, 146–147
  selecting (F2), 317
  Simple Query wizard, selecting in, 150
  size, 49, 67, 94, 328
  sorting, 131–132
  types of, 48–51, 65–66
  typing in, 83
  width, changing, 106–108
File
  Close, 14
  Exit, 21
  Export, 294
  Get External Data, Import, 292
  New, 56–60

Open, 13, 81, 84
   Page Setup, 209–213
file formats
   Access, 13
   importing, 290–291, 293
file size, reducing, 328
filenames, 329
Fill/Back Color, 234–235
Filter by Manufacturer, labels, 217
filters
   Advanced Filter/Sort, 140–145
   Excluding Selection, 137–138
   Filter For, 133
   by Form, 134–137
   input masks, 96–101
   versus queries, 141 *See also* queries
   by Selection, 133–134
   types of, 132
   window, 142
Find command. *See also* filters; queries
   and Replace, 192–193
   using (Ctrl+F), 128–131
Find Duplicates Query Wizard, 158
Find Unmatched Query Wizard, 158
First function, 177
first page, headers and footers on, 250, 255,
   261
Fit view, 207–208
Fixed format, 93
Flat effect
   forms, 287
   Page Header, 256
   report borders, 239
   table cells, 115
flat file databases
   converting to relational, 297–300
   versus relational, 52–54
folders
   opening databases, 81
   organizing, 330
   saving databases, 58
Font/Fore Color, 234–235

fonts
   mailing labels, 218
   reports, 234–235, 239
   tables, 114
footers
   date and time, inserting in, 261
   group, 251–254
   page breaks, 244–245, 253–254, 256–257
   pages including, 248–251, 254–255, 257
   summaries, including in, 259–261
foreign key, 72, 76
Format
   Align, 243
   Datasheet, Cell Effect, 114–115
   Font, 114
   Freeze Columns, 113
   Hide Columns, 112
   Snap to Grid, 243
   Unfreeze Columns, 113
   Unhide Columns, 112
   Vertical Spacing, 244
formats, field
   calculated, 183
   changing, 90–91
   customized, 96
   Date/Time, 94–95
   Number and Currency, 92–94
   searching for, 130
   Text and Memo, 92
   Yes/No, 95–96
formats, file
   Access, 13
   importing, 290–291, 293
formatting reports
   aligning elements, 243–244
   AutoFormat, 242–243
   borders, 237–239
   color, setting, 234–235
   Design view, opening in, 230
   designing tables for, 55–56
   font setting, 234–235, 239
   grouping records, 251–254

formatting reports *(continued)*
  images, adding, 245
  Label Wizard, 215–220
  moving elements, 235–237
  page breaks, 244–245, 253–254, 256–257
  Page Setup, 209–213
  previewing layout, 240–241
  Print Preview, 206–209
  printing, 17–18, 209, 253–254
  Report Wizard, 227–228
  sections, 230–232, 247–251
  spacing, 237
  styles, 59
  text alignment, 240
  toolbar, 233–234
formatting tables
  color settings, 115
  fonts, 114
  gridlines, removing, 115
  height, row, 108–109
  saving changes, 105
  three-dimensional effects, 114–115
  width, column, 106–108
forms
  advantages of, 278
  AutoForms, 284
  color and background styles, 281
  creating using Form Wizard, 279–282
  exporting to HTML, 274
  filtering, 132–138, 140–145
  formatting, 285–287
  moving fields, 286
  searching, 128–131
  tab order, changing, 287–288
  types of, 282–283
  window, 28–29
formulas, creating, 181–182, 188–190
FoxPro
  exporting to, 294
  files, importing, 290–293
freezing columns, 112–113
full names, combining fields for, 186–187
functions, calculation, 176–177, 189

• *G* •

General Date format, 94
General Number format, 93
General tab, Field Properties, 89–90
General Templates, 57
Get External Data, 292
glossary, 46–48, 119
graphics, adding, 60, 245
graphs, 220–222, 283
Greater Than or Equal To criteria, 144
greater than symbol (>)
  Advanced Filter/Sort criteria, 144
  formatting text, 92
  input masks, 99
  validation rules, 102
grid, snapping to, 243
Grid Settings, Page Setup, 212–213
gridlines, removing, 115
Group By, 172, 177
group headers and footers
  adding, 252–253
  formatting, 256–257
  pages appearing on, 249–251
grouping
  queries, 173–176
  report fields, 224–226
  report records, 251–254

• *H* •

handwriting recognition, 107
headers
  date and time, inserting, 261
  formatting, 258–259
  page breaks, 244–245, 253–254, 256–257
  pages including, 248–251, 254–255, 257
height, records, 108–109
help
  Answer Wizard, 37
  Contents tab, 36
  Index tab, 38–39

Office Assistant, 25, 33–35
   toolbar screen tips, 30–31
   web sites, 39–40
   What's This?, 39
hiding columns, 110–112
highlighting, 4
horizontal spacing, reports, 244
HTML
   converting to, 270–273
   exporting to, 295
   file format, 291
   templates, 274
HTML 4 for Dummies, 270
Hyperlink fields
   about, 50
   adding, 267
   indexing, 77
   as primary fields, 70
hyperlinks
   formatting, 268
   forms and reports, adding to, 274
   opening, 269
   tables, adding to, 267
   types of, 266–267

• *I* •

images, adding, 60, 245
importing data, 290–293, 296
Index tab, help topics, 38–39
indexing fields, 77–78
Inprise web site, 325
input masks, 96–101
Insert
   Date and Time, 261
   New Record, 82–84
   Page Numbers, 261
   Picture, 245
   Rows, 119
installation, troubleshooting, 325–326
integer division, 190
IntelliMouse, 104–105, 107

internet
   converting databases for, 265–266,
      270–273
   hyperlinks, adding, 50, 266–269, 274
   support web sites, 39–40
Internet Explorer, 266
Internet For Dummies, The, 40
Interval, grouping on, 253
intranets, 270
introductory screens, 14–15, 26–27, 60
italic fonts, 114, 239

• *J* •

James, Steve, 270
Justified forms, 283

• *K* •

Kaufeld, John, 40
Keep Together, 253–254, 256
key, foreign, 72, 76
key, primary
   Paradox tables, troubleshooting, 291
   queries, role in, 154
   relational databases, 72–73, 75
   setting, 70–72
key field, 53, 72. *See also* key, primary
keyboard shortcuts
   common, 317–320
   tables, moving through, 104–105
   using, 4
keywords, help topics, 38–39

• *L* •

label markers, report
   alignment, 240, 243
   borders, 237–239
   color, changing, 234–235
   defined, 231
   font settings, 239

label markers, report *(continued)*
  formatting headers and footers, 257–259
  moving, 235–237
Label Wizard, 215–220
labels, mailing
  creating, 215–220
  names for, 186–187
landscape orientation, 211, 227
Language toolbar, speech recognition,
    309–310
Last function, 177
layout, reports
  aligning elements, 243–244
  AutoFormat, 242–243
  borders, 237–239
  color, setting, 234–235
  Design view, opening in, 230
  designing tables for, 55–56
  font setting, 234–235, 239
  grouping records, 251–254
  images, adding, 245
  Label Wizard, 215–220
  moving elements, 235–237
  page breaks, 244–245, 253–254, 256–257
  Page Setup, 209–213
  previewing layout, 240–241
  Print Preview, 206–209
  printing, 17–18, 209, 253–254
  Report Wizard, 227–228
  sections, 230–232, 247–251
  spacing, 237
  styles, 59
  text alignment, 240
  toolbar, 233–234
layout, tables
  color settings, 115
  fonts, 114
  gridlines, removing, 115
  height, row, 108–109
  saving changes, 105

three-dimensional effects, 114–115
  width, column, 106–108
left-aligning text, 240
Lernout & Hauspie. *See* speech recognition
Less Than or Equal To criteria, 144
less than symbol (<)
  Advanced Filter/Sort criteria, 144
  formatting text, 92
  input masks, 99
  validation rules, 102
Levine, John, 40
Levine, Margaret, 40
line breaks (Ctrl+Enter), 318
line charts, 220–222
lines
  forms, adding to, 286–287
  moving, 235–237
  reports, adding to, 237–239, 244
linking. *See also* hyperlinks
  files, 290–293, 296
  images, 245
  tables, 72–77
linking field, 72, 83. *See also* primary key
listservs, 40
logical operators
  AND, 163–166, 168–169
  BETWEEN, 165
  Advanced Filer/Sort criteria, 144–145
  mathematical, 190
  OR, 163–164, 167–169
  validation rules, 102
Long Date format, 94
Long Integer setting, 94
Look in, 81, 129, 131
Lookup Wizard, 50
Lotus 1-2-3, 291
lowercase
  formatting text, 92
  searching for, 130

• M •

mailing labels
  creating, 215–220
  names for, 186–187
mailing lists, support, 40
main window, 24–25
Make-Table query, 194–195
many-to-many relationships, 73
many-to-one relationships, 73
margins, reports, 210
markers, report
  alignment, 240, 243
  borders, 237–239
  color, changing, 234–235
  defined, 230–231
  font settings, 239
  moving, 235–237
  spacing, 237
masks, input, 96–101
Match, 130, 131
Max, 177, 226–227
Medium Date format, 94
Memo fields
  formatting, 92
  indexing, 77
  as primary keys, 70
  using, 49
memory requirements, speech recognition, 306
menus
  context-sensitive, 31
  keyboard shortcuts, 4
  speech recognition, accessing with, 312–313
  troubleshooting, 324
Merant web site, 325
microphone, speech recognition
  speaking into, 307–308
  turning on or off, 309

Microsoft Excel
  exporting to, 245
  files, importing, 291–293
Microsoft IntelliMouse, 104–105, 107
Microsoft Office
  2002 Resource Kit, 274–275
  Assistant, 25, 33–35
  exporting to, 245
  XP, features of, 107
Microsoft SQL Server, terminology, 47
Microsoft Windows
  For Dummies books on, 24, 58
  shutting down, 21
  Start menu shortcuts, adding, 9–11
  taskbar, 24–25
  versions supported, 1
Microsoft Word, exporting to, 245
Min, 177, 226–227
MOD operator, 190
money
  Currency field, 49
  decimal places, 93, 94, 321–322
month format, 94
More Files, 12, 80
mouse
  Microsoft IntelliMouse, 104–105, 107
  using, 3–4
moving
  boxes, 235–237
  columns, 109–110
  between fields, 104–105
  form fields, 286
multifield key, 70
multiple tables
  deleting records from, 196
  queries, 153–162
  reports, 222–228
  updating records in, 198
multiplying, 188

• N •

name tags, creating, 186–187, 215–220
naming
  fields, 52, 122–124
  files, 329
  primary keys, 71
navigating tables, 103–105
network drives, opening databases on, 81
new
  database, 56–60
  fields, 59, 62, 118–120
  Object bar button, 26
  records, 82–84
  tables, 59, 61–67
newsgroups, 40
No duplicates, 78
Not Equal To criteria, 144
Number fields
  about, 49, 51
  automatic rounding, 321–322
  data validation, 101–102
  decimal places, 93–94, 321–322
  formats, 92–94
  grouping, 253
  versus Text fields, 328
numbers, sorting, 131–132

• O •

Object Linking and Embedding (OLE)
  fields, 50, 70, 77
  inserting, 245
Objects bar, 13–14, 26
ODBC files, 290
Office, Microsoft
  2002 Resource Kit, 274–275
  Assistant, 25, 33–35
  exporting to, 245
  XP, features of, 107
older versions, Access files, 13

OLE objects
  fields, 50, 70, 77
  inserting, 245
one-to-many relationships, 73, 75–76, 196
one-to-one relationships, 73, 196
online database publishing, 265–266,
    270–273
online help
  Answer Wizard, 37
  Contents tab, 36
  Index tab, 38–39
  Office Assistant, 25, 33–35
  toolbar screen tips, 30–31
  web sites, 39–40
  What's This?, 39
open
  Object bar button, 26
opening
  Access 2002, 9–11
  databases, 12–13, 79–82, 84
  troubleshooting, 325–326
operators
  AND, 163–166, 168–169
  BETWEEN, 165
  Advanced Filer/Sort criteria, 144–145
  mathematical, 190
  OR, 163–164, 167–169
  validation rules, 102
optimizing databases, 302–303
optional information, input masks, 99–100
OR
  Advanced/Filter Sort criteria, 144–145
  versus AND, 163–164
  combining with AND, 168–169
  queries, using in, 167
  validation rules, using in, 102
Or tab, Filter by Form, 136–137
Oracle
  files, importing, 290, 292–293
  terminology, 47
orientation, page, 211, 227

• P •

padding fields, 92
page breaks
   adding, 244–245
   Force New Page option, 256–257
   Keep Together option, 253–254
Page Down key, 104–105
Page Footer, 250–251, 254–256
Page Header, 250, 254–256
page numbers, inserting, 261
page orientation, 211, 227
Page Setup, 209–213
Page tab, 210–211
Page Up key, 104–105
paper size, selecting, 211
Paradox
   exporting to, 294
   files, importing, 290–293
   troubleshooting, 325
parent tables, 75–76. *See also* relational
      databases
parentheses in input masks, 99
Paste Table As, 192
Percent format, 93
percentages, converting to decimals, 181
Performance Analyzer, 302–303
PgDn key, 104–105
PgUp key, 104–105
Phillips, R. Michele, 40
phone numbers
   fields for, 51
   input masks for, 96–101
phone support, 41
pictures, adding, 60, 245
pie charts, 220–222
Pivot Chart forms, 283
Pivot Table forms, 283
placeholders, creating, 93
plus sign, 27
pop-up menus, 32
portrait orientation, 211, 227

postal codes
   fields for, 51
   input masks for, 96–98
pound sign (#), 164–165
preview, print, 206–209, 240–241
previewing query results, 194–195
primary key
   Paradox tables, troubleshooting, 291
   queries, role in, 154
   relational databases, 72, 73, 75
   setting, 70–72
Print Data Only, 210
Print Preview, 206–209, 240–241
printer, choosing, 211
printing reports, 18, 209. *See also* page
      breaks
prior versions, Access files, 13
publishing, online, 265–266, 270–273

• Q •

queries
   Advanced Filter/Sort, 140–145
   AND, 163–166, 168–169
   Append, 194
   calculated fields, creating, 180–183,
      185–186
   Count, 173–175, 177
   Crosstab, 175–176
   date, 164
   defined, 140–141
   Delete, 194–196
   Detail, 157
   documenting, 327–328
   editing, automated, 192–193
   field box, resizing, 184
   filtering, 132–138, 142
   Find Duplicates, 158
   Find Unmatched, 158
   functions, 176–177
   grid, 147–149
   grouping, 173–176

queries *(continued)*
  Make-Table, 194–195
  multiple calculations, 184–185
  multiple-table, 153–162
  OR, 163–164, 167–169
  previewing results, 194–195
  primary key, role in, 154
  Query View button, 194–195
  reports based on, 205–206
  Run button, 194–195
  saving, 161
  Select, 145–148, 171–173
  Simple Query Wizard, 149–151, 155–157
  sorting results, 147, 149, 160
  speeding up, 77–78
  Summary, 157
  Top Value setting, 146
  totals, adding to, 171–173
  Totals row, adding to, 172
  troubleshooting, 322–323
  Update, 194, 197–200
  window, 29–30
question mark (?)
  input mask code, 100
  What's This? help, 39
quotation mark, in input masks, 99

• R •

Raised effect
  forms, 287
  Page Header, 256
  report borders, 238–239
  tables, 114–115
Rathbone, Andy, 24, 58
records
  adding, 82–84
  counting, 173–175
  defined, 47
  deleting, 86, 329
  duplicate. *See* redundant data

editing, 17, 85
  filtering, 132–138
  height, changing, 108–109
  indexing, 77–78
  keyboard shortcuts for, 318–319
  missing, troubleshooting, 323
  moving between, 104–105
  primary key, 70–72
  searching, 128–131
  sorting, 131–132
  undoing changes, 87
Records menu
  Advanced Filter/Sort, 143–145
  Filter by Form, 134–137
  Filters, 132
  Sort command, 131
redundant data
  Find Duplicates Query Wizard, 158
  flat file versus relational databases, 52–53
  indexes, 78
  preventing, 77–78
  primary keys, 72
  Table Analyzer, 298
referential integrity, 76, 196
relational databases
  converting flat files to, 297–300
  creating, 72–77
  deleting records from, 86, 196
  versus flat file, 52–54
  queries, 153–162
  Table Wizard, creating with, 63–64
  updating records in, 198
Relationships window, 27, 56, 74–77
remainders, division, 190
Remove Filter button, 134, 137
renaming fields, 122–124
reorganizing fields, 109–110
repeated data
  Find Duplicates Query Wizard, 158
  flat file versus relational databases, 52–53
  indexes, 78

preventing, 77–78
primary keys, 72
Table Analyzer, 298
Replace command, 128–131, 192–193
Report Footer, 250–251
Report Header, 250
reports
   aligning elements, 243–244
   AutoFormat, 242–243
   borders, 237–239
   Chart Wizard, 220–222
   color, setting, 234–235
   creating with AutoReport, 204–206
   Database Documenter, 301–302
   date and time, inserting, 261
   Design view, opening in, 230
   designing tables for, 55–56
   documenting, 327–328
   e-mailing, 209
   filtering, 133
   font setting, 234–235, 239
   footers, 248–251, 254–255, 257, 259–261
   Formatting toolbar, 233–234
   grouping records, 251–254
   headers, 248–251, 254–255, 257, 258–259
   HTML, exporting to, 274
   images, adding, 245
   Label Wizard, 215–220
   Microsoft Office, exporting to, 245
   moving elements, 235–237
   page breaks, 244–245, 253–254, 256–257
   Page Setup, 209–213
   previewing layout, 240–241
   Print Preview, 206–209
   printing, 18
   Report Wizard, 222–228
   sections, 230–232, 247–251
   spacing, 237
   styles, 59
   text alignment, 240
required information, input masks, 99–100
resizing fields
   height, 108–109
   width, 106–108

restoring databases, 20
right-aligning text, 240
right-clicking
   with mouse, 4, 32
   with speech recognition, 313
rounding, decimal places, 93–94, 321–322
Row Spacing, reports, 212
rows (records)
   adding, 82–84
   counting, 173–175
   defined, 47
   deleting, 86, 329
   duplicate. *See* redundant data
   editing, 17, 85
   filtering, 132–138
   height, changing, 108–109
   indexing, 77–78
   keyboard shortcuts for, 318–319
   missing, troubleshooting, 323
   moving between, 104–105
   primary key, 70–72
   searching, 128–131
   sorting, 131–132
   undoing changes, 87
Run button, queries, 194–195
Running Sum, 260–261

• S •

Save as/Export, 209
Saved Record, editing, 17
saving
   automatic, 19–20, 83
   databases, 58–59
   filenames, 329
   Filter by Form searches, 137
   filters as queries, 145
   formatting changes, 105
   queries, 161
   records, 83
   tables, 67, 105

screen tips, toolbar, 30–31
scrolling, 104–105, 112–113
searching. *See also* filters; queries
  for databases, 84
  Find command (Ctrl+F), 128–131
  Replace command, 192–193
  Search Fields as Formatted, 130
sections, report. *See also* footers; headers
  grouping, 251–254
  markers, 230–231
  resizing, 254, 257
  types of, 231–232, 247–251
Select queries, 145–148, 171–173
Selection, Filter by, 133–134
semicolons in input masks, 100
Send as mail message, 209
Shadowed effect
  forms, 287
  report borders, 239
shipping labels
  creating, 215–220
  names for, 186–187
shortcuts
  keyboard, 4, 317–320
  Start menu, adding, 9–11
  tables, moving through, 104–105
Show Table, 74–75
Simple Query Wizard
  multiple-table queries, 155–157
  single-table queries, 149–151
Single Field Size setting, 94
size
  field, 49, 67, 94
  file, 328
  menu, formatting reports, 243–244
  paper, 211
Snap to Grid, 243
Social Security numbers
  fields for, 51
  input masks for, 92, 96–98
sorting
  calculation results, 172
  fields, 131–132

filter results, 143–144
  mailing labels, 219
  primary key, 70–72
  query results, 147, 149, 160
  reports, 224–226
  speeding up, 77–78
Sorting and Grouping, reports, 251–254
spaces, adding, 92
spacing, report settings, 212–213, 237, 244
special characters
  Advanced Filter/Sort criteria, 144
  ampersand (&), 187–188
  exclamation point (!), 189
  formatting text, 92
  input mask codes, 99–101
  pound sign (#), 164, 165
  square brackets ([ ]), 180–181
  text formatting, 92
  validation rules, 102
special effects
  form borders, 287
  Page Header, 256
  report borders, 238–239
  table cells, 114–115
speech recognition
  command mode, 312–313
  dictation mode, 309–311
  errors, correcting, 311–312
  preparing for, 305–308
  spelling mode, 310, 312
  system requirements, 306, 314
  troubleshooting, 314
spell checker, 300
spelling mode, speech recognition, 310, 312
spreadsheets, importing from, 291–293
SQL Server, terminology, 47
square brackets ([ ]), 180–181
Standard format, 93
Start menu, adding shortcuts to, 9–11
Start of Field, Match, 131
starting Access, 9–11, 325–326
startup screens, 14–15, 26–27, 60
static HTML conversion, 270–271
Status bar, 24–25

styles, fonts, 114
subfolders, organizing, 330
subtracting, 188
Sum
  queries, 171–173, 177
  reports, 226–227
  Running, 260–261
Summary Options, Report Wizard, 226–227
Summary query, 157
Sunken effect
  forms, 287
  Page Header, 256
  report borders, 238–239
  tables, 114–115
support, customer, 39–41
switchboards, 14–15, 26–27, 60
symbols
  Advanced Filter/Sort criteria, 144
  ampersand (&), 187–188
  exclamation point (!), 189
  formatting text, 92
  input mask codes, 99–101
  pound sign (#), 164–165
  square brackets ([ ]), 180–181
  text formatting, 92
  validation rules, 102
system requirements
  Internet Explorer, 266
  Microsoft Access, 1
  speech recognition, 306

• T •

Tab order, forms, 287–288
tables
  analyzer, 297–300
  backing up, 192
  child, 75–76 *See also* relational databases
  color settings, 115
  copying, 192
  creating in Datasheet view, 65
  creating in Design view, 65–67
  creating using Database Wizard, 59
  creating using Table Wizard, 61–64
  datasheet view, 27–28
  Datasheet view, displaying in, 103–105
  defined, 47–48
  deleting fields, 121–122
  Design View, displaying in, 89–90
  designing, 55–56
  documenting, 327–328
  exporting, 293–295
  Expression Builder, 189
  fields. *See* fields
  filtering, 132–138, 140–145
  font settings, 114
  formatting, changing, 105
  gridlines, removing, 115
  height, changing, 108–109
  importing, troubleshooting, 325
  indexing, 77–78
  input masks, adding to, 100
  linking, 72–77
  opening, 14, 79–82
  parent, 75–76 *See also* relational
    databases
  pasting, 192
  primary key, 70–72
  records. *See* records
  relationships. *See* multiple tables;
    relational databases
  samples, 64
  searching, 128–131
  sorting, 131–132
  three-dimensional formatting, 114–115
  troubleshooting, 325
  width, changing, 106–108
Tabular forms, 282
Tabular reports
  creating, 204–206
  moving elements on, 237
  orientation, 211
  sections, 248–249
Task Pane, 11–12, 58, 80

taskbar, Windows
  adding shortcuts to, 9–11
  using, 25
technical support, 39–41
telephone numbers
  fields for, 51
  input masks for, 96–101
telephone support, 41
templates
  database, 57
  HTML, 274
terminology, 46–48, 119
text boxes, report
  alignment, 240, 243
  borders, 237–239
  color, changing, 234–235
  defined, 230
  font settings, 239
  moving, 235–237
  resizing, 237
Text fields
  about, 49–51
  calculated, 186–187, 188
  formats, 92
  grouping, 253
  input masks, 96–101
  versus Number fields, 328
text files, importing, 291–293
thousands separator, 93
three-dimensional effects
  form borders, 287
  Page Header, 256
  report borders, 238–239
  table cells, 114–115
time, inserting in
  Date/Time fields (Ctrl+;), 85, 317
  reports, 261
Title bar, 24–25
titles, report, 248
Tittel, Ed, 270
toolbars
  Formatting, reports, 233–234

speech recognition, accessing with,
  312–313
  using, 30–31
Tools
  Analyze Documenter, 301–302
  Analyze Performance, 302–303
  Analyze Table, 297–300
  Office Links, 245
  Relationships, 74
  Speech, 307, 309
Top Value setting, 146
Total row, using with
  Count queries, 173–175
  Select queries, 171–173
training, speech recognition, 307–309
troubleshooting
  automatic rounding, 321–322
  menus, 324
  queries, 322–323
  records, missing, 323
  speech recognition, 314
  starting program, 325–326
  tables, 325
  validation rules, 324
  wizards, 326
True/False fields. *See* Yes/No fields
TrueType fonts, 114
typing, 83, 318
typo checker, 300

underlined text, 239
underscore, 100
Undo
  changes to records, 17
  keyboard shortcut (Ctrl+z), 319
  Saved Record, 83
unfreezing columns, 112–114
Unhide Columns, 112
universal product code (UPC), 328
Unknown fields, creating, 93

Unmatched Query Wizard, 158
UPC (universal product code), 328
Update query, 194, 197–200
uppercase
   formatting text, 92
   searching for, 130
Use Specific Printer, 211
Usenet, 40
Utility buttons, 24–25

• *V* •

validation, data, 101–102, 324
versions
   Access, opening older files, 13
   Internet Explorer, 266
   Windows, supported, 1
vertical spacing, reports, 244
View
   Pages, 208, 209
   Sorting and Grouping, 251–254
   Tab Order, 288
views. *See* windows
voice recognition
   command mode, 312–313
   dictation mode, 309–311
   errors, correcting, 311–312
   preparing for, 305–308
   spelling mode, 310, 312
   system requirements, 306, 314
   troubleshooting, 314

• *W* •

web sites
   Borland Database Engine (BDE), 325
   converting databases to, 265–266,
      270–273
   hyperlinks, adding, 50, 266–269, 274
   Office 2002 Resource Kit, 274–275
   support, 39–40
What's This? Help, 39
Where, 177

Whole Field, Match, 130
width
   border, 238
   field, 106–108
windows
   database, 26
   datasheet, 27–28
   Filter, 142
   form, 28–29
   main, 24–25
   navigating through, 104–105
   query, 29–30
   Relationships, 27, 56, 74–77
   resizing, 25
   speech recognition, accessing with, 312
Windows, Microsoft
   For Dummies books on, 24, 58
   shutting down, 21
   Start menu shortcuts, adding, 10–11
   taskbar, 24–25
   versions supported, 1
wizards, troubleshooting, 326
Word, exporting to, 245

• *X* •

X button, Object bar, 26
XML, 291, 295
XY charts, 221–222

• *Y* •

Yes/No fields
   about, 50
   formats for, 95–96
   as primary keys, 70

• *Z* •

zip codes
   fields for, 51
   input masks for, 96–98
zoom command, 207–208

Notes

Notes

Notes

Notes

Notes

Notes

Dummies Books™
Bestsellers on Every Topic!

GENERAL INTEREST TITLES

BUSINESS & PERSONAL FINANCE

Title	Author	ISBN	Price
Accounting For Dummies®	John A. Tracy, CPA	0-7645-5014-4	$19.99 US/$27.99 CAN
Business Plans For Dummies®	Paul Tiffany, Ph.D. & Steven D. Peterson, Ph.D.	1-56884-868-4	$19.99 US/$27.99 CAN
Business Writing For Dummies®	Sheryl Lindsell-Roberts	0-7645-5134-5	$16.99 US/$27.99 CAN
Consulting For Dummies®	Bob Nelson & Peter Economy	0-7645-5034-9	$19.99 US/$27.99 CAN
Customer Service For Dummies®, 2nd Edition	Karen Leland & Keith Bailey	0-7645-5209-0	$19.99 US/$27.99 CAN
Franchising For Dummies®	Dave Thomas & Michael Seid	0-7645-5160-4	$19.99 US/$27.99 CAN
Getting Results For Dummies®	Mark H. McCormack	0-7645-5205-8	$19.99 US/$27.99 CAN
Home Buying For Dummies®	Eric Tyson, MBA & Ray Brown	1-56884-385-2	$16.99 US/$24.99 CAN
House Selling For Dummies®	Eric Tyson, MBA & Ray Brown	0-7645-5038-1	$16.99 US/$24.99 CAN
Human Resources Kit For Dummies®	Max Messmer	0-7645-5131-0	$19.99 US/$27.99 CAN
Investing For Dummies®, 2nd Edition	Eric Tyson, MBA	0-7645-5162-0	$19.99 US/$27.99 CAN
Law For Dummies®	John Ventura	1-56884-860-9	$19.99 US/$27.99 CAN
Leadership For Dummies®	Marshall Loeb & Steven Kindel	0-7645-5176-0	$19.99 US/$27.99 CAN
Managing For Dummies®	Bob Nelson & Peter Economy	1-56884-858-7	$19.99 US/$27.99 CAN
Marketing For Dummies®	Alexander Hiam	1-56884-699-1	$19.99 US/$27.99 CAN
Mutual Funds For Dummies®, 2nd Edition	Eric Tyson, MBA	0-7645-5112-4	$19.99 US/$27.99 CAN
Negotiating For Dummies®	Michael C. Donaldson & Mimi Donaldson	1-56884-867-6	$19.99 US/$27.99 CAN
Personal Finance For Dummies®, 3rd Edition	Eric Tyson, MBA	0-7645-5231-7	$19.99 US/$27.99 CAN
Personal Finance For Dummies® For Canadians, 2nd Edition	Eric Tyson, MBA & Tony Martin	0-7645-5123-X	$19.99 US/$27.99 CAN
Public Speaking For Dummies®	Malcolm Kushner	0-7645-5159-0	$16.99 US/$24.99 CAN
Sales Closing For Dummies®	Tom Hopkins	0-7645-5063-2	$14.99 US/$21.99 CAN
Sales Prospecting For Dummies®	Tom Hopkins	0-7645-5066-7	$14.99 US/$21.99 CAN
Selling For Dummies®	Tom Hopkins	1-56884-389-5	$16.99 US/$24.99 CAN
Small Business For Dummies®	Eric Tyson, MBA & Jim Schell	0-7645-5094-2	$19.99 US/$27.99 CAN
Small Business Kit For Dummies®	Richard D. Harroch	0-7645-5093-4	$24.99 US/$34.99 CAN
Taxes 2001 For Dummies®	Eric Tyson & David J. Silverman	0-7645-5306-2	$15.99 US/$23.99 CAN
Time Management For Dummies®, 2nd Edition	Jeffrey J. Mayer	0-7645-5145-0	$19.99 US/$27.99 CAN
Writing Business Letters For Dummies®	Sheryl Lindsell-Roberts	0-7645-5207-4	$16.99 US/$24.99 CAN

TECHNOLOGY TITLES

INTERNET/ONLINE

Title	Author	ISBN	Price
America Online® For Dummies®, 6th Edition	John Kaufeld	0-7645-0670-6	$19.99 US/$27.99 CAN
Banking Online Dummies®	Paul Murphy	0-7645-0458-4	$24.99 US/$34.99 CAN
eBay™ For Dummies®, 2nd Edition	Marcia Collier, Roland Woerner, & Stephanie Becker	0-7645-0761-3	$19.99 US/$27.99 CAN
E-Mail For Dummies®, 2nd Edition	John R. Levine, Carol Baroudi, & Arnold Reinhold	0-7645-0131-3	$24.99 US/$34.99 CAN
Genealogy Online For Dummies®, 2nd Edition	Matthew L. Helm & April Leah Helm	0-7645-0543-2	$24.99 US/$34.99 CAN
Internet Directory For Dummies®, 3rd Edition	Brad Hill	0-7645-0558-2	$24.99 US/$34.99 CAN
Internet Auctions For Dummies®	Greg Holden	0-7645-0578-9	$24.99 US/$34.99 CAN
Internet Explorer 5.5 For Windows® For Dummies®	Doug Lowe	0-7645-0738-9	$19.99 US/$28.99 CAN
Researching Online For Dummies®, 2nd Edition	Mary Ellen Bates & Reva Basch	0-7645-0546-7	$24.99 US/$34.99 CAN
Job Searching Online For Dummies®	Pam Dixon	0-7645-0673-0	$24.99 US/$34.99 CAN
Investing Online For Dummies®, 3rd Edition	Kathleen Sindell, Ph.D.	0-7645-0725-7	$24.99 US/$34.99 CAN
Travel Planning Online For Dummies®, 2nd Edition	Noah Vadnai	0-7645-0438-X	$24.99 US/$34.99 CAN
Internet Searching For Dummies®	Brad Hill	0-7645-0478-9	$24.99 US/$34.99 CAN
Yahoo!® For Dummies®, 2nd Edition	Brad Hill	0-7645-0762-1	$19.99 US/$27.99 CAN
The Internet For Dummies®, 7th Edition	John R. Levine, Carol Baroudi, & Arnold Reinhold	0-7645-0674-9	$19.99 US/$27.99 CAN

OPERATING SYSTEMS

Title	Author	ISBN	Price
DOS For Dummies®, 3rd Edition	Dan Gookin	0-7645-0361-8	$19.99 US/$27.99 CAN
GNOME For Linux® For Dummies®	David B. Busch	0-7645-0650-1	$24.99 US/$37.99 CAN
LINUX® For Dummies®, 2nd Edition	John Hall, Craig Witherspoon, & Coletta Witherspoon	0-7645-0421-5	$24.99 US/$34.99 CAN
Mac® OS 9 For Dummies®	Bob LeVitus	0-7645-0652-8	$19.99 US/$28.99 CAN
Red Hat® Linux® For Dummies®	Jon "maddog" Hall, Paul Sery	0-7645-0663-3	$24.99 US/$37.99 CAN
Small Business Windows® 98 For Dummies®	Stephen Nelson	0-7645-0425-8	$24.99 US/$34.99 CAN
UNIX® For Dummies®, 4th Edition	John R. Levine & Margaret Levine Young	0-7645-0419-3	$19.99 US/$27.99 CAN
Windows® 95 For Dummies®, 2nd Edition	Andy Rathbone	0-7645-0180-1	$19.99 US/$27.99 CAN
Windows® 98 For Dummies®	Andy Rathbone	0-7645-0261-1	$19.99 US/$27.99 CAN
Windows® 2000 For Dummies®	Andy Rathbone	0-7645-0641-2	$19.99 US/$27.99 CAN
Windows® 2000 Server For Dummies®	Ed Tittel	0-7645-0341-3	$24.99 US/$37.99 CAN
Windows® ME Millennium Edition For Dummies®	Andy Rathbone	0-7645-0735-4	$19.99 US/$27.99 CAN

Dummies Books™
Bestsellers on Every Topic!

GENERAL INTEREST TITLES

FOOD & BEVERAGE/ENTERTAINING

Bartending For Dummies®	Ray Foley	0-7645-5051-9	$14.99 US/$21.99 CAN
Cooking For Dummies®, 2nd Edition	Bryan Miller & Marie Rama	0-7645-5250-3	$19.99 US/$27.99 CAN
Entertaining For Dummies®	Suzanne Williamson with Linda Smith	0-7645-5027-6	$19.99 US/$27.99 CAN
Gourmet Cooking For Dummies®	Charlie Trotter	0-7645-5029-2	$19.99 US/$27.99 CAN
Grilling For Dummies®	Marie Rama & John Mariani	0-7645-5076-4	$19.99 US/$27.99 CAN
Italian Cooking For Dummies®	Cesare Casella & Jack Bishop	0-7645-5098-5	$19.99 US/$27.99 CAN
Mexican Cooking For Dummies®	Mary Sue Miliken & Susan Feniger	0-7645-5169-8	$19.99 US/$27.99 CAN
Quick & Healthy Cooking For Dummies®	Lynn Fischer	0-7645-5214-7	$19.99 US/$27.99 CAN
Wine For Dummies®, 2nd Edition	Ed McCarthy & Mary Ewing-Mulligan	0-7645-5114-0	$19.99 US/$27.99 CAN
Chinese Cooking For Dummies®	Martin Yan	0-7645-5247-3	$19.99 US/$27.99 CAN
Etiquette For Dummies®	Sue Fox	0-7645-5170-1	$19.99 US/$27.99 CAN

SPORTS

Baseball For Dummies®, 2nd Edition	Joe Morgan with Richard Lally	0-7645-5234-1	$19.99 US/$27.99 CAN
Golf For Dummies®, 2nd Edition	Gary McCord	0-7645-5146-9	$19.99 US/$27.99 CAN
Fly Fishing For Dummies®	Peter Kaminsky	0-7645-5073-X	$19.99 US/$27.99 CAN
Football For Dummies®	Howie Long with John Czarnecki	0-7645-5054-3	$19.99 US/$27.99 CAN
Hockey For Dummies®	John Davidson with John Steinbreder	0-7645-5045-4	$19.99 US/$27.99 CAN
NASCAR For Dummies®	Mark Martin	0-7645-5219-8	$19.99 US/$27.99 CAN
Tennis For Dummies®	Patrick McEnroe with Peter Bodo	0-7645-5087-X	$19.99 US/$27.99 CAN
Soccer For Dummies®	U.S. Soccer Federation & Michael Lewiss	0-7645-5229-5	$19.99 US/$27.99 CAN

HOME & GARDEN

Annuals For Dummies®	Bill Marken & NGA	0-7645-5056-X	$16.99 US/$24.99 CAN
Container Gardening For Dummies®	Bill Marken & NGA	0-7645-5057-8	$16.99 US/$24.99 CAN
Decks & Patios For Dummies®	Robert J. Beckstrom & NGA	0-7645-5075-6	$16.99 US/$24.99 CAN
Flowering Bulbs For Dummies®	Judy Glattstein & NGA	0-7645-5103-5	$16.99 US/$24.99 CAN
Gardening For Dummies®, 2nd Edition	Michael MacCaskey & NGA	0-7645-5130-2	$16.99 US/$24.99 CAN
Herb Gardening For Dummies®	NGA	0-7645-5200-7	$16.99 US/$24.99 CAN
Home Improvement For Dummies®	Gene & Katie Hamilton & the Editors of HouseNet, Inc.	0-7645-5005-5	$19.99 US/$26.99 CAN
Houseplants For Dummies®	Larry Hodgson & NGA	0-7645-5102-7	$16.99 US/$24.99 CAN
Painting and Wallpapering For Dummies®	Gene Hamilton	0-7645-5150-7	$16.99 US/$24.99 CAN
Perennials For Dummies®	Marcia Tatroe & NGA	0-7645-5030-6	$16.99 US/$24.99 CAN
Roses For Dummies®, 2nd Edition	Lance Walheim	0-7645-5202-3	$16.99 US/$24.99 CAN
Trees and Shrubs For Dummies®	Ann Whitman & NGA	0-7645-5203-1	$16.99 US/$24.99 CAN
Vegetable Gardening For Dummies®	Charlie Nardozzi & NGA	0-7645-5129-9	$16.99 US/$24.99 CAN
Home Cooking For Dummies®	Patricia Hart McMillan & Katharine Kaye McMillan	0-7645-5107-8	$19.99 US/$27.99 CAN

TECHNOLOGY TITLES

WEB DESIGN & PUBLISHING

Active Server Pages For Dummies®, 2nd Edition	Bill Hatfield	0-7645-0603-X	$24.99 US/$37.99 CAN
Cold Fusion 4 For Dummies®	Alexis Gutzman	0-7645-0604-8	$24.99 US/$37.99 CAN
Creating Web Pages For Dummies®, 5th Edition	Bud Smith & Arthur Bebak	0-7645-0733-8	$24.99 US/$34.99 CAN
Dreamweaver™ 3 For Dummies®	Janine Warner & Paul Vachier	0-7645-0669-2	$24.99 US/$34.99 CAN
FrontPage® 2000 For Dummies®	Asha Dornfest	0-7645-0423-1	$24.99 US/$34.99 CAN
HTML 4 For Dummies®, 3rd Edition	Ed Tittel & Natanya Dits	0-7645-0572-6	$24.99 US/$34.99 CAN
Java™ For Dummies®, 3rd Edition	Aaron E. Walsh	0-7645-0417-7	$24.99 US/$34.99 CAN
PageMill™ 2 For Dummies®	Deke McClelland & John San Filippo	0-7645-0028-7	$24.99 US/$34.99 CAN
XML™ For Dummies®	Ed Tittel	0-7645-0692-7	$24.99 US/$37.99 CAN
Javascript For Dummies®, 3rd Edition	Emily Vander Veer	0-7645-0633-1	$24.99 US/$37.99 CAN

DESKTOP PUBLISHING GRAPHICS/MULTIMEDIA

Adobe® In Design™ For Dummies®	Deke McClelland	0-7645-0599-8	$19.99 US/$27.99 CAN
CorelDRAW™ 9 For Dummies®	Deke McClelland	0-7645-0523-8	$19.99 US/$27.99 CAN
Desktop Publishing and Design For Dummies®	Roger C. Parker	1-56884-234-1	$19.99 US/$27.99 CAN
Digital Photography For Dummies®, 3rd Edition	Julie Adair King	0-7645-0646-3	$24.99 US/$37.99 CAN
Microsoft® Publisher 98 For Dummies®	Jim McCarter	0-7645-0395-2	$19.99 US/$27.99 CAN
Visio 2000 For Dummies®	Debbie Walkowski	0-7645-0635-8	$19.99 US/$27.99 CAN
Microsoft® Publisher 2000 For Dummies®	Jim McCarter	0-7645-0525-4	$19.99 US/$27.99 CAN
Windows® Movie Maker For Dummies®	Keith Underdahl	0-7645-0749-1	$19.99 US/$27.99 CAN

Dummies Books™
Bestsellers on Every Topic!

GENERAL INTEREST TITLES

EDUCATION & TEST PREPARATION

Title	Author	ISBN	Price
The ACT For Dummies®	Suzee Vlk	1-56884-387-9	$14.99 US/$21.99 CAN
College Financial Aid For Dummies®	Dr. Herm Davis & Joyce Lain Kennedy	0-7645-5049-7	$19.99 US/$27.99 CAN
College Planning For Dummies®, 2nd Edition	Pat Ordovensky	0-7645-5048-9	$19.99 US/$27.99 CAN
Everyday Math For Dummies®	Charles Seiter, Ph.D.	1-56884-248-1	$14.99 US/$21.99 CAN
The GMAT® For Dummies®, 3rd Edition	Suzee Vlk	0-7645-5082-9	$16.99 US/$24.99 CAN
The GRE® For Dummies®, 3rd Edition	Suzee Vlk	0-7645-5083-7	$16.99 US/$24.99 CAN
Politics For Dummies®	Ann DeLaney	1-56884-381-X	$19.99 US/$27.99 CAN
The SAT I For Dummies®, 3rd Edition	Suzee Vlk	0-7645-5044-6	$14.99 US/$21.99 CAN

AUTOMOTIVE

Title	Author	ISBN	Price
Auto Repair For Dummies®	Deanna Sclar	0-7645-5089-6	$19.99 US/$27.99 CAN
Buying A Car For Dummies®	Deanna Sclar	0-7645-5091-8	$16.99 US/$24.99 CAN

LIFESTYLE/SELF-HELP

Title	Author	ISBN	Price
Dating For Dummies®	Dr. Joy Browne	0-7645-5072-1	$19.99 US/$27.99 CAN
Making Marriage Work For Dummies®	Steven Simring, M.D. & Sue Klavans Simring, D.S.W	0-7645-5173-6	$19.99 US/$27.99 CAN
Parenting For Dummies®	Sandra H. Gookin	1-56884-383-6	$16.99 US/$24.99 CAN
Success For Dummies®	Zig Ziglar	0-7645-5061-6	$19.99 US/$27.99 CAN
Weddings For Dummies®	Marcy Blum & Laura Fisher Kaiser	0-7645-5055-1	$19.99 US/$27.99 CAN

TECHNOLOGY TITLES

SUITES

Title	Author	ISBN	Price
Microsoft® Office 2000 For Windows® For Dummies®	Wallace Wang & Roger C. Parker	0-7645-0452-5	$19.99 US/$27.99 CAN
Microsoft® Office 2000 For Windows® For Dummies® Quick Reference	Doug Lowe & Bjoern Hartsfvang	0-7645-0453-3	$12.99 US/$17.99 CAN
Microsoft® Office 97 For Windows® For Dummies®	Wallace Wang & Roger C. Parker	0-7645-0050-3	$19.99 US/$27.99 CAN
Microsoft® Office 97 For Windows® For Dummies® Quick Reference	Doug Lowe	0-7645-0062-7	$12.99 US/$17.99 CAN
Microsoft® Office 98 For Macs® For Dummies®	Tom Negrino	0-7645-0229-8	$19.99 US/$27.99 CAN
Microsoft® Office X For Macs® For Dummies®	Tom Negrino	0-7645-0702-8	$19.95 US/$27.99 CAN

WORD PROCESSING

Title	Author	ISBN	Price
Word 2000 For Windows® For Dummies® Quick Reference	Peter Weverka	0-7645-0449-5	$12.99 US/$19.99 CAN
Corel® WordPerfect® 8 For Windows® For Dummies®	Margaret Levine Young, David Kay & Jordan Young	0-7645-0186-0	$19.99 US/$27.99 CAN
Word 2000 For Windows® For Dummies®	Dan Gookin	0-7645-0448-7	$19.99 US/$27.99 CAN
Word For Windows® 95 For Dummies®	Dan Gookin	1-56884-932-X	$19.99 US/$27.99 CAN
Word 97 For Windows® For Dummies®	Dan Gookin	0-7645-0052-X	$19.99 US/$27.99 CAN
WordPerfect® 9 For Windows® For Dummies®	Margaret Levine Young	0-7645-0427-4	$19.99 US/$27.99 CAN
WordPerfect® 7 For Windows® 95 For Dummies®	Margaret Levine Young & David Kay	1-56884-949-4	$19.99 US/$27.99 CAN

SPREADSHEET/FINANCE/PROJECT MANAGEMENT

Title	Author	ISBN	Price
Excel For Windows® 95 For Dummies®	Greg Harvey	1-56884-930-3	$19.99 US/$27.99 CAN
Excel 2000 For Windows® For Dummies®	Greg Harvey	0-7645-0446-0	$19.99 US/$27.99 CAN
Excel 2000 For Windows® For Dummies® Quick Reference	John Walkenbach	0-7645-0447-9	$12.99 US/$17.99 CAN
Microsoft® Money 99 For Dummies®	Peter Weverka	0-7645-0433-9	$19.99 US/$27.99 CAN
Microsoft® Project 98 For Dummies®	Martin Doucette	0-7645-0321-9	$24.99 US/$34.99 CAN
Microsoft® Project 2000 For Dummies®	Martin Doucette	0-7645-0517-3	$24.99 US/$37.99 CAN
Microsoft® Money 2000 For Dummies®	Peter Weverka	0-7645-0579-3	$19.99 US/$27.99 CAN
MORE Excel 97 For Windows® For Dummies®	Greg Harvey	0-7645-0138-0	$22.99 US/$32.99 CAN
Quicken® 2000 For Dummies®	Stephen L. Nelson	0-7645-0607-2	$19.99 US/$27.99 CAN
Quicken® 2001 For Dummies®	Stephen L. Nelson	0-7645-0759-1	$19.99 US/$27.99 CAN
Quickbooks® 2000 For Dummies®	Stephen L. Nelson	0-7645-0665-x	$19.99 US/$27.99 CAN

Dummies Books™
Bestsellers on Every Topic!

GENERAL INTEREST TITLES

CAREERS

Title	Author	ISBN	Price
Cover Letters For Dummies®, 2nd Edition	Joyce Lain Kennedy	0-7645-5224-4	$12.99 US/$17.99 CAN
Cool Careers For Dummies®	Marty Nemko, Paul Edwards, & Sarah Edwards	0-7645-5095-0	$16.99 US/$24.99 CAN
Job Hunting For Dummies®, 2nd Edition	Max Messmer	0-7645-5163-9	$19.99 US/$26.99 CAN
Job Interviews For Dummies®, 2nd Edition	Joyce Lain Kennedy	0-7645-5225-2	$12.99 US/$17.99 CAN
Resumes For Dummies®, 2nd Edition	Joyce Lain Kennedy	0-7645-5113-2	$12.99 US/$17.99 CAN

FITNESS

Title	Author	ISBN	Price
Fitness Walking For Dummies®	Liz Neporent	0-7645-5192-2	$19.99 US/$27.99 CAN
Fitness For Dummies®, 2nd Edition	Suzanne Schlosberg & Liz Neporent	0-7645-5167-1	$19.99 US/$27.99 CAN
Nutrition For Dummies®, 2nd Edition	Carol Ann Rinzler	0-7645-5180-9	$19.99 US/$27.99 CAN
Running For Dummies®	Florence "Flo-Jo" Griffith Joyner & John Hanc	0-7645-5096-9	$19.99 US/$27.99 CAN

FOREIGN LANGUAGE

Title	Author	ISBN	Price
Spanish For Dummies®	Susana Wald	0-7645-5194-9	$24.99 US/$34.99 CAN
French For Dummies®	Dodi-Kartrin Schmidt & Michelle W. Willams	0-7645-5193-0	$24.99 US/$34.99 CAN

TECHNOLOGY TITLES

DATABASE

Title	Author	ISBN	Price
Access 2000 For Windows® For Dummies®	John Kaufeld	0-7645-0444-4	$19.99 US/$27.99 CAN
Access 97 For Windows® For Dummies®	John Kaufeld	0-7645-0048-1	$19.99 US/$27.99 CAN
Access 2000 For Windows For Dummies® Quick Reference	Alison Barrons	0-7645-0445-2	$12.99 US/$17.99 CAN
Approach® 97 For Windows® For Dummies®	Deborah S. Ray & Eric J. Ray	0-7645-0001-5	$19.99 US/$27.99 CAN
Crystal Reports 8 For Dummies®	Douglas J. Wolf	0-7645-0642-0	$24.99 US/$34.99 CAN
Data Warehousing For Dummies®	Alan R. Simon	0-7645-0170-4	$24.99 US/$34.99 CAN
FileMaker® Pro 4 For Dummies®	Tom Maremaa	0-7645-0210-7	$19.99 US/$27.99 CAN

NETWORKING/GROUPWARE

Title	Author	ISBN	Price
ATM For Dummies®	Cathy Gadecki & Christine Heckart	0-7645-0065-1	$24.99 US/$34.99 CAN
Client/Server Computing For Dummies®, 3rd Edition	Doug Lowe	0-7645-0476-2	$24.99 US/$34.99 CAN
DSL For Dummies®, 2nd Edition	David Angell	0-7645-0715-X	$24.99 US/$35.99 CAN
Lotus Notes® Release 4 For Dummies®	Stephen Londergan & Pat Freeland	1-56884-934-6	$19.99 US/$27.99 CAN
Microsoft® Outlook® 98 For Windows® For Dummies®	Bill Dyszel	0-7645-0393-6	$19.99 US/$28.99 CAN
Microsoft® Outlook® 2000 For Windows® For Dummies®	Bill Dyszel	0-7645-0471-1	$19.99 US/$27.99 CAN
Migrating to Windows® 2000 For Dummies®	Leonard Sterns	0-7645-0459-2	$24.99 US/$37.99 CAN
Networking For Dummies®, 4th Edition	Doug Lowe	0-7645-0498-3	$19.99 US/$27.99 CAN
Networking Home PCs For Dummies®	Kathy Ivens	0-7645-0491-6	$24.99 US/$35.99 CAN
Upgrading & Fixing Networks For Dummies®, 2nd Edition	Bill Camarda	0-7645-0542-4	$29.99 US/$42.99 CAN
TCP/IP For Dummies®, 4th Edition	Candace Leiden & Marshall Wilensky	0-7645-0726-5	$24.99 US/$35.99 CAN
Windows NT® Networking For Dummies®	Ed Tittel, Mary Madden, & Earl Follis	0-7645-0015-5	$24.99 US/$34.99 CAN

PROGRAMMING

Title	Author	ISBN	Price
Active Server Pages For Dummies®, 2nd Edition	Bill Hatfield	0-7645-0065-1	$24.99 US/$34.99 CAN
Beginning Programming For Dummies®	Wally Wang	0-7645-0596-0	$19.99 US/$29.99 CAN
C++ For Dummies® Quick Reference, 2nd Edition	Namir Shammas	0-7645-0390-1	$14.99 US/$21.99 CAN
Java™ Programming For Dummies®, 3rd Edition	David & Donald Koosis	0-7645-0388-X	$29.99 US/$42.99 CAN
JBuilder™ For Dummies®	Barry A. Burd	0-7645-0567-X	$24.99 US/$34.99 CAN
VBA For Dummies®, 2nd Edition	Steve Cummings	0-7645-0078-3	$24.99 US/$37.99 CAN
Windows® 2000 Programming For Dummies®	Richard Simon	0-7645-0469-X	$24.99 US/$37.99 CAN
XML For Dummies®, 2nd Edition	Ed Tittel	0-7645-0692-7	$24.99 US/$37.99 CAN

Dummies Books™
Bestsellers on Every Topic!

GENERAL INTEREST TITLES

THE ARTS

Art For Dummies®	Thomas Hoving	0-7645-5104-3	$24.99 US/$34.99 CAN
Blues For Dummies®	Lonnie Brooks, Cub Koda, & Wayne Baker Brooks	0-7645-5080-2	$24.99 US/$34.99 CAN
Classical Music For Dummies®	David Pogue & Scott Speck	0-7645-5009-8	$24.99 US/$34.99 CAN
Guitar For Dummies®	Mark Phillips & Jon Chappell of Cherry Lane Music	0-7645-5106-X	$24.99 US/$34.99 CAN
Jazz For Dummies®	Dirk Sutro	0-7645-5081-0	$24.99 US/$34.99 CAN
Opera For Dummies®	David Pogue & Scott Speck	0-7645-5010-1	$24.99 US/$34.99 CAN
Piano For Dummies®	Blake Neely of Cherry Lane Music	0-7645-5105-1	$24.99 US/$34.99 CAN
Shakespeare For Dummies®	John Doyle & Ray Lischner	0-7645-5135-3	$19.99 US/$27.99 CAN

HEALTH

Allergies and Asthma For Dummies®	William Berger, M.D.	0-7645-5218-X	$19.99 US/$27.99 CAN
Alternative Medicine For Dummies®	James Dillard, M.D., D.C., C.A.C., & Terra Ziporyn, Ph.D.	0-7645-5109-4	$19.99 US/$27.99 CAN
Beauty Secrets For Dummies®	Stephanie Seymour	0-7645-5078-0	$19.99 US/$27.99 CAN
Diabetes For Dummies®	Alan L. Rubin, M.D.	0-7645-5154-X	$19.99 US/$27.99 CAN
Dieting For Dummies®	The American Dietetic Society with Jane Kirby, R.D.	0-7645-5126-4	$19.99 US/$27.99 CAN
Family Health For Dummies®	Charles Inlander & Karla Morales	0-7645-5121-3	$19.99 US/$27.99 CAN
First Aid For Dummies®	Charles B. Inlander & The People's Medical Society	0-7645-5213-9	$19.99 US/$27.99 CAN
Fitness For Dummies®, 2nd Edition	Suzanne Schlosberg & Liz Neporent, M.A.	0-7645-5167-1	$19.99 US/$27.99 CAN
Healing Foods For Dummies®	Molly Siple, M.S. R.D.	0-7645-5198-1	$19.99 US/$27.99 CAN
Healthy Aging For Dummies®	Walter Bortz, M.D.	0-7645-5233-3	$19.99 US/$27.99 CAN
Men's Health For Dummies®	Charles Inlander	0-7645-5120-5	$19.99 US/$27.99 CAN
Nutrition For Dummies®, 2nd Edition	Carol Ann Rinzler	0-7645-5180-9	$19.99 US/$27.99 CAN
Pregnancy For Dummies®	Joanne Stone, M.D., Keith Eddleman, M.D., & Mary Murray	0-7645-5074-8	$19.99 US/$27.99 CAN
Sex For Dummies®	Dr. Ruth K. Westheimer	1-56884-384-4	$16.99 US/$24.99 CAN
Stress Management For Dummies®	Allen Elkin, Ph.D.	0-7645-5144-2	$19.99 US/$27.99 CAN
The Healthy Heart For Dummies®	James M. Ripple, M.D.	0-7645-5166-3	$19.99 US/$27.99 CAN
Weight Training For Dummies®	Liz Neporent, M.A. & Suzanne Schlosberg	0-7645-5036-5	$19.99 US/$27.99 CAN
Women's Health For Dummies®	Pamela Maraldo, Ph.D., R.N., & The People's Medical Society	0-7645-5119-1	$19.99 US/$27.99 CAN

TECHNOLOGY TITLES

MACINTOSH

Macs® For Dummies®, 7th Edition	David Pogue	0-7645-0703-6	$19.99 US/$27.99 CAN
The iBook™ For Dummies®	David Pogue	0-7645-0647-1	$19.99 US/$27.99 CAN
The iMac For Dummies®, 2nd Edition	David Pogue	0-7645-0648-X	$19.99 US/$27.99 CAN
The iMac For Dummies® Quick Reference	Jenifer Watson	0-7645-0648-X	$12.99 US/$19.99 CAN

PC/GENERAL COMPUTING

Building A PC For Dummies®, 2nd Edition	Mark Chambers	0-7645-0571-8	$24.99 US/$34.99 CAN
Buying a Computer For Dummies®	Dan Gookin	0-7645-0632-3	$19.99 US/$27.99 CAN
Illustrated Computer Dictionary For Dummies®, 4th Edition	Dan Gookin & Sandra Hardin Gookin	0-7645-0732-X	$19.99 US/$27.99 CAN
Palm Computing® For Dummies®	Bill Dyszel	0-7645-0581-5	$24.99 US/$34.99 CAN
PCs For Dummies®, 7th Edition	Dan Gookin	0-7645-0594-7	$19.99 US/$27.99 CAN
Small Business Computing For Dummies®	Brian Underdahl	0-7645-0287-5	$24.99 US/$34.99 CAN
Smart Homes For Dummies®	Danny Briere	0-7645-0527-0	$19.99 US/$27.99 CAN
Upgrading & Fixing PCs For Dummies®, 5th Edition	Andy Rathbone	0-7645-0719-2	$19.99 US/$27.99 CAN
Handspring Visor For Dummies®	Joe Hubko	0-7645-0724-9	$19.99 US/$27.99 CAN

Notes

Notes